The Alaska Travel Journal of

Archibald Menzies,

1 7 9 3 - 1 7 9 4

Discovery Deptford
Thursd: night Oct.ʳ 22
795

Dear Sir

I have the pleasure of acquainting
you with our safe arrival here this moment
from our long and fatiguing Voyage, after
some tedious delays, both in the Shannon
and long Reach, for you must know
that as we drew nearer home every
moment's delay seemed to lengthen in
an increased ratio, with the pressing
anxiety of knowing something of the
fate, & welfare of our Friends after
so long an Absence. — And as I have
                                              not

country, so the same cause of del
prevails still — I do not think how
I shall wait much longer, unless
s. macelim rae. 7 py. 3. as you
drawing, and this was my pro
wishing to have it altered alter
be done it must remain as it
                          Thursd May 17.

The Alaska Travel Journal of
Archibald Menzies,

1 7 9 3 - 1 7 9 4

with an introduction and annotation by
Wallace M. Olson

and a list of the botanical collections by
John F. Thilenius

University of Alaska Press
Fairbanks, 1993

Library of Congress Cataloging-in-Publication Data

Menzies, Archibald, fl. 1763.
    The Alaska travel journal of Archibalc Menzies, 1794-1794 / with
an introduction and annotation by Wallace M. Olson ; with a list of
botantanical terms by John Thilenius.
      p. cm.
    Includes bibliographical references and index.
    ISBN 0-912006-70-6
    1. Alaska--Description and travel--To 1867. 2. Botany--Alaska.
3. Menzies, Archibald, fl. 1763--Diaries. I. Olson, Wallace M.
II. Thilenius, John F. II. Title.
F907.M45 1993
917.9804' 1--dc20   93-1334
                                                            CIP

Printed in the United States by
            McNaughton & Gunn, Inc.

This publication was printed on acid-free paper that meets the minimum
requirements of American National Standard for Information Sciences-
Permanence for Paper for Printed Library Materias, ANSI Z39.48-1984.

Publication coordination, design and production by
            Deborah Van Stone.

Frontispiece: *Letter from Menzies to a friend showing a sample
of his handwriting. The letter was written aboard the* Discovery *at
Deptford, Thursday night, October 22, 1795, when he had returned
from the Vancouver expedition which he describes as a "long and
fatiguing Voyage." (Courtesy British Museum, Natural History.)*

*Dedicated to my wife, Marie,
for her help and encouragement
and to
Dr. W. Kaye Lamb,
a true gentleman and superb scholar.*

Contents

List of Illustrations
and Maps

The Alaska Travel Journal of Archibald Menzies, 1793–1794 Errata

Page 70—Read *whose name is* in line 14 instead of *who name is.*
Bibliography page 227, under de Laguna, Frederica entry add:

1960 *The Story of a Tlingit Community: A Problem in the Relationship Between Archaeological, Ethnological, and Historical Methods.* Bureau of American Ethnology, Bulletin No. 17. Smithsonian Institution, Washington, D.C.

1972 *Under Mount St. Elias: The History and Culture of the Yakutat Tlingit.* Smithsonian Contributions to Anthropology, Number 7. (3 volumes). Smithsonian Institution, Washington, D.C.

Acknowledgements

I want to express my sincere thanks to the following people and organizations who have contributed to the publication of this journal:

The Archives of British Columbia for allowing me to use their microfilm copy of the transcription of the 1793 portion of the journal.

The National Library of Australia for granting permission to publish portions of Menzies' 1794 journal, and to Graeme Powell of that library for his assistance.

The British Museum (Natural History) and particularly Dr. David Galloway, head of the Lichen Section, for providing information on Menzies and his collection. And to Dr. Eric Groves, now retired from the museum, for details on Menzies' contributions to botany.

The Linnean Society of London for granting permission to include a photograph of their portrait of Menzies in this book.

Dr. Lydia Black for her transcriptions of Russian names and information concerning the Russian companies in Alaska in the late eighteenth century.

Dr. Robert Wolfe of the Alaska Department of Fish and Game for coming to my rescue with maps of Alaska and to Point Stephens Press for their graphics and preparation of the maps for publication.

Dr. John Thilenius for his research regarding the botanical terms and taxonomic information. Without his help, I would have remained lost in the world of botanical terms.

Dr. Ole Mathiesen, Dr. Frederica de Laguna, Dr. Richard Dauenhauer and Nora Marks Dauenhauer for their technical advice and expertise.

The Tlingit, Haida and Tsimshian informants whose comments regarding the journal were most informative.

The University of Alaska Southeast for permitting me to use my research time to work on the transcription and annotation.

Debbie Van Stone and the University of Alaska Press for being so helpful and encouraging in the process of publication.

And most of all, Dr. W. Kaye Lamb, for his help in transcription and his time and patience with me over the past few years. He deserves all the credit for keeping the research on the right course. Any errors or misinterpretations in the text are entirely my own.

Thank you very much.

Wallace M. Olson
Professor of Anthropology
University of Alaska Southeast

Introduction

In my anthropological research regarding the Tlingit Indians of Southeastern Alaska, I have found that the reports and journals of early visitors to the Northwest Coast are important sources of information regarding conditions in the 18th and 19th centuries. Oftentimes these writings describe the people, their language, behavior, technology, settlements and dress. The journal of Captain George Vancouver has proven to be a valuable resource. I have been using the latest edition of his report entitled *A Voyage of Discovery to the North Pacific Ocean and Round the World, 1791-95*, with an introduction and appendixes, edited by W. Kaye Lamb. This four-volume work was published by the Hakluyt Society of London in 1984. Dr. Lamb has provided both a comprehensive introduction and made extensive annotations regarding the account. To supplement Vancouver's narrative, Dr. Lamb examined all of the available journals and records of the officers and crew members of the ships *Discovery* and *Chatham*. Among those journals was that of Archibald Menzies, the botanist and surgeon of the expedition.

In several places, Dr. Lamb quoted statements from Menzies' journal for the 1794 season. I was surprised to see these references because other writers did not know if Menzies had compiled a journal for that final year of exploration. For instance, in Bern Anderson's book, *The Life and Voyages of Captain George Vancouver: Surveyor of the Sea* (1960:174), he describes how Menzies climbed Mauna Loa in Hawaii, and then goes on to say, "Unfortunately, Menzies' journal ends with the return from the peak to his camp at the snow line, and there is no record of his opinions and observations for the rest of the voyage." In 1987,

D. J. Galloway and E. W. Groves, botanists at the British Museum of Natural History, published a brief biography of Menzies in the Archives of Natural History journal. On page twenty-three of that biography, they write, "The manuscript journal of Archibald Menzies' *Discovery* journey consists of a single volume which unfortunately ends abruptly at 16 February 1794. As up to that date his entries are full and detailed, one cannot but suspect there to have been originally a further portion dealing with the events for the remainder of the voyage." It is not too surprising that others did not know about the final segment of the journal, because it is in the National Library of Australia. I will explain later how it came to be there.

When I met with Dr. Lamb, he explained that he had examined the 1794 portion of Menzies' journal in Australia, and the Library had graciously provided him with a photocopy of the original handwritten text. Dr. Lamb then gave me a copy of his photocopy, from which I have transcribed and annotated the text for the spring and summer of 1794.

For the survey of 1793 in southern Southeastern Alaska, Dr. Lamb directed me to a microfilm copy of a typewritten transcription in the British Columbia Provincial Archives in Victoria. It is simply numbered "M 1405" with no indication of who made the typed transcription. Galloway and Groves (1987:5) mention that "Menzies' journal kept during the *Discovery* voyage is in the British Library, London (Add Ms 32641) with a copy in the Archives of the Linnean Society, also in London." In 1923, the Archives of British Columbia published *Menzies' Journal of Vancouver's Voyages, April to October, 1792*, edited by Dr. C. F. Newcombe. Apparently, he used a typewritten transcription prepared by someone for the Linnean Society. Since I was unable to determine who had made the transcription, Dr. Lamb carefully examined my transcription and compared it with a photocopy of the original handwritten text which is in the British Library. After checking my text, he concluded that it is an accurate transcription of the original journal.

What we have today is not the rough copy written aboard the ship, but a "clean copy" produced later. In a letter dated December 20, 1989, Graeme Powell, Manuscript Librarian, National

Library of Australia, wrote to me saying, "I expect you realize that, although evidently in Menzies' handwriting, the journal is not the original, but appears to have been copied after the voyage. The watermark on the paper is dated 1798." It is not known when Menzies actually completed his entire, "clean copy" of his journal.

Wallace M. Olson
Professor of Anthropology
University of Alaska Southeast

Brief Biography of
Archibald Menzies

The inscription for plot 706 in All Souls Cemetery, Kensal Gardens, London, reads as follows:

> Archibald Menzies....many years a surgeon in the Royal Navy in which station he served in the fleet commanded by Admiral Rodney on the 12th of April 1782. He afterwards twice circumnavigated the globe first with Captain Colnett, and again in the voyage of discovery under the orders of Captain Vancouver as the naturalist to that expedition.
>
> He added greatly to the knowledge then possessed of the natural productions, especially the plants, of the various countries visited. After practicing his profession for many years in London, he retired to Notting Hill where he died on the 15th February 1842 aged 88. Sincerely respected and deeply regretted by his numerous friends (Galloway and Groves, 1987:34).

Archibald Menzies, son of James and Anne Menzies, was born at Styx House in the parish of Weem, near Aberfeldy, Perthshire, Scotland. He was baptized at the local parish church on March 15, 1754. He left home to enter the Royal Botanic Garden at Edinburgh where his older brother William was already employed (Galloway and Groves, 1987:3). While attending the University of Edinburgh as a student of medicine, he was greatly influenced by Dr. John Hope, Regius Professor of Botany (Newcombe, 1923:vii). In 1778, he traveled through the Highlands and the Hebrides and became

1

an assistant to a surgeon at Carnavon. In 1781 he was qualified as a surgeon (Galloway and Groves, 1987:3; Newcombe 1923: vii).

Entering the Royal Navy as an assistant surgeon, he served aboard the *Nonsuch* under Captain Truscott and took part in Admiral George Brydges Rodney's victory over the Comte de Grasse, near the coast of Dominica, West Indies, in April 1782. His next voyage to the New World came in May, 1784, when he sailed to Nova Scotia as the surgeon on the *Assistance* (Newcombe, 1923:viii; Galloway and Groves, 1987:3). It was during this voyage that he first corresponded with Sir Joseph Banks, the well known botanist, administrator, supporter of Kew Gardens, and influential friend of King George III (Galloway and Groves, 1987:36; Lamb, 1992:2). Menzies sailed along the eastern seaboard of North America to the West Indies, collecting seeds and botanical specimens along the way. He sent part of his collection to Banks. In his letters, it is clear that although his training was in surgery and medicine, his great love was botany. Two weeks after his return to England in August of 1786, he made plans for a voyage around the world with James Colnett (Galloway and Groves, 1987:8). Since this was to be a commercial voyage, Menzies took a leave of absence from the Royal Navy.

Colnett had served as a midshipman with Captain James Cook on the *Resolution* and was promoted to the rank of First Lieutenant. Two ships, the *Prince of Wales* and the *Princess Royal*, set sail on October 15, 1786. Since their main purpose was to purchase furs, they were not allowed to collect "curiosities." Banks prevailed upon the ship's owner, Richard Cadman Etches, and an exception was granted for Menzies to collect plants and other curiosities beneficial to science. Dr. C. F. Newcombe points out that "Menzies' first voyage to the coast is referred to in a few places, and, meagre though they be, add something to the imperfect knowledge of it...Very little is known of Colnett's voyage of this year [1788]." (Newcombe, 1923:xiv). Colnett's journal (n.d.) is fairly complete, but has only a brief reference to Menzies' presence aboard the vessel. Groves (1992:3-4) says that Menzies "undoubtedly kept a personal journal during this voyage but this, as far as is known, has not survived....There exists no complete roster of plants collected for the whole of this voyage."

Portrait of Archibald Menzies by Eden Upton Eddis.
(Courtesy of the Linnean Society of London.)

James Johnstone was Colnett's second in command, and later served under Captain George Vancouver on the great survey. Johnstone and Menzies had served together in Nova Scotia in 1783 and were united again on the Colnett expedition. They remained on friendly terms and that may explain why Menzies had access to Johnstone's reports during the Vancouver expedition. In fact, when Menzies later served aboard the *Sans Pariel*, Johnstone was again one of the officers (Vancouver, 1798(1984):255).

After stopping in South America, the ships reached Nootka on Vancouver Island in July 1787 and continued trading along the Northwest Coast until fall. They then sailed to Hawaii for the winter months (Newcombe, 1923:8,9,11-12). By March of 1788, they were back on the coast and began trading in Prince William Sound where they anchored at Port Etches and Snug Corner Cove (Colnett, n.d., Newcombe, 1923:xiv). After a brief stop at Yakutat Bay, they continued along the outside coast to Cape Edgecumbe and present day Sitka. In his journal, Vancouver mentions that Johnstone had been in Port Mulgrave (Yakutat) in 1788. Also, in a journal entry for August 9, 1793, Menzies mentions that in his attempt to learn about the Natives' language, he asked them to "repeat their Numerals, which I found to be exactly the same with those I formerly collected at Cape Edgecumbe & Port Mulgrave."

At the end of the 1788 season, Johnstone, with Menzies on board, took the *Prince of Wales* back to England, arriving there in July 1789. By October 8th of that same year, he was busy securing an appointment for a second voyage around the world (Galloway and Groves, 1987:14). The British Admiralty had begun preparations for a major survey of the Northwest Coast under the command of Henry Roberts in the vessel *Discovery*. Roberts resigned the appointment and was replaced by George Vancouver, who had been promoted to the rank of Commander. The other ship, the *Chatham*, was under the command of Lieutenant W. R. Broughton. Their expedition had two objectives. The first was to conclude an agreement over the "Nootka Controversy" which arose when Spanish forces seized three British ships in Nootka harbor in 1789. Captain Colnett, the commander in charge of the ships, was taken prisoner. The ensuing dispute nearly erupted

into war before a settlement was achieved. Vancouver's assign-
ment was to accept the transfer of Nootka to Great Britain.

The second objective was to make a complete survey of the
Northwest Coast in search of the legendary "Northwest Passage."
The legend was that at about 55° North there existed a passageway across North America linking the Pacific and Atlantic Oceans.
Captain Cook and others had searched for the elusive waterway,
but found no sign of it. Vancouver's task was to explore every
navigable waterway leading north or east that might be the
entrance to the Northwest Passage. It was to be a long voyage. The
two ships left England in April 1, 1791 and did not return home
until September 1795 (Anderson, 1960:48,212).

Following their homecoming, Menzies resumed his military
service at the end of November 1796 and served most of the next
three years aboard the *Princess Augusta* (Lamb, 1992:18). In 1799
he was awarded the Medical Doctor Degree *honoris causis* by
Aberdeen University (Galloway and Groves, 1987:36) and was
appointed surgeon aboard the *Sans Pariel*, serving under Lord
Hugh Seymour, and in that capacity he spent the next three years
in the West Indies. Soon after his return to England in 1802 he was
married. (Galloway and Groves, 1987:26, 36). He and his wife,
Janet, had no children.

He practiced surgery at 6 Chapel Place, Oxford Street, but he
was in poor health, suffering from attacks of asthma. Menzies
expressed a desire to produce a systematic report of his collection
but work and poor health prevented him from publishing papers
or his journals from the Vancouver survey, except for some
accounts of his travels in Hawaii (Galloway and Groves, 1987:26).
He was generous in allowing others access to his botanical collection and even shared some specimens with fellow scientists
(Galloway and Groves, 1987:25)

Although there are no geographic places in Alaska today com-
memorating Archibald Menzies, some features bore his name for
a brief period of time following his voyage with Colnett. Early fur
traders called what is now Chatham Strait, "Menzies' Strait," and
for a few years, traders referred to Cape Ommaney as "Menzies's
Cape" (Orth, 1971:201,724). In British Columbia, at least four
geographical features have been named in his honor.

According to Groves (1992:26), "Apart from the genus *Menziesia* created by Sir James E. Smith (1791, fasc.III) there have been nearly a hundred flowering plant taxa, whether it be species, sub-species or varieties which have celebrated him in epithet 'menziesii.' Not all have survived as by the law of priority in botany names of earlier authors may have superceded him." Dr. David Galloway, of the British Museum, Natural History (personal communication) said that Menzies made a major contribution to the field of lichen studies. Although he was never an officer of the Linnean Society of London, he was respected as one of its "elder statesman" (Groves, 1992:26).

He retired in 1826, at age 72 and lived at Notting Hill but maintained a great interest in botany and corresponded with many other scientists regarding ferns and mosses (Galloway and Groves, l987:32). His wife died on September 23, 1836 at age 66. Menzies lived alone for the next six years. After writing out his will on February 14, 1842, he died the following day at 88. He was buried in the plot next to his beloved wife (Galloway and Groves, l987:40).

In 1992, Eric Groves (personal communication) tried to identify Menzies' grave at All Souls' Cemetery, but said that the plot was so overgrown that it was almost impossible to determine which grave was that of Archibald Menzies.

The Vancouver Expedition

Vancouver, Banks and Menzies

George Vancouver, son of John Jasper Vancouver and Bridget Berners, was born at King's Lynn, Norfolk, on June 22, 1757. His father was of Dutch ancestry, a member of the van Coeverden family. The young Vancouver first went to sea in 1772 aboard the *Resolution* under the command of Captain James Cook. As they matured into officers, the midshipmen were trained in the skills of seamanship and navigation. Over the next 19 years, as trust and loyalty developed between the midshipmen, Vancouver became friends with several of the men who later served with him, namely, Joseph Whidbey, Peter Puget, Joseph Baker and Zachary Mudge (Vancouver, 1798(1984):2, 3, 28). Others in the expedition, including Menzies and James Johnstone, were not chosen by Vancouver but received their appointments through influential associates.

There has been some debate about the personality traits of Vancouver and his behavior on this expedition. Dr. John Naish, retired naval surgeon (1992:1), mentions his "failures of temperament and his proneness to violent outbursts of temper." Throughout his biography of Vancouver, Bern Anderson (1960) proposes that the Captain's irascibility was due to a hyperthyroid condition known as Grave's disease. Anderson suggests that Vancouver's moodiness and hyperactivity followed at times by complete exhaustion, shows a progressive development of the illness so that in the final year of exploration, the Captain seldom shared in the boat surveys. On the other hand, Naish (1992) suggests that Vancouver's personality can best be understood not as a result of physical illness but as a result of his early life experiences. His mother died just before he first went to sea at the age of 15. His formative, adolescent years were spent in the "harsh time-ridden discipline of the quarter deck and the midshipmen's mess....Such an upbringing with its emphasis on exactitude, obedience and punishment for misdemeanour is precisely that which would intensify already existing obsessional characteristics" (Naish, 1992:1-2). He goes on to list a series of emotional outbreaks on the voyage, including several altercations with Menzies over a plant-frame on the quarter deck.

Naish has examined the records regarding Vancouver's health (Naish, 1992), and is convinced that Vancouver's ill health was due to "Bright's Disease or Chronic Glomerulo-nephritis." He points out that individuals with chronic kidney infection may continue to live for upwards of 20 years after the onset of the problem. After taking command of the *Discovery* at the age of 33, Vancouver's health seems to have deteriorated until he died at the end of his 41st year. For the last two and half years of his life he was almost an invalid (Naish, 1992:1).

To appreciate Menzie's position and activities on the Vancouver expedition, it is necessary to understand the influential role that Sir Joseph Banks had in the planning of the voyage and Menzies' journal. Banks was born in 1743 to a well-to-do family in Linconshire, England. He attended Harrow and Eaton schools and was not interested in most subjects, but at 14 became fascinated with botany. His father died in 1761, and the family moved to Chelsea where the young Banks met William Alton, who was in charge of the Royal Botanic Gardens at Kew. King George III had a great interest in botany, and in time, he and Banks became friends. Before long, Banks was advising the King in matters related to botany and gardens. In 1764, when Banks came of age and took possession of his family's estate, he began to implement his plan to collect plants from around the world and bring them to Kew Gardens. At age 23, he was elected to the prestigious Royal Society (Lamb, 1992:1-2).

The Royal Society recommended that Banks accompany Captain James Cook on his first voyage of discovery to the South Pacific. Banks was joined by D. C. Solander, a noted botanist and pupil of Linnaeus, H. Sporing, A. Buchan and S. Parkinson. It is estimated that Banks spent £10,000 on the expedition, an immense amount of money in those days (Price, 1971:17). When they returned in 1771, "he and Solander, not Cook, were greeted as the conquering heroes. The King received Banks before Cook, and one newspaper actually identified Cook as a person who had 'sailed around the Globe' with Solander and Banks" (Lamb, 1992:2).

Captain Cook was soon off on his second voyage of discovery. His journal with its "nautical terminology and details; its abbreviations, and its chaotic spelling and punctuation, was unfit for publication..."(Price, 1971:97). Cook's journal, along with that of Joseph Banks, was turned over to Dr. John Hawkesworth for editing and publication. As A. Grenfell Price (1971:97) describes it, "Hawkesworth appears to have given more weight in his volume to the journals of the 'gentleman Joseph Banks Esquire' than to the those of the unlettered sailor who commanded the expedition [Cook]." The fact that Banks' journal played such a large part in the edited version of Cook's report was to have an impact on the publication of Vancouver's journal and indirectly on Menzies' as well.

Banks wanted to sail with Cook on his second voyage, but his excessive demands for accommodations for himself and his staff had created some resentment among the naval officers. Banks then began to sponsor other botanists to help collect for Kew Gardens (Lamb, 1992:3).

Banks insisted that Menzies be given special consideration on the voyage. Before Vancouver assumed command of the *Discovery*, and while Captain Roberts was in charge, Banks had insisted that a special frame, eight feet by twelve feet, with glass panes, be constructed on the quarter deck to hold botanical specimens collected on the expedition. This plant frame was to be a source of irritation to Vancouver throughout the voyage. By the fall of 1793, Menzies was complaining to Vancouver that the "fowls have been in it again last night, and have done irreparable damage." He requested that the box be covered with strong netting and that a man be assigned to watch after the plant frame (Lamb, 1992:12).

Originally, Menzies had requested an appointment as the ship's surgeon. He explains in his journal for December 1790 that "as a state of tedious suspense was more intolerable to me, than the hardships of a long voyage…I requested leave of the Treasury to go out as Surgeon of the Discovery, promising at the same time that my vacant hours from my professional charge, would be chiefly employed…in making such collections and observations as might elucidate the natural history of the Voyage" (Lamb, 1992:8).

Banks and the Secretary of State became involved regarding Menzies' appointment. According to Lamb (1992:8) "Some of Banks rough notes include the earliest reference to a Menzies journal; he was 'To deliver his journal to his employers on his return Provided that [it] was thought proper for Publication, he should be allowed to publish it for his own benefit.' The term 'employers' is ambiguous, but in Bank's mind it was certainly intended to mean the Secretary of State." The Secretary of State agreed to the appointment of Menzies as Surgeon and his salary was to be £80 a year.

It appears that Vancouver objected to Menzies' appointment, and so a compromise was reached. Alexander Cranstoun was appointed surgeon and Menzies was made a supernumerary as a botanist, and it was only later in the journey that he was made surgeon on the *Discovery* (Vancouver, 1798(1984):31). His salary was increased to £150, but he had to pay for his mess and other services (Lamb,1992:9) It is not surprising then, that there were some disagreements between Menzies and Vancouver. Anderson (1960:46) suggests that Vancouver's resentment was directed more at Banks' interference than at Menzies personally. Banks was suspicious of Vancouver and warned Menzies by writing "How Capt Van will behave to you is more than I can guess unless I was to judge by his Conduct towards me which was not such as I am used to receive from Persons in his situation" (Lamb, 1992:9). Banks directed Menzies to keep a journal along with all specimens collected, but also warned him that it would be imprudent of Vancouver to put obstacles in his way, but "I trust he will have too much good sense to destruct it if he does the instances whatever they are will of course appear as they happened in your Journal which as it will be a justification of you will afford ground for impeaching the propriety of his conduct which for your sake I shall not Fail to make use of" (Lamb, 1992:10). Even though there were these differences prior to departure, and some minor problems over messing arrangements for Menzies, the early part of the voyage seems to have gone well. In fact, when he became sick, Vancouver chose Menzies rather than Cranstoun to act as his personal physician (Lamb, 1992:10).

Outside of the disputes described above, Vancouver and Menzies seem to have had a mutual respect for each others' expertise. Menzies, Vancouver's senior by three years, had already spent several years at sea, and proved to be a very competent surgeon and physician. With his medical training, Menzies probably understood that Vancouver was in poor health, and that the burden of enforcing discipline among 145 men for four years, may have pushed the captain to his emotional limits.

The Vessel and Crew

The *Discovery's* overall length was 99' 2" with a breadth of 28' 3". The space between decks was 6' 2". The hull was sheathed with planks and covered with sheets of copper for protection. When fully loaded, the ship drew 15' 6". The *Chatham*, on the other hand, was only 53' long on the keel, 21' 6" wide and was rated at 131 tons compared to the *Discovery* 330 tons (Vancouver, 1798(1984):36-37).

Throughout the voyage, the officers and crew lived in very restricted quarters, working closely with each other every day for four years. Among the crew, the Lieutenants were Mudge, Puget and Baker while Whidbey was the Master. As mentioned earlier, these men had served with Vancouver during their early days in the navy. There were sixteen marines, and the rest were midshipmen, crew and seamen. The full complement of the *Discovery* was one hundred men. The smaller *Chatham* was originally under the command of Lieutenant W. R. Broughton, and James Hanson was the Lieutenant with Johnstone as the Master. There were forty-two other crew members including eight marines (Vancouver, 1798(1984):279-80). One must remember that much of the room on the ships was used for storage, armament, sails and work areas, leaving little room for living quarters (Vancouver, 1798(1984):34). The ventilation on the lower decks was very bad, and at times the odors became unbearable. Occasionally, Vancouver ordered the living areas washed down with vinegar, and smudge fires set to clear the air.

During the survey, it became obvious that the two larger vessels were not suitable for exploring the intricate inside waterways of the Northwest Coast. The usual procedure was to locate a secure anchorage for the *Discovery* and *Chatham*, and then send out small boats for the actual reconnaissance. Normally, the boats were provisioned for two weeks, after which time they returned to the ships to resupply. The smaller boats—the launch, cutters and yawls—had both sails and oars, but in many places the entire survey was carried out by rowing. These small boats, with a crew of twelve or fifteen, were vulnerable to attack by the Indians, who were well equipped with firearms, telescopes and metal weapons.

The 1792-1793 Survey

The *Discovery* and *Chatham* set out from Falmouth, England, on April 1, 1791. After stopping by the Canary Islands and the Cape of Good Hope, they continued on to Australia, New Zealand, Tahiti and Hawaii. They spent the first half of March, 1792 in Hawaii, and on the 16th of that month, departed for the Northwest Coast. Land was sighted on April 18th about 110 miles north of San Francisco (Anderson, 1960:69).

From May 1 to August 19, 1792, they conducted boat surveys of Puget Sound, Port Orchard, the Gulf of Georgia and Johnstone Strait up to Queen Charlotte Sound. Menzies spent much of the season in the boat surveys studying the plants and animals of the area (Anderson, 1960:94-96).

On August 28th, the *Discovery* and *Chatham* dropped anchor at Friendly Cove in Nootka Sound where they were enthusiastically welcomed by the Spanish Naval Commander of San Blas, Mexico, Don Juan Francisco de la Bodega y Quadra. He had been designated the official representative of the Viceroy of New Spain, Don Juan Vicente de Guemes Pacheco de Pedilla, Count of Revilla Gigedo. With his gracious hospitality, the Spanish Commander won the friendship and respect of Vancouver and his officers (Anderson, 1960:97-100). In the following year, Vancouver named a large island in Southeastern Alaska Revilla Gigedo (Revillagigedo Island) in honor of the Viceroy.

While at Nootka, Menzies was appointed surgeon for the *Discovery*, replacing Alexander Cranstoun who been ill for some time and had requested to be sent home aboard the supply ship the *Daedalus* (Anderson, 1960:113). In mid-October, the two ships began their journey south to investigate the mouth of the Columbia River. They proceeded on to California and Hawaii, and remained there from February 22 to the end of March, 1793 (Anderson, 1960:114,152).

The plan for 1793 was to continue the survey from where they had left off in August of the previous year. After stopping off in Nootka Sound, the *Discovery* joined the *Chatham* in late May at Restoration Cove in Burke Channel in British Columbia. They explored Milbanke Sound by boat, and then continued northward. In July, the ships were met by Captain Brown with his three vessels, the *Butterworth*, the *Prince Lee Boo*, and the *Jackal*. The Captain directed them to a safe anchorage later named Observatory Inlet (Anderson, 1960:152-159). (See Maps 1 and 2.) Since the present work focuses on Menzies' travels through Alaska, the accounts of the survey along the coast of British Columbia, Canada, have not been included.

Menzies' Journal:
Its Composition and Botanical Collections

For the most part, Menzies' handwriting is very legible. There are a few difficulties in transcribing the text due to his personal writing style and the customs of the eighteenth century writers. Spelling was not as fixed as it is today, and so there are occasional variations in the spelling of the same term and some spellings have changed over the past 200 years. In his journal, for instance, Menzies writes the word "examined" as "examind," "examin'd," "examinid," and "examined." Dr. Lamb also notes that Menzies repeatedly spells the name of the vessel *Butterworth* as *Buttersworth*. Menzies also capitalizes in a rather erratic manner, sometimes capitalizing in mid-sentence a word which today would be in the lower case. His formation of the letter "C" varies in size so that at times it is uncertain whether or not he meant the word to be capitalized. His punctuation does not always follow the modern style and some of his words appear with superscript letters. A few terms in the journal are no longer in use or were peculiar to mariners of his day. Menzies underlined words in his journal to add emphasis or note Latin names. Those words have been italicized in this volume.

In his 1923 edition of Menzies' journal, Dr. Newcombe (1923: 132-152) included an Appendix of "Plants Collected by A. Menzies on the North-West Coast of America." It is subdivided into lists of ferns and flowering plants, mosses, lichens and marine algae. Dr. Newcombe attempted to reconcile, as best he could, the journal entries and the specimens in the collection, but he had only limited success in his efforts. Over the past 20 years, Eric Groves, now retired from the Botany Department of the Natural History Museum in London, has searched out information regarding Menzies' non-lichen specimens which he collected on this voyage. Groves (1992:3-4), states with regard to specimens collected by Menzies on his 1786-88 voyage with Colnett that:

> There exists no complete roster of plants collected for the whole of this voyage (or indeed for that of Vancouver which will be dealt with later). What dried material has survived is scattered throughout the cabinets of at least three major herbaria...The label accompanying each specimen gives the clue as to its provenance but unfortunately not all possess precise data...There still remains a number of such plants that bear no further detail than 'West Coast of North America.'

During the first season with Vancouver, as they traveled around the world past the Cape of Good Hope and on to Australia, New Zealand and to the Northwest Coast, Menzies collected and recorded many plants. His journal for this period lists many plants including 30 trees and shrubs (Groves, 1992:10; Newcombe, 1923:49). In the 1793 season, Menzies continued to collect specimens and mentions some of them in his journal. During the final season in Alaskan waters during the summer of 1794, only a relatively few plants are noted in the journal. It may be that since he had already noted certain species either on his 1778 voyage with Colnett, or during the earlier part of the survey of the Northwest Coast, that Menzies decided not to list the same plants in his journal for Alaska. Groves (Personal Communication) is continuing his search for specimens from Menzies' collections on the Northwest Coast, but finds it difficult to try and piece together the journal reports, the remaining specimens and their provenance. The many specimens collected by Menzies are now stored in the major herbaria of the British Museum, Kew, Edinburgh and the Linnean Society. There are smaller collections at Oxford, Cambridge, Manchester and Liverpool (Groves, 1992:25). It may be impossible now to determine precisely which plants Menzies collected in Alaska, or if plants are from Alaska, whether they were gathered during his voyage with Colnett or Vancouver.

There appear to be some discrepancies with the collections themselves. For instance, Dr. Newcombe (1923:146) says "Much doubt is felt however, as to the authenticity of some of the localities given for Menzies' plants." He indicates that the collection records state that the specimens were collected by Menzies in "Behrings' Straits." But as Newcombe (1923:146) goes on to say, "No evidence has come to light that he collected anywhere near Behring's Straits and Nelson's plants may have become mixed with his."

Faced with these difficulties, Dr. John F. Thilenius went through the journal entries for the 1793 and 1794 seasons in Alaska and researched every taxon. His work has been incorporated here as an Appendix of Botanical Collections. Dr. Thilenius was unable to examine the actual specimens, so in some instances he made an educated guess concerning the plant which Menzies mentions. Eric Groves, through his continuing research on Menzies' collection, has been able to supplement the information contained in the journal itself. In his 1992 paper, he shows how it may be possible to identify which plants may have been collected at certain times by Menzies. For example:

> When the ships were at their last NW anchorage of the third season in Ship Cove, Port Conclusion, Menzies

botanized in the neighbourhood. On the 2 August he walked through some of the forest on the sides of the adjacent hills. He met here and there with swamps and clear spots. Of his dried specimens extant only three can be attributable to his Port Conclusion stay and possibly to this particular day's excursion. These are the Fringed Grass-of-Parnassus *Parnassia fimbriata* and two louseworts *Pedicularis palustris var.wlassoviana* and *P. menziesii* all from damp areas (Groves, 1992:21).

Since Dr. Thilenius researched only those plants actually mentioned in the journal, the other plants listed by Groves have not been included in the Appendix.

Descriptions of the Native People and Their Languages

During the 1793 season, the expedition traveled among three Indian groups, the Tsimshian, the Tlingit and the Haida. The Tsimshian lived in northern British Columbia and were neighbors to both the Haida and Tlingit. In the Tsimshian stories recorded by Barbeau and Beynon (1987), there are many accounts of trade and warfare between the Tsimshian and Tlingit. There appears to have been a special relationship between the Tsimshian and the Tlingit of the Stikine River. One story (Barbeau and Benyon, 1987:187-190) tells of the Tsimshian joining with the Stikine Tlingit to attack the Tlingit of Sitka. A famous leaders of the Stikine Tlingit was Chief Shakes. The oral tradition is that the name *Shakes* (variants, *Saiks*, *Ceks*) is a Tsimshian name taken by a great Tlingit spokesman. In one of the stories collected by Barbeau and Beynon (1987:189), Chief Shakes reportedly used Tsimshian expressions to direct his warriors. The name Shakes has remained in use among the Tlingit to the present time. An elderly, knowledgeable Tlingit, Mrs. Cecilia Kunz (personal communication), said that Tlingit often used Tsimshian words, in spite of the fact the two languages are actually from different language families.

During the late 1700s, the Haida Indians were expanding northward into what is now Southeastern Alaska from their homeland in the Queen Charlotte Islands. Some eventually settled on the eastern shore of Prince of Wales Island at the site of the village of Old Kasaan. Vancouver apparently met these Haida when he anchored in Port Stewart. As with the Tsimshian, the Tlingit traded and fought with the Haida.

The 1794 survey began in Cook Inlet where they met Aleut, Eskimos and Tanaina Athabaskan Indians. Afterwards, when the expedition moved to Prince William Sound, they were again in Eskimo territory. But, by this time, the Russians had established bases in this area and were using both Eskimos and Aleuts as hunters. The Eyak Indians lived just to the east of Prince William Sound, but there is no indication that the surveyors met with the Eyak.

As they proceeded southward to Port Mulgrave, the present site of Yakutat, they moved into Tlingit territory for the remainder of their last summer of exploration.

From the descriptions given by Menzies and Vancouver, it is difficult to determine whether the people they described at any one time were Indians, Eskimos or Aleuts. For example, among the Eskimo, both men and women wore lip plugs or labrets. With the Tanaina and Tlingit, women used the labret. Eskimos, Aleuts, Tanaina and Tlingits all made skin boats (Osgood, 1937; de Laguna, 1972). Even the spruce root baskets of the Chugach Eskimos are quite similar to those produced by the Tlingit Indians. And so, the question of whether the people were Indians or Eskimos cannot be ascertained from the descriptions of their appearance or technology.

In some cases, Eskimos, Eyak and Tlingit inhabited specific territories, so when we know the exact place the boats were at a given time, we can be quite sure which people they had met. Languages are usually the principal indicators of ethnic identity. As they traveled through these various groups, the Native terms recorded reflect the linguistic variations of each area. The translation of the Native terms or expressions entails a myriad of problems. One basic question is how to relate the written form of the word to sounds actually spoken. Menzies and Vancouver were recording the words as they heard them based on the English sound system. But English has several sounds not used in Tlingit,

Haida or Tsimshian, and those languages have sounds that are foreign to speakers of English. When they heard entirely new sounds and words, they recorded them as best they could, but since they were not trained linguists, it is oftentimes uncertain what the Natives said.

Beyond the written record of the terms, many other factors are unknown. For example, what language were the Natives speaking? Were they speaking their own tongue, or what they thought was English, French or Spanish as they had heard it from traders? They might even have been speaking some words in the Chinook Jargon—a trade language used on the Northwest Coast. However, Dr. Dale Kinkade, Professor of Linguistics at the University of British Columbia (personal communication, 1992) says that "Chinook jargon seems an unlikely source for anything in Ketchikan in 1794." From all indications, Professor Kinkade is correct although the Chinook Jargon was later used is some parts of Alaska, perhaps as early as 1800. To make matters even more complicated, the Indians may have been speaking a combination of all these tongues. Vancouver (1798(1984):994,998) mentions, for instance, that the Indians frequently used the words *Winnee watter* when they wanted to trade, and that if the ship did not trade, they cried out *Pusee* and *Peshack* as terms of disapproval. It is possible that the Indians were trying to repeat some English expression which they had heard the traders call out when they first met the Natives. Mrs. Gertrude Johnson (personal communication), a Tsimshian, suggested that *watter* may have been the Tsimshian expression *wa'da* meaning "trade." The Chinook Jargon did have an expression like "wawa" meaning to talk or speak (Shaw, 1909:29). The Tlingit language has no frontal sounds like those in English written as "p" or "b," but in the Chinook tongue, *Pasese* or *Paseesie* means "a blanket or woolen cloth," and *Peshak* means "bad," so if they were using Chinook they may have been indicating they wanted blankets or woolen cloth and that refusing to trade was "bad" (Shaw, 1909).

A peculiar problem arises when the expedition approached the Nass River and later met an important person from the Stikine River. In both cases, Vancouver (1798(1984):985) mentions that the people used the term *Ewen*, for example, *Ewen Nass*. Vancouver then says that "The word *Ewen* we understood to signify great, or powerful; as *Ewen Smoket*, a great chief." According to David and Annabelle Peele who are speakers of Haida (personal communication), the modifier *u-en* means large or great. The Tlingit word for "large, great" is *tlein*. But in Tlingit grammar, an adjective such as this always follows the noun, so their expression would have been *Naas-tlein*. In Tsimshian, the expression *u-i* is sometimes used to indicate "great, important." For instance, in referring to Chief Shakes, his name is always given as "We [*u-i*] Shakes" (Keithahn, 1981:5). According to Mrs. Gertrude Johnson, the expression *u-i* is used to indicate honor and importance. And so, even though the people were undoubtedly Tlingit and Nass is a Tlingit name, it seems that they were using combinations of Haida and Tsimshian expressions as well to describe themselves or communicate with the explorers.

With all of these uncertainties, the translation of any of the Indian terms is only an approximation at best and in many cases, all we can do is to guess its meaning.

History of Menzies' Manuscript

Lamb's 1992 paper gives an excellent summary of the events surrounding Menzies journal and the following information has been gleaned from his presentation.

Menzies did not know at the outset that the Admiralty had instructed Vancouver to impound all journals and logs prepared by "the officers, petty officers and gentlemen on board the *Discovery*." He became concerned about this on the final portion of the voyage and wrote to Banks on April 28, 1795 "…when the Journals of the Voyage &c. are demanded by Captain Vancouver, I mean to seal up mine, & address them to you, so that I hope you will receive them" (Lamb, 1992:13). Matters turned worse once the plant frame had been left open and the rain damaged the plants. There was a heated exchange between Vancouver and Menzies, and Vancouver accused Menzies of having treated him with "great contempt and disrespect" and asked that Menzies be tried by court martial. Menzies wrote a letter to Banks giving his interpretation of the events and said that he had:

cooly & without either *insolence* or *contempt* complained
to Captain Vancouver of being unjustly used in this
proceeding. He immediately flew in a rage, and his
passionate behaviour, and abusive language on the
occasion, prevented any further explanation - and I was
put under Arrest, because I would not retract my expression, while my grievance still remained unredressed
(Lamb, 1992:13).

According to Speck(1970:149), Menzies later apologized and
Vancouver dropped the charges, and they reached a reconcilia-
tion.

As to the journals, Menzies replied to Vancouver's order that he
turn them over, that:

I have received your Order of this day's date, Addressed
to me as Surgeon of His Majesty's Sloop *Discovery*:
demanding my Journals, Charts, drawings etc of the
voyage, but I can assure you that, in that capacity, I kept
no other Journals than the Sickbook which is ready to be
delivered if you think this is necessary.... I therefore beg
leave to acquaint you that I do not conceive myself
authorized to deliver these Journals etc. to anyone till
they are demanded of me, by the Secretary of State for
the home department, agreeable to the tenor of my
instructions (Lamb, 1992:14).

It appears that after March, 1796, when Vancouver was ordered to prepare his journal for publication, he learned that there
was a scheme to include Menzie's journals in the project just as
Banks' journal had been included in Cook's report. Vancouver
countered this proposal by saying that Menzies' report should not
be included, nor should he share in any profits from the publication. He wrote to the Earl of Chatham, the First Lord of the
Admiralty telling him that since Menzies had been amply paid for
his work, the results of his efforts were the property of the
government (Lamb, 1992:17). Vancouver's protest was successful,
and it appears that Banks then wanted to have Menzies complete

his journal and rush it to publication before Vancouver could complete his own account (Lamb, 1992:13).

On September 14, 1795, Menzies wrote to Banks that:

> I am present hard at work, in bringing the clean copy of my Journal of the Voyage, & I am much affraid, I shall require the indulgence of a few months after I get back home to have it compleated; as I am but a very slow hand at the pen, & our constant & frequent movements during the Voyage, took up much of my time on Shore, in examining the different countries we visited (Vancouver, 1798(1984):1631-32).

But Menzies needed an income, and so he resumed his service with the Navy and served aboard the *Princess Augusta*, while at the same time continuing to work on a "clean copy" or copy ready for publication, based on his original notes. On January 3, 1798, Menzies wrote to Banks saying:

> I received your kind letter this morning and return my sincerest thanks for your kindly admonitions & solicitations respecting the finishing of my Journal before Captain Vancouver's is published. It is what I most ardently wish, for more reasons than one, and therefore have lately applied to it very close. - I generally get up at five in the morning and continue at it, with as little interruption as possible till six or seven in the evening daily. The volume I am now at work upon (and which is nearly finished) I once thought would include the whole of the remainder of the Narrative, but I find' it will not, though it is much larger than either of those you have got. A desire of making it a full and continued narrative of the Voyage and my being but a slow hand at the pen, are the principal reasons for it taking so much of my time in finishing, but the most fagging part of it is nearly over, and can assure you that I will continue with unremitting application until the whole is accomplished (Lamb, 1992,18).

After Vancouver's death on May 12, 1798, his brother John, who had been helping him, completed his manuscript and *A Voyage of Discovery* was published in the fall of 1798. It now appears that when Menzies failed to publish a journal before Vancouver, that the relationship between Banks and Menzies began to cool. Apparently they gave up their plans to publish Menzies' account. Banks had in his possession at least three of Menzies' journals which recorded his activities up to February 16, 1794 (Lamb, 1992:19). This, then, accounts for the fact that only three of the four volumes of Menzies' journal were among Banks' papers when he died in 1820. They remained as part of Bank's estate until they were sold at Sotheby's in 1886. The three volumes were purchased by the British Museum and are now classified as Add. Ms. 32641 in the Manuscript Department of the British Library (Lamb, 1992:19).

When Menzies returned from his duties as surgeon aboard the *Sans Pareil* in 1802, he was in ill health. Evidently he kept the final portion of his journal. It is not clear what happened to the manuscript after his death in 1842. In 1875, George Robertson, a publisher in Melbourne, Australia, hired Augustus Petherick to go to London to buy books and manuscripts related to the history and exploration of Australia and New Zealand. Petherick obtained a copy of the final volume of Menzies' journal which covers the last year of the voyage. In 1909, Petherick's collection went to the National Library of Australia, and this is where the final portion of Menzies' journal is kept today (Lamb, 1992:21).

According to Lamb (1992) many people have commented on the paucity of botanical material in Menzies' journal, particularly in the latter years. More than likely, in addition to his journal, Menzies kept other notes regarding his botanical collections and activities. He may have planned to publish a separate botanical report and limit his journal to an account of the voyage, much as Banks had done for his voyage with Captain Cook.

Although Menzie's journal may be limited in botanical information, it is an important contribution to the ethnological and historical record of the Northwest Coast and Alaska.

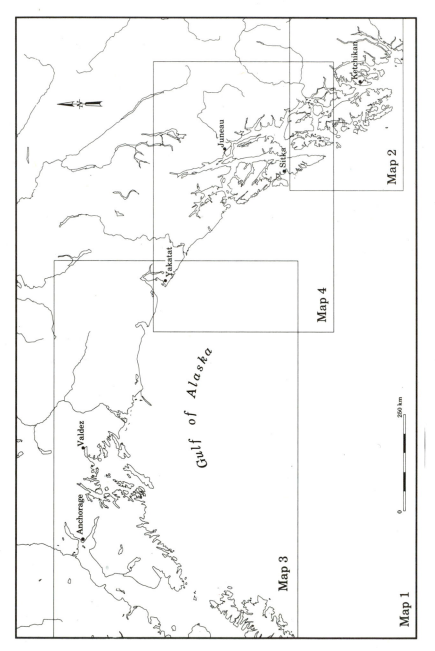

Map of area surveyed in Alaska by Captain George Vancouver.

Menzies' Journal 1793*

Synopsis

After returning to the Northwest Coast and Nootka in 1793, Vancouver resumed his survey of the British Columbia coast on May 29th. They began at Burke Channel and continued northward to Bentinck Arm, Milbanke Sound and Bank's Island. After two months, they had worked their way up to a point about twenty nautical miles west of the present city of Prince Rupert, British Columbia. According to Vancouver's Journal (1798(1984):983) on Sunday July 21st, the ships had passed to the west of Porcher and Stephen Islands. Menzies' Journal begins now as they approached the Tree Nob Island area. (See Map 2.)

---

*(Transcript of the original in the British Library, folios 330-354.)

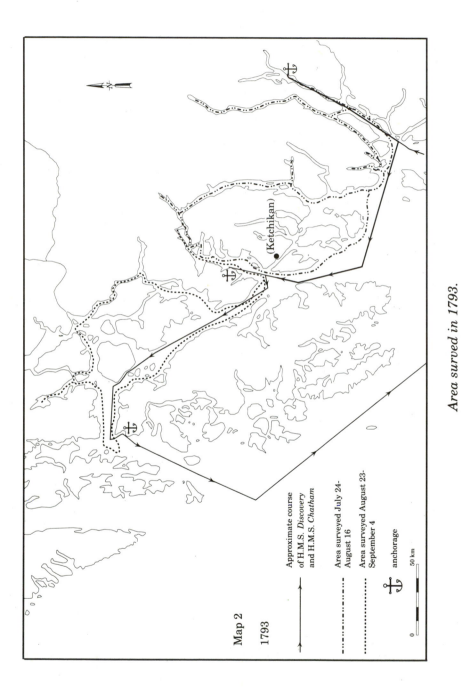

(Ketchikan)

Map 2
1793

Approximate course
of H.M.S. *Discovery*
and H.M.S. *Chatham*

Area surveyed July 24-
August 16

Area surveyed August 23-
September 4

anchorage

0   50 km

Area surved in 1793.

[July, 1793]

20th The shore to the Eastward of us was now become more rugged & dreary & more numerously interspersd with naked rocky islets, we passed a cluster of these about a league from the shore which gave us but a very indifferent idea of the safety of the Navigation, especially in such thick weather which had the appearance of becoming even more unfavorable & tempestuous, and though we were nearly abreast of the opening which Mr. Whidbey had explord with the Boats yet we could not make it out distinctly; In this state of dubiousness & apparent danger we were about putting our head to the Southward to stand back the way we came to have more sea room, when a Whale Boat was seen rowing towards us from the eastern shore, we immediately brought to, to give her time to join us, which she soon accomplished, when we found that she belongd to the Ship Buttersworth, which with her two Tenders the Jackall & Prince Lee Boo were then at anchor within a range of the Islands to the North East of us, where we were assurd by the Gentleman that came in the Boat there was good shelter from the storm that threaten'd, & he very kindly offering to conduct us in by the safest Channel, his good offices were accepted of & in about two hours after, we both anchord close to these Vessels,[1] when we were saluted by the Buttersworth by seven Guns for which Compliment we returnd five; Thus were we reliev'd from our state of anxiety & embarrassment through the friendly attention of Mr. Brown Commander of the Buttersworth in sending his Boat to our assistance the moment he observd us, & which was the more pleasing as we by this means shunned a strong gale which blew in the night time from the South east accompanied with rain & dirty weather.[2]

---

1. Dr. Lamb calculates, from the information in Vancouver's journal, that the ships were anchored at Rushton Island (Vancouver, 1798(1984):983 footnote).

2. Howay (1973) Lists the following ships as trading on the Northwest Coast in 1793. Some of these vessels were trading in what is now Southeastern Alaska. *Amelia* (American), *Butterworth, Prince Lee Boo, Jackal* (under Captain Brown, British), *L'Emilie* (French), *Hancock* (American), *Iphigenia* (Portuguese), *Jane* (American), *Jefferson* (American), *La Flavie* (French), *Margaret* (American), *Prince William Henry* (British), *Resolution* (American), *Three Brothers* (British), *Lady Washington* (American). The presence of these ships in the region explains why so many trade goods were found among the Indians at this time.

The part of our examination we were now entering on was very interesting Being according to the modern Spanish Charts about the entrance of the *Straits of De Fonta*[3] which from the incoherent accounts that have been given of it in former times, has been treated by some Geographers either as a forgery or a fabulous story, while others have strenuously endeavourd by collateral circumstances to give it a probable degree of authenticity; And we find the Spaniard who visited this part of the Coast so late as last Year in the Frigate Aranzazu under the Command of Lt Commaño, put so much credit in this ancient discovery that they mark it down in their Chart of this part of the Country a very conspicuous Channel under that name, which they tracd as far as 55 ½° N. & where they left off the Channels continued running Inland without any apparent signs of termination.

As Mr. Brown's Vessels had been employd a great part of this summer in collecting Furs through this interior part of the Country, we eagerly enquird of him & his Officers about the appearance & extent of the interior inlets, & their information not only corroborated the accounts we had from the Spaniards at Nootka that this part of the Country much intersected with spacious Channels apparently penetrating to a considerable distance inland, but their Vessels being smaller they pursued these Channels further than the Spaniards in different directions; One of the Tenders had pursued a Channel to the Northwestward as far as Latitude of 56° 20' N. where through a wide opening they had sight of the Ocean: This information was so far interesting to us, that to whatever distance we might be led inland, it was pleasing to know, we should find a passage out to Sea so far to the Northward.

About 8 or 9 leagues NNE of our present situation they found several large Channels branching inland, one of these which went about North by East they said the Natives called *Nass*[4] & always

---

3. Supposed entrance to the Northwest Passage.

4. The Nass River was a meeting place for the Tsimshian, Haida and Tlingit Indians, especially during the times when the Eulachon, or "candlefish" runs occurred. The oil from this fish was so highly prized for food and as a trade item, that some Natives refer to it as "liquid gold." Some of the Tlingit Raven stories speak of the creature at the "head of the Nass" who kept the sun and moon in boxes. According to Cecilia Kunz (personal communication), the word *Nass* is

spoke of it as leading to a very remote distance, up which they
often made Voyages in their Canoes that took them two or three
Moons to perform: This information greatly excited our curiosity
more especially as the informants had an opportunity from their
trafic & intercourse with the Natives to become so far acquainted
with their manners & language that they were confident they
perfectly understood their meaning in this particular; & that we
might not be at a loss in finding out this great Nass, Mr. Brown
was so obliging as to send with us next day one of his Tenders the
Prince Lee Boo to point it out to us.

The Buttersworth had lately got upon some Rocks where she
receivd considerable damage which they were now repairing &
refitting her & the other Vessels for quitting the Coast & proceeding with their Cargo of Furs to China; Mr. Brown himself informd
us that they had collected upwards of three thousand Sea Otter
Skins chiefly about this part of the Coast & might have collected
a great many more had they proper articles of trade to purchase
them but they traded till they consumd the Articles which took
best amongst the Natives & were now obligd to leave them.

21st In the forenoon of the 21st the weather became fair but cloudy
with the wind from the South West quarter. At eleven we both
weighd & quitted our Anchorage which was well shelterd by a
surrounding group of Islands which I believe obtaind the name of
Brown's Islands, we were accompanied by the Prince Lee Boo who
was directed to go a head & we followd her to the Northward; We
were nearly abreast of the place where Mr. Whidbey left off the
Continental shore in his last boats cruize & as we got in with it,
he landed occasionally in a boat to take the necessary bearings as
we saild along the shore to the Northward with a pleasant light
breeze Our Latitude at noon was 54° 16' N. and we soon after got
into a wide sea of some leagues across; Towards evening we enterd

a Tlingit term referring to the stomach. Naish and Storey (1976:47) only give
one word similar to "Nass" and it is the term *naasi*, meaning "intestine." In a
footnote in Vancouver's Journal (1798(1984):985) Dr. Lamb mentions that
Archdeacon Collinson, who was well acquainted with the languages of this
area, says that it is a Tlingit word meaning "stomach." The term may have been
derived from the fact that at the mouth of the Nass there are many winding
channels, convoluted like intestines.

the Channel which the Natives had pointed out as leading to *Nass* & a little after dusk anchord under a small Island close to the eastern shore about two leagues up.[5]

At the entrance of this Channel we passed an opening leading to the South east ward in which one of Mr. Brown's Tenders found a considerable Village situated like a Fortress[6] upon the summit of a projecting Rock about two leagues up, the Inhabitants of which were so turbulent & daring in their insults, that they found it necessary to cannonade their Village in order to repress their conduct.

We brought the continental shore to this opening & its Mountains here assumd a less rugged appearance than what we had lately been accustom'd to view, no beds of Torrents or rude precipices interrupted the gradual ascent which was every where cloth'd with an even & continued surface of Pinery to the very summits of the Mountains.

Having no further occasion for the Prince Lee Boo she was dismiss'd to rejoin the Buttersworth & as they were immediately to proceed to Canton in China we embracd the opportunity of sending Letters by her to be forwarded from thence to England to acquaint Government with our progress in this intricate scene of operation which on the part of the Officers & Men requir'd no small degree of fortitude & perseverance to encounter.

22nd Early in the morning we weighd & stood up a Channel between two & three miles wide steering about North half East with a moderate breeze from South West & pleasant weather. The Island we anchord under on the preceeding evening was computed to be in the Latitude of 54° 47' N. & Longitude 229° 48' E. after passing an opening on the eastern shore We at Noon observ'd in Latitude 54° 58' N & soon after we found the Arm divide on each

---

5. Vancouver's charts which accompany his journal show his course and nearly all of the places they anchored.

6. Along the Northwest Coast, and particularly among the Tlingit, there were several fortified and safe places. Later the boat surveys reported seeing several of these abandoned forts. The Tlingit term *nu* (sometimes written *noo*) means a safe place, and is also used to indicate a fortified settlement. The number of forts observed is an indication of the warfare and raiding that was common in this region at this time.

side sending a branch to the Northwestward & another to the eastward; from this last we had a strong current in ripplings & whirlpools, & its water was remarkably pale and brakish joining with that in the main arm in muddy patches. We enterd this Eastern Arm[7] & brought to while a boat was sent to examine a Bay on the north shore for Anchorage, but not finding a situation sufficiently eligible we stood on again in the main arm leading to the Northward which still preservd nearly the same direction.[8]

Having but a light breeze from the Southward in the afternoon we were baffled in our progress by what we conceivd to be the meeting of two Tides which often deprivd the helm of its due influence on the Vessel. We continued under Sail till about dusk when we anchord on the east shore for the night which was calm & fair. As we were quitting the eastern opening three Canoes came out to us containing about a dozen of Men,[9] who appeard stout & robust & had an air of confidence in approaching us that would indicate they were not unaccustom'd to such Visitants; several of them were dress'd in European Cloaths & had their Spears pointed with iron:[10] Their Canoes were shap'd like those we saw behind Banks's Isles. - We had this day run about ten leagues in the direction of North half East by Compass, & as we advancd in the afternoon the Mountains on both sides became more dreary & rugged, apparently compsd of huge barren rocks with stinted Pines issuing from the Crevices thinly scatterd, &

---

7. Portland Inlet, named after the Bentinck family, the Dukes of Portland.

8. They were entering Observatory Inlet.

9. This area is the historic boundary between the Tsimshian and Tlingit Indians.

10. The presence of iron among the Indians of the Northwest Coast has prompted some controversy among scholars. Many suggest that the Natives obtained iron from shipwrecks while others say it was spread through trade. There is no doubt, however, that soon after contact with Europeans, many Indians had iron weapons. In his diary of 1792, the Spanish explorer Caamaño comments "Everyone carries a sheath knife slung around the neck. This is a well sharpened dagger, consisting of a blade some twelve inches long and four in width...These knives were so well fashioned and finished, that at first I felt sure they were not of native manufacture, but later I found that the Indians make them themselves quite easily from the iron they obtain by barter, heating it in the fire and forging it by beating it with stones in the water" (Wagner, 1938: 203).

towards the summits quite destitute of Vegetation & in many places cover'd with snow.[11]

23rd As it was not intended to go higher up the Arm with the Vessels until it was further explor'd, a boat was sent on the morning of the 23d to search for a harbour for them to remain in with a proper situation for erecting the Observatory to ascertain the rate of the Time keepers & having found a convenient place in a small Bay surrounded with a fine beach on the opposite shore, we immediately remov'd thither with both Vessels & Moor'd.[12] - This being about the beginning of the Spawning season for the Salmon on this Coast, a stream of fresh water that emptied into the bay swarm'd with them, though there was scarcely water sufficient to cover them, so that they could be caught with the hand in any quantity we chose; in shooting the Seine across the entrance of this Stream it surrounded such a prodigious quantity of these Salmon that it was impossible to haul them all on shore without endangering the Seine, they therefore took what quantity they pleas'd & sufferd the rest to escape:[13] A few Natives who were employd in catching Salmon on this Stream left the place in a Canoe when they saw us come into the Bay without coming near us. In the middle of the day the Thermometer was at 61 degrees. About three in the afternoon Mr. Johnstone set off with two boats arm'd & victuall'd for ten day with orders to return back to the South east opening where he was to begin & explore that & the different openings & bays on the east side of the Channel, so as to trace the continental shore as far as the Vessels. The Markee & Observatory were sent on shore & erected together with the Astronomical Instruments & Time-keepers accompanied by a guard of four Marines under the Command of Mr. Whidbey, who was to carry on the Astronomical Observations & ascertain the rate of the Time-keepers by equal Altitudes.

---

11. The climate was probably much cooler than at present. The "little Ice Age" which began about 2500 years ago, was coming to a close.

12. The passageway was named Observatory Inlet and on his chart, Vancouver identifies "Salmon Cove."

13. In a footnote in Vancouver's journal (1798(1984)990), Lamb mentions that others in the expedition were amazed at the number of fish taken. One account says that in a single set of the seine, they captured 2,000 salmon.

24th Early on the morning of the 24th Capt. Vancouver set out with two boats well manned armed & victualled with a fortnights provision to explore and survey the Channel to the Northward of the Vessels; In this expedition he was accompanied in the Pinnace by Mr. Puget Commander of the Chatham, & as the inland direction of the Channel was likely to afford a variety of soil and situation favorable to my pursuits I embark'd in the Launch with Mr. Swaine who was accompanied by some of the Gentlemen viz the Honble Mr. Pitt & Mr. Sykes.

The morning was foggy & unfavorable when we left the Vessels but soon clear'd up, & we pursued the Channel to the Northward which preservd nearly the same direction as before, but soon became much wider & interspers'd with Islands cover'd with Pines. On the Eastern shore we saw a great Smoke & expected to meet some of the Natives, but on approaching it, we found the wood had been set on fire & saw nobody near it.

After going about ten miles we found the Channel divide, one branch winded round to the North east ward which we pursued about four leagues where it terminated in some low land[14] from which we were visited by a few Natives in two Canoes who were very urgent for our landing at their habitations, we however returnd back without stopping to the division of the Arm where we encampd for the night.

25th Early next morning we enterd the other Channel which at first was very narrow by what we found to be a long Island in mid-channel; we pursued it about ten Miles in a northerly direction, when we found it also terminate,[15] & returning back along the western shore of it we enterd a Creek opposite to the long Island, where a fine clear spot coverd with grass, encouragd us to pitch our Tents for the night in a situation we thought sufficiently secure by its elevation from the reach of the Tide, but in this we were mistaken, for in the night time it suddenly overflowd the place we reposd on, & obligd us to quit it in the utmost confusion.[16]

---

14. Alice Arm.

15. Hastings Arm.

16. Some waterways in this latitude have extreme tides that fluctuate from a +21 feet to -5 feet.

26th On the 26th we continued our return along the western shore which here formed a considerable track of low land wooded with Pines, & arrivd at the Vessels by noon after finishing what was expected from the report we had from Mr. Brown & his Officers to penetrate a great way inward; the information however was not to be discredited until all its branches were examin'd, those two we had just finish'd terminated about seven leagues beyond the situation of the Vessels. Having replenishd the two Boats with what provisions we had expended, so as to compleat our stock for a fortnight's allowance, we set out again after dinner to the southward along the western shore of the Channel, which was now presumd to be the continental shore, & after going about three leagues we brought to in a Sandy Cove for the Night which prov'd wet and uncomfortable.

27th We started again by the dawn of next day & soon reachd the north west opening which we had passed about noon on the 22d in the Vessels, & whose North point[17] as well as the eastern opening we then found to be exactly in the 55th degree of North Latitude.[18] We enterd this opening & followd it to the North west ward about five Miles, when we found it join into another Channel, running nearly parallel with the one we had quitted. At this juncture we fell in with a small party of the Natives whom we eagerly interrogated in the best manner we could about *Nass*, but all of them who seem'd to comprehend us pointed back the way we came to the eastern opening which was not yet examined, so that we had now little doubt of its laying in that direction to whatever extent it might run, & as it lay within the limits of Mr. Johnstone's orders we were equally confident that he would give a faithfull account of it as far as he could trace it in the boats. By prevailing on some of these Natives to repeat their numerals, we found they spoke a broken dialect of what we call the Woaganian language or that which is spoke along the Coast between Admiralty Bay & Queen

---

17. Point Ramsden, named for Jesse Ramsden who was a famous manufacturer of navigational instruments such as the sextants used by the expedition (Vancouver, 1798(1984:993).

18. This is the entrance to Portland Canal, the present boundary between the U.S. and Canada.

Charlotte's Isles, of which we had a short Vocabulary; On our reciting the numerals of Nepean's Sound & those of Queen Charlotte's Isles they perfectly understood both & pointed in the direction in which each were used.[19]

From this place we pursued the Channel[20] to the Northward which was found unbranchd & in general about a mile & half wide, running in a waving northerly direction between high rugged mountains whose summits were coverd with perpetual snow, while their sides were thinly scatterd with a forest of Pine trees; nearly opposite to the Vessels it bent its course towards the other Channel so as to be scarcely at that place five miles apart, yet a snowy ridge of Mountains of considerable height intervend.

We were this & the following four days employd in exploring this Channel which by an observation of Capt. Vancouver's with the quick silver horizon hear the head of it was found to terminate about the Latitude of 55° 45' N. that is about 40 miles to the Northward of where we enterd it.[21] In our return the last day we din'd in a small Creek on the Western shore, where in a fresh water brook we found the Salmon so plenty that we took what number we pleasd of them with our hands, they were so easily

---

19. Menzies was apparently adept at learning languages. One technique he used to identify a language was to have people count to ten. In this locality, he was at the juncture of the Tsimshian, Haida and Tlingit, all of whom speak entirely different languages. The Natives were correct in pointing towards the Queen Charlotte Islands in response to his counting in Haida. Menzies' term, *Woaganian* is somewhat puzzling because later on he says that it "implies friendship." He uses the term to identify Indians who live between Port Mulgrave (Yakutat) and the Queen Charlotte Islands, i.e. the Tlingit. There are several expressions which Menzies may have heard and recorded as "Woagan." One expression is "a'wu-a-kaan" meaning "in the middle," that is, people who are qualified to welcome or greet individuals on either side (Anna Katzeek, personal communication). Another possibility is that it comes from the Tlingit expression for deer, "guwakaan." (Cecilia Kunz, personal communication). The term for deer was used in peace making ceremonies for those who were go-betweens to formalize a peace treaty. A "guwakaan" was expected to be peaceful and friendly. The term may also be extended to mean a hostage. It may have been the Tlingit way of asking for a hostage while trading. It is possible that Menzies heard one of these greetings and recorded it as "Woagan," and used it as the name for the Tlingit people.

20. Portland Canal.

21. Site of the present town of Hyder, Alaska.

taken that many of them fall a prey to Eagles & to Bears Foxes & other Animals, as we found both sides of the Brook strewd with parts of them that appeard to be the Leavings of these Animals; They were of a different kind from the common English Salmon & by no means so well flavor'd, yet in our situation they afforded a seasonable & desirable refreshment of which we availd ourselves whenever we could meet with them.[22] - We saw no Natives up this Channel nor any thing else different from what has already been observ'd.

[In the manuscript, there is a small space here—Editor][23]

August 1st Having returnd the last evening in July to the place where we enterd the Channel, we encampd on the opposite shore, & the first morning of Augt being a little foggy we breakfasted before we set out as we were to enter on new ground in continuing the examination of the Channel to the south ward;[24] After it cleard up we continued rowing along the Western shore till about noon when our Latitude was 54° 55' North, at this time we came to a small narrow opening[25] out of which this Tide came so rapid that it baffled all our endeavours to enter it till the Tide slacken'd, & we then got up a small Creek leading to the northward about four Miles; While we were at dinner in this Creek, we were visited by two Canoes & five of the Natives from the head of it, who pressd us much to visit their habitations, & by their promising us Sea Otter Skins as an allurement, they seemd to be pretty well acquainted with what best suited Europeans of their commodi-

---

22. Menzies is very correct in his observation. The Atlantic salmon are of the genus *Salmo*, while the Pacific salmon are classed as *Onchorynchus*.

23. At this time, a discrepancy develops between Menzies' journal and that of Vancouver. What Vancouver has occurring on August 1st, for instance, Menzies has on the following day, August 2nd. This time difference continues until August 9th, at which time both journals give the same descriptions for the same date. The variations in the accounts may be partially due to the fact that Vancouver was compiling his record after his return to England, while Menzies was preparing his "clean copy" some time later, perhaps as much as three years after the events.

24. They now continued into Pearse Canal, the southern extension of Portland Canal. They passed to the north and west of Pearse and Wales Islands.

25. Hidden Inlet.

ties; as we saw several rillets at the head of the Creek we doubted
not but there was a small party employ'd in curing & drying fish
for winter store; On coming back to the narrow entrance of the
Creek we found the Tide rushing into it so rapid that we were
obligd to lay by till its strength abated & then pursued our
progress to the Southward passing a small Island at the entrance
of the Creek & after rowing about a league crossed over to the
eastern shore where we put up in a small Bay for the night; Soon
after we perceivd that we were followd by one of the Canoes that
visited us at dinner time with a chorus of women singing as the
approachd our encampment; They brought several Sea Otter
Skins which they sold to Captain Vancouver for blue Cloth, but
would not take Iron or Copper for them in any shape; All the
women had their lower lips pierc'd & stretch'd round oval pieces
of wood as already describ'd,[26] they staid in a Cove close by us all
night, & were very clamorous & noisy, being join'd by another
Canoe in the night time; they wanted to disturb us, all for the
purpose of traficing for their Furs.

2nd Next morning we found on board the Canoe which came in the
night time, a large fresh killed Bear, the whole party were anxious
to have it purchasd as an article of refreshment, but there being
no higher offers for it than a piece of blue cloth about the Value of
a Sea Otter Skin the Natives would not part with it for that price,
& they soon after parted with us, while we continued exploring to
the Southward: The Land now before us & on both sides was much
lower & not near so rugged & mountainous as we found it towards
the head of this long Arm, After going about a league & half from
our resting place we found the Channel divide sending a branch
off on each side, we enterd that going off to the westward which
was narrow & not above a league long when it joind in with a small

---

26. Apparently, the Tlingit women who came to trade wanted cloth rather than
metal tools. Since women made the clothing, they were probably more interested in what they could use rather than the metal which the men wanted for
tools. The lip ornament is known as a "labret" and was normally worn by the
upper class Tlingit women as a status symbol. Nearly every explorer who came
to this region commented on the effect that the labret had on the women's
appearance.

Arm running nearly parallel to the one we quitted,[27] in this we first turnd to the Northward among a cluster of Islands which occupied us a good part of the day, & among which we saw a great number of Sea Otters attending their young & gamboling about with them in the Water, hence it is probable that these Animals always visit the interior Channels to Cub & rear their young until they acquire strength sufficient to encounter the boisterous Ocean. After examining these Islands which render the head of this Arm very intricate we returnd back and continued our route to the South west ward in this small Arm which we found strewd with a number of Islands & rocky Islets. In the evening as we were following the starboard shore we came to a small opening going off to the Northward about a quarter of a mile wide & nine fathoms deep, the Launch which was at this time ahead, enterd it, & was drawing smoothly down towards a rapid fall when called back by Capt Vancouver who thought it unsafe to explore it, we however in the Launch did not see the danger so glaring, but should soon have plung'd into it, had we not been recalld just in time to recover ourselves from the impetuosity with which we were drawing towards it:[28] After passing this opening we found the Arm take a short turn to the Southward & join the Channel we quitted in the morning, which was here strewd with a numerous group of large & small Islands,[29] the adjacent country being of a very moderate height & densely wooded with Pines.

3rd After setting out on the morning of the 3d we found the shore we were following took a turn round to the westward by a narrow Channel on the inside of some Islands which soon brought us into a wide Sound of several miles across[30] strewd over with a number of Islands; A little way off the entrance of this Sound we saw a

27. They were traveling through Edward Passage into Fillmore Inlet.

28. The entrance to Willard Inlet which has extremely strong tidal currents and whirlpools.

29. They were traveling through Tongass and Sitklan Passages.

30. Vancouver named this feature Cape Fox in honor of the Right Honorable Charles James Fox (Vancouver, 1798(1984):1001).

naked group of rocky islets & the Shores are every where so lin'd with them that it requires the utmost caution to enter any of these Channels with large Vessels & indeed to attempt is scarcely at all advisable.

We turnd to the Northward up this Sound which we found soon narrowd & divided into a number of small Creeks in different directions interspersd with Islands, but the principal branch[31] was about a mile wide & went to the Northward about three leagues where it terminated among some low land; there were several Islets near the end of it & we saw some dogs on shore but no Natives; Having a good deal of thick foggy weather we were not able to finish the examination of this little Sound[32] till the afternoon of next day when we reachd an Island off the western point of it, on which we din'd.

We were now got as far to the Southward as the entrance of the Channel in which the Vessels lay,[33] & after all our laborious & fatiguing examination not above 4 or 5 leagues to the Westward of it, having trac'd one Channel near 70 miles besides the collateral branches - We considered the Island on which we now were in the Latitude of 54° 45' North. To the Westward of us was a very spacious & wide Channel running to the Northward,[34] but the Weather was so thick & foggy that we had no distinct view of its extent or western boundaries. After dinner finding the weather was not likely to clear up & that the situation we were in was not eligible for remaining all night being too much expos'd, we removd to the Continental Shore where we soon got a small Cove & pitchd our Tents; The trees here being small & stunted the wood was thin and easily penetrated had the Weather been favorable, but it continued foggy with rain all day. We found here plenty of the Ledum palustre[35] which was collected for tea, the Kalmia glauca, two new species of *Orchis* & a new species of *Ophrys*.

---

31. Nakat Inlet.

32. Nakat Bay.

33. Portland Inlet.

34. Revillagigdeo Channel.

35. See Appendix.

5th On the 5th though the weather was still foggy with rain we got away after breakfast with a light breeze in our favor along the continental shore which now trended about North by West true & appeard dreary rocky & indented, & having gone about nine or ten Miles under the disagreeable circumstances of rainy weather & thick fog which renderd our progress hazardous & doubtfull we at last found ourselves among a cluster of Islands[36] where the intervening Channels were full of danger from peeked[37] Rocks breakers & Shoals, on account of which & as the Weather was not likely to clear up we pitchd our Tents on one of these Islands for the night; We knew we were now in a large spacious Channel though from the thickness of the Weather we obtain but very imperfect glances of its opposite shores.

6th The weather being somewhat clearer & fairer we set off next morning by the dawn of day & we now had an opportunity of viewing the prospect around us; To the southward the eye glanc'd over a wide spacious sea to meet distant land & islands; To the westward the land appeard in general low & broken with some round hills & a ridge of mountains extended to the northward commencing nearly opposite to us about the Latitude of 55 degrees North; To the Northward the wide Channel seemd to terminate in various openings among low land.

Soon after our departure we enterd a Channel about a league from these Islands going off to the Eastward within the entrance of which Capt. Vancouver observd at noon for the Latitude & made it 55° 4' North. This Channel divided into several branches hemmed in on both sides by steep rugged heights coverd with patches of Snow;[38] These branches employd us this & the following

---

36. They had passed by the point of land which Vancouver named Foggy Point, and proceeded north across Very Inlet, probably camping on one of the Delong Islands.

37. "peaked."

38. They were entering Boca de Quadra, between Kah Shakes and Quadra points. Vancouver's journal gives a much more detailed account of the exploration of this inlet.

day in exploring during which the Weather was mostly favorable.[39]

8th On the morning of the 8th we came out of what we took to be Quadra's Sound by the Spaniards though differing from them a good deal in the Latitude of its entrance; We proceeded to the Northward & soon after went into another Arm leading to the North east ward, which took us up the whole of this day in examining & in which we staid for the night in a very indifferent situation.[40]

9th Early next morning we came out of the Arm & followd the continental shore to the Northward by a very narrow Channel with shallow water, though the low land that was seen three days ago & which we now found to be an Island; On getting on the Northern side of them a remarkable picturesque pinnacle presented itself to our view in mid-channel about two miles off, its appearance excited our curiosity & we directed our course towards it where we landed, kindled a fire & breakfasted at the bottom of it on a small flat sandy Island coverd with loose stones; from the middle of this a rugged spire or pinnacle rose to about 250 feet high on a base the diameter which did not exceed one fourth of its height, it was composd of dark porous rock much resembling Lava which seem'd to be intermix'd & cemented by Volcanic Dregs;[41] On the South side of it I enter'd a cavity where the rocks & stones which compos'd it were very loose & mix'd with red ochreous earth that bore evident marks of having undergone the action of fire, so that we had little doubt of this remarkable pinnacle being reared at some distant period by some volcanic evolution.

39. According to Vancouver, on the morning of August 7th, they had come out of Boca de Quadra and stopped at Slate Island. The southern point was named for a midshipman, Mr. Sykes, while the northern point was named after the Commissioner of Nootka and Commander of San Blas, Jose Manual de Alva (Vancouver, 1798(1984):1004).

40. They also explored Smeaton Bay.

41. Vancouver (1798(1984):1006) records that this "singular rock, which from its resemblance to the Light House off Plymouth, I called New Eddystone."

Here we were visited by three Canoes with a few Men in them but no Women from the eastern shore, they were very urgent for us to go to their Village where they promisd us we should get plenty of Furs; I got two or three of these Natives to repeat their Numerals which I found to be exactly the same with those I formerly collected at Cape Edgecumbe & Port Mulgrave & I also found that they understood those of Queen Charlotte's Isles & intermix'd many words of that language in their common conversations, but they knew nothing of the language spoke about Banks's Islands & Nepean's Sound; They called the pinnacle by the name of *Shekil*.[42] They behav'd quiet & peaceably till a little after our departure when we observd one of them hastily putting on his war dress & brandishing his Spear & Dagger on parting with the Pinnace, the cause of which conduct we were not able to account for as we could not find that any one of the party had given him the least offence, unless he might have taken umbrage on finding that we were not going to the Village, we however took no notice of it, but pursued our course for an Arm which opend to the North east of us, which we soon after enterd & having examin' it[43] we put up late at night in a small Creek where the Shores were so rocky as to be very difficult of access.

10th We came again into the large Channel on the morning of the 10th & though it was sometimes hazy we had the pinnacle in view, which made a very conspicuous appearance most part of the forenoon while we were making progress to the Northward. We breakfasted at the entrance of an opening[44] which we did not examine & passed another about noon when our Latitude was 56° 36 44' North. Captain Vancouver was now desirous of pushing forward to examine for a sea passage in case he should be obligd to bring the Vessels thus far, though from the paleness of the Water in both these Arms it was not probable that either of them went far; the Water too appeard whitish the whole way across the

---

42. Although the term the Tlingit used is uncertain, it may have been *shaa gil* meaning high mountain cliff, or high rock.

43. Rudyerd Bay.

44. Walker Cove.

large Arm which was in some places about a league wide so that the general opinion was that we should soon come to the termination of it. In the afternoon we went about four leagues & brought up in the evening near a point where the Arm took a turn to the North east & sent off a branch to the South West.[45]

11th Next morning we pursued the North East Channel for a little distance in order to form some judgment how far it was likely to run & in about two leagues we found it terminate near the Latitude of 56° North in a low marshy flat Country back'd at some distance by high mountains; Finding this to be the case we turnd back & enterd the South West branch where about noon when our Latitude was 55° 54' North we came to the remains of a large Village situated on a high rock projecting over the side of the Arm & well constructed to guard against any attack of a hostile tribe with their usual Weapons; We were at first puzzled to find the entrance to this fortress till we observd a Tree laid slant from the rock on the land side with notchd steps that led to a small portal capable only of admitting one person at a time, over which a scaffold was erected very well adapted to defend the entrance by a small party with their long spears; A considerable space was cleard behind this Village by cutting down large Trees for the purpose of building it & to afford a temporary situation for some scattering Huts for the Natives to live in while this laborious work was accomplishing; On one side of the Rock the houses were supported by Posts & floor'd over with cross spars; These Houses were built of logs of wood & were of a quadrangular figure raised six or eight feet high with a roof slanting to both sides; We saw laying by the Rock the remains of two broken Canoes, & the whole place was so filled with rubbish & filth & the stench issuing from it so intolerable that we could not stay long to examine it, & as it did not seem to be deserted many months, it is probable that this circumstance alone may have obligd its inhabitants to change

---

45. At this point Behm Canal divides. Vancouver may have named the northeast point to honor John Fitzgibbon, while the southwest point was named Whaley. The northeast arm he called Burroughs Bay, while the southwest branch leads to Behms Narrows (Vancouver, 1798(1984):1009-1010).

their situation. If we might judge from comparing the extent of this Village with others we have seen inhabited on this Coast, it was capabale of containing 4 or 500 people perfectly secure from any invading Tribe.

After leaving this spot in following the Arm to the Southward we soon passed another small opening on our right[46] & several on our left; The former by the direction it took seemd to join another opening which we passed on our right soon after;[47] In the dusk of the evening we found the Arm turn to the Southward & become more spacious at which direction we were not displeased, in the North West corner of this bending there appeard to be a deep Bay among some low land,[48] but from the dimness of the Weather we could not judge how far it might penetrate. After turning our face to the Southward we brought up for the night in a small sandy Bay on the eastern shore.

12th As we were now upwards of 120 miles from the Vessels in the nearest direction we knew of, & as two days over & above the time we had been Victualled for was elapsd, it may naturally be supposd that we were anxious to return by the shortest passage; for this purpose we set out early in the morning of the 12th along the eastern shore to the Southward of this large Channel, exploring it as we went on. After breakfast we crossed a deep Bay or opening going to the Eastward where we saw some Smoke from which a few Canoes were seen coming out towards us, but we kept rowing on after the Pinnace without altering our course or waiting for them in the least; four of these Canoes containing about 36 Natives approachd the Launch, carolling & holding up Sea Otter Skins with all the alluring signs of friendship; As soon as they joind us, they threw two of these Skins into the boat & took the first things that were offerd in return with apparent satisfaction without driving a bargain for them as the Natives we had hitherto met with generally did; after which some more were offerd, in doing which, they crouded close in at different times to take hold

---

46. Anchor Pass.

47. Bell Arm, north of Bell Island.

48. Spacious Bay.

of the Boat, but as they were at first easily kept off by gentle admonition, we thought only that their eagerness for Trafic might induce them to be thus forward. One of the Canoes was manned with about double the number of any of the rest, & appeard to be under the direction of an *old woman* who steerd it & was the only female of the whole party.[49] Finding that we would not wait to trade with them, this large Canoe attempted to stop our progress by paddling across our Bow, on which a musket was pointed at them with menacing threats that it would be instantly fir'd if they did not desist, this had the desir'd effect to make them back astern & aw'd every one in the Canoe but the surly old woman who kept growling all the while for having thus missed her aim. When this Canoe first joind us we observd a man standing up in the forepart of it armed with a Musket which he handled with apparent ease, looking now & then very cunningly at the priming as if he intended to impress us with the idea that it was in good order & that he knew how to use it; this bravado we little regarded any further than observing that the author of it had the most savage sullen coutenance, disfigurd with the loss of an eye, of any in the whole Canoe, which would probably mark him out as first victim to our vengeance if any thing further should happen that would lead us to chastise their temerity. At the time the large Canoe was attempting to cross our Bow the others were observd crouding close on our quarters, but some menacing threats made them also drop astern, & after this none of them were sufferd to approach the Boat. It was now deem'd necessary to get all the Arms out of the Arm Chest & in order not to alarm the Natives with any hostile preparations, they were all secretly loaded by the Gentlemen while the men kept rowing as we were resolvd not to be the first aggressors but be prepard & watchfull over their conduct that we might punish any further attempts with deserved severity, for the Musket that was pointed at them would do but little execution as it was only loaded with small shot, but now all the fire Arms were loaded with ball cartridges & laid down in the bottom of the boat quite ready at hand; The Natives kept following us all this while

---

49. The Tlingit are matrilineal. Early explorers and traders noted that many times old women controlled the trade, seemingly in charge of entire expeditions.

& approachd now & then the stern of the boat to offer Skins fish & other Articles for Sale, but as they were easily kept at due distance by gentle means, we encouragd their orderly disposition by distributing presents amongst them.

The Pinnace at this time accompanied by two small Canoes was near a mile a head & about landing at a point to take Angles, when the large Canoe left us & paddled to her with great speed being invited as we thought by the vociferous bawlings of those about her, the other three Canoes soon after followd her, parting with us in the most friendly manner, so that we were again ready to attribute their first turbulent disposition to a desire for trafic, which having met with timely check had brought them to a more peaceable behaviour towards us; A good looking man about the prime of life stood up in the middle of the last Canoe that quitted us -decently dreased in red cloth & who by his general deportment appeard to be the only Chief in the party, he seemd very quiet & friendly all along, & before he went away he presented us with some fish & berries which were accepted of & to establish a friendly intercourse some presents were given him in return.

The Pinnace was about quitting the Point after Capt Vancouver had taken the Angles, when we approachd her & were alarmd at seeing her closely surrounded by the Natives brandishing their Spears, though we were uncertain what they were about till Lieutenant Puget called out to us to fire upon the Natives, that they were attacking the Pinnace; we were then within pistol shot of them with all our Arms at hand & already loaded; on seeing our promptitude they dropped their Spears & kept waving their hands at us calling out *Woagan*, a word which implies friendship, notwithstanding which we instantly obeyd the order & dischargd a Volley amongst them, on which the greatest part of them plung'd into the Water & those that were able swam to the shore leaving their canoes adrift; others paddled to the shore expos'd to a heavy firing, among these we observd the old woman left alone in the large Canoe which she very coolly securd before she retreated to a place of safety for herself. As it was necessary to punish these Natives with severity to deter them & others from such rash attempts in future we continued firing at them from the Launch with Muskets & Wall pieces till those that reachd the shore escapd into the Wood & hid themselves behind Trees & Rocks. The pinnace having pulled immediately off from the scene of action made us apprehensive that some lives were lost or in imminent danger in her, which made us the more anxious to punish the authors of such cruel & savage barbarity by committing every depredation against them, & as their Canoes were in our power, Mr. Swaine hail'd the Pinnace to ask Capt Vancouver if he would destroy them, he answerd to let them alone till he join'd us, on which we lay by, firing a Musket now & then whenever any of them were seen stirring in the wood, for when they saw us approach their Canoes they began throwing stones from behind the Rocks & discharg'd a Musket or two at us, neither of which did us any injury; The old woman was discover'd in the Crevice of a Rock watching her Canoe & one of the party had his Musket levell'd at her, but as it was found that she had so far escap'd the general firing, he was prevaild upon to desist from taking his aim at this famous heroine, who was sufferd to remain in her retreat without further molestation.[50]

When the Pinnace joind us again we were informd that two of her Crew were severely wounded, but so far did the bravery of these men overcome their sufferings, that they conceald their situation from their Officers till sometime after they removd from the scene of action; On examining these men one of them was found to have a deep lacerated wound at the top of his left thigh near the course of the femoral artery; the other had his left thigh piercd through the middle by a Spear but luckily neither of these wounds appeard dangerous & after cleaning & dressing them I was enabled to sooth their minds with a favorable report of them.[51]

On seeing these wounds most of the party were fir'd with indignation at the perpetrators & anxious to renew their resentment in destroying at least their Canoes, which would probably be a more severe & general punishment than any yet inflicted, but Capt Vancouver was afraid that in attempting this object some

50. Vancouver (1798(1984):1015) named this place Traitors' Cove and Escape Point. Later, they anchored up directly across from here in Port Stewart.

51. One of these men was Robert Betton, sail maker and Vancouver named Betton Island in his honor.

more of the party might get wounded which might prove a serious loss to us on acount of our distance from the Vessels & our provisions being nearly expended, these prudential considerations had their full sway & we immediately proceeded on our way to the Southward, leaving these Natives who were at this time making lamentable noise in the wood & bemoaning no doubt the consequences of our just resentment & their own rashness for which we had reason to believe they had already sufferd pretty severly, but when we consider their unprovok'd attack & the manner in which they were proceeding to butcher the Pinnace's Officers & Crew in cold blood we can hardly think any punishment too severe for such diabolical treachery. Lenity on such occasions assumes the aspect of a crime, as Savages are apt to construe it into a Victory obtaind over their opponents, & which afterwards stimulates them to the perpetration of cruelties with the most audacious temerity, but as a just resentment, a timely & severe chastisement would readily check their treacherous conduct & deter them from committing actions so disgracefull to humanity.

Of the manner in which the Natives attack'd the Pinnace, Mr. Puget now inform'd us of the following particulars. That they were at first join'd by a few Natives in two Canoes, amongst whom they distributed some trifling presents with which they were so well pleasd that they invited others from the shore who kept joining them as they approachd the Point; They now observd that these Canoes were all well stor'd with implements of War, such as Lances Spears Daggers &c But the friendly behaviour of the Natives had lulled our party into a state of perfect security so that these appearances had excited no kind of suspicion or alarm to induce them to take the necessary precautions, for they trusted that even the appearance of their strength would always intimidate the Natives from putting any hostile plan in execution. When the Natives perceivd the intention of landing they became more assiduous in impressing a favorable idea of their friendship repeating often the word *Woagan* & offering very eagerly Skins fish & other articles for Sale, though at the same time they kept calling out in a vociferous manner to those round the Launch who were about a mile astern & who on this intimation quitted her & paddled with all their strength towards the Pinnace & on ap-

proaching her it was observd they threw some dogs they had into
the Water; On landing the Natives clos'd in on both sides of the
Pinnace, but shewd not the least inclination to pilfer, on the
contrary they endeavord to engage their attention by advanta-
geous offers of trafic, till the rest of the Natives stole upon them,
without their perceiving the increase of their number. In this
manner they continued to trade for fish & other articles till the
bearings were taken & till then they carried on their dissimula-
tion with wonderfull success, but in endeavouring to shove the
Pinnace off from the shore they found her so entangled with the
Canoes crouding close on both sides that they were under the
necessity of using some little force to clear a space for the Oars; At
this time the large Canoe push'd directly across the boat's stern
under the guidance of an old woman, who in this situation fasten'd
her Canoe to the Boat by means of the lead line, so as to prevent
their getting clear & increase their embarrassments; A Young
Man who appeard to be a Chief with his War dress on & a Mask
resembling a fox's head, jump'd into the Boat, & to make him quit
it Capt Vancouver went forward with a Musket in his hand, on
which all the Natives instantly arm'd themselves & brandishd
their daggers & spears pointing them from every direction into the
Boat; The party now became too late sensible of their alarming
situation, & as the Launch was too far off to give them immediate
assistance, it was necessary for their safety to keep the Natives at
parley till she should come up & in this they succeeded so far as
to ward off the attack for a few minutes; they got the Chief to quit
the Pinnace, & the Arms were laid down on both sides by agreement, so that every thing bore an amicable appearance; but the
restless tongue of the old woman in the large Canoe kept alive that
eagerness they first discoverd for the attack, & as fast as the
Natives on one side of the Boat were prevaild on to lay down their
arms, those on the other side brandishd theirs holding the points
of them within a yard of our peoples breasts; At this time they
became so daring that one of them wrench'd a musket from the
Canopy rods to which four were suspended with their Cartridge
Boxes to be in readiness, & though they might easily have punishd
the person who committed this robbery, yet from the number
about them & the situation they were in thought it prudent to take

no notice of it; this encouragd others to begin their depredations, two other Muskets were taken from the Rods & a fowling piece belonging to Capt Vancouver together with the Cartridge boxes; In this critical situation their only resource was in the arm chest which could not immediately be got at, so that they were entirely at the mercy of the Natives suing as it were for their lives & endeavoring by every fair means to keep off the attack; In this they observd they were assisted by the young Chief who was exerting his influence to pacify his people, but still the old woman kept persuading them to renew their depredations which unfortunately for both parties they again commencd, for as one of the seamen was clearing away to get at the Arm chest a Spear touchd his breast but catching it in his hand he broke off the force of the blow which however was repeated & wounded him terribly in the thigh; Another Seaman that was assisting him was wounded at the same time in the manner already describ'd. As the attack was now begun by brandishing their Spears on all sides, & the Launch having arriv'd within pistol shot, orders were given to fire upon the Natives as already mentiond; at this time there were about 50 of them round the Pinnace & it is suppos'd that six or eight of them were killed besides several wounded, but the exact number of either could not be ascertained. When the attack was thus began neither of the Pinnace's Wall pieces would go off, & the only remaining Arms they had at hand were a brace of pistols a blunderbuss & a fowling piece; As soon as they had dischargd these, they retird some distance out in the Arm to prepare themselves, not a little pleasd at their miraculous escape, & it was not till then that the two wounded men made their situation known to their Officers.

The circumstances attending this skirmish shew the necessity of being watchfull & guarded amongst Savages who are always ready to unite in taking any favorable advantage of strangers when they think they can do it with impunity, but who are easily aw'd & kept under due subjection by a steady temperate & cautious conduct or by a manly & ready opposition to their treachery. We had reason to believe that it was this very Tribe who cut off the Columbia's small boat & murderd her Crew about two

Years before as we were informd by the Commander of that Vessel when we met him near the entrance of the Streights of Juan de Fuca that the Castrophe happend near this situation, & we had no doubt but their success in that fatal instance renderd them more daring in their present attempt upon the Pinnace, which we have no doubt would have been cut off in the same manner had she not been releivd from the impending catastrophe by the timely aid & prompt assistance of the Launch.[52]

The point at which this skirmish happen'd is in the Latitude of 55° 36' North about 25 leagues inland from the exterior coast due West of it, & what we suppose to be Cape Commaño was on the opposite side of the Channel about three leagues to the South West of us, so that we were now nearly in the situation where the Spaniards left off their researches last year & in the very channel which they took to be the Straits of De Fonta, but from what we had seen of it we had little reason to think that the few branches which we had left unexplord were likely to penetrate much further inland.

13th When we came opposite to Cape Commaño we found the Shore we were on turning[53] to the South east ward which we pursued till we crossed the Channel we went to the Northward in & by that means surrounded a considerable group of large Islands; We then enterd the Channel we came out of on the 4th instant & by that returnd to the Vessels, making all the haste we could not only on account of the scanty state of our provisions, but also for the sake of our wounded Men, who we endeavourd to nurse in the best manner we were able & had the satisfaction to find that they

52. The Tlingit were bellicose and, when they saw that they had the advantage, were not afraid to attack Europeans but when outnumbered, they were friendly and helpful. Vancouver (1798 (1984):1016) blames some of the Natives' animosity on the fact that traders had previously promoted intra-group competition for goods, and in some cases had bombarded villages.

53. Vancouver (1798(1984):1018) named the southern point in honor of Senor Ambrosio O'Higgins de Vallenar, "the president of Chili [sic]." The survey party was now moving down Duke of Clarence Strait (presently Clarence Strait). On his chart, Vancouver's Clarence Strait includes what is today called Sumner Strait.

kept tolerably easy, so that we had no occasion to touch or dress their wounds till they arrivd on board on the morning of the 16th after being absent 21 days on a fortnight's provision.[54]

16th We now learnd that Mr. Johnstone having finishd the task assign'd to him returnd to the Vessels with the two Boats on the 7th day after his departure & it is to himself we are chiefly indebted for the following particulars relative to their expedition.

After they set out from the Vessels it was the intention to go streight back to the place where the Continental shore was left off, & from thence to trace it on to the Vessels, but in this they were oppos'd by such a strong fiery breeze from the Southward, that their utmost efforts in rowing & sailing made but a slow progress against it, & from their Boats being deeply loaded & the Channel so rough they shippd a great deal of water & ran no little risk of having their provisions spoil'd or even of swamping the Boats; this enducd Mr. Johnstone on coming opposite to the eastern opening which the Natives called *Nass* to enter it with a view to explore it, till the Weather became more favorable for proceeding to the Southward; they first examind a large Bay on the South side & were proceeding on to the Eastward but soon found themselves in shoal water, on which they stood directly across the Channel in a depth sufficient for Boats only, till they approachd the North side when they suddenly deepn'd their soundings from five feet to five & six fathoms, & as suddenly shoal'd again into an extended flat along shore, which prevented them from getting the Boats sufficiently near to the land for the night, they were therefore oblig'd to come to with grapnells & sleep in the Boats on the second evening after their departure, they were then about five or six

---

54. They sailed around Gravina Island, rather than down Tongass Narrows where today the city of Ketchikan is located. Vancouver named the island they had circumnavigated in honor of Conde de Revilla Gigedo, Viceroy of New Spain. The waterway surrounding the island he named in honor of Magnus von Behm, Governor of Kamchatka, where he had visited in 1779 (Vancouver, 1798 (1984:1019). The southern tip of Annette Island was named in honor of Alexander Davison, the captain of their supply ship, the *Daedalus*. Later, he named Cape Northumberland and Duke Island for the Percy family, the Dukes of Northumberland.

miles up the opening which from every appearance they conceivd
to be a *river* as the Water was perfectly fresh & the ebb tide came
out of it with much greater rapidity than the flood went in, which
was an evident proof that it discharged a considerable body of
water.

When they enter'd the opening they were joind by a small part
of the Natives from the North side of it, who followd them very
peaceably till they brought to in the evening, & were then very
easily prevaild upon to retire from the boats that the Crews might
enjoy their repose in quietness; but they return'd again in the
middle of the night with a considerable reinforcement in several
Canoes & greatly alamrd the whole party who thought that they
were approaching with hostile designs to surprise them in their
sleep, but when they were made to understand that their visit at
that time of the night was highly displeasing, they quietly retir'd
again after throwing into one of the Boats three or four Salmon by
way of an apology for their intrusion at so unseasonable an hour.

From the shallowness of this river it was deemd unnecessary to
pursue it further, & in this we have not the least doubt but Mr.
Johnstone strictly complied with his general instructions, yet had
he known at the time that this was the opening the Natives called
Nass it is probable curiosity would have prompted him to trace it,
to know how far their information concerning it was likely to be
true, for though it might not appear as eligible navigation for large
Vessels at its entrance, which is the case with many Rivers, yet it
might issue from or communicate with some interior Lake extending to a considerable distance inland & thereby afford a sufficient
scope for a Voyage of two or three Moons in Canoes as reported by
the Natives; in this case to ascertain the direction & extent of such
an opening would not merely be an object of curiosity, but might
in the end turn out the greatest utility to the commercial interest
of our Colonies on the opposite side, by directing the adventurous
& persevering views of the Canadian & Hudson's Bay Traders to
a part of the Coast where their laudable endeavours would most
likely succeed in penetrating across by an interior chain of Lakes
& Rivers, & by that means they might be enabled to draw yearly
from this Coast the greatest part of its rich & valuable Furs, for

which purpose the entrance of the present opening could not be better situated, as from all accounts this is the most abundant part of the Coast for Furs of superior quality.[55]

We cannot therefore help regretting that this River or whatever it is, had not been pursued a little further, as the examination of it might in this respect prove of some consequence to future adventurers, at the same time we candidly confess that our curiosity concerning it is in a great measure excited from the reports of the Natives, whose accounts of the extent & termination of the Channels we seldom found fallacious when we were capable of comprehending their meaning. In these suggestions we are far from ascribing any blame to Mr. Johnstone, on the contrary we have the fullest confidence that he faithfully executed his orders whatever they were.

We leave it to the researches of Geographers & future investigators to ascertain how far this may be considered as the river Parmentier of De Fonta,[56] its being in the Latitude of 55° North instead of 53° may be considered as an error easily committed in transcribing these figures if they are carelessly wrote.

Mr. Johnstone now directed his course as first intended down the southern Channel, & for this purpose the two Boats started with the ebb tide a little before day light & the breeze against them not being near so fresh they reachd in the evening the Island where we parted with *the Prince Lee Boo* & where they encampd on the third night. Next day they enterd the opening where we left off the continental shore & which they pursued in a south east direction for about ten leagues with a favorable breeze that brought them in the afternoon to the head of it, which they found surrounded by a small extent of level land coverd with wood & backd by high mountains; The Shores of this Channel were streight & rose steep to a considerable height on both sides, & contrary to what they met in the last opening, the Soundings were

55. The expedition did not know that on July 20, 1793, Alexander MacKenzie of the North West Company had reached the coast at North Bentnick Arm of Burke Channel, about the same time that Vancouver was anchored nearby (Anderson, 1960:156).

56. De Fonte had claimed to have sailed up the coast to the river Los Reyes and up this river twenty leagues to Lake Belle (Vancouver, 1798(1984):1024 footnote).

deep & the Water saltish to the very extremity. They returnd back about three leagues from the head of the Arm & stopped for the night at the entrance of a small branch going off to the north east, which next forenoon they explor'd four about three leagues, where it terminated; In this Armlet they saw the remains of an uninhabited Village which looked like a strong fortress situated on the top of a Rock naturally difficult of access & defended by a Parapet wall of Trees laid horizontally one over the other to about a mans height & enclosing a space near 300 yards in circuit which was renderd level on the inside by a platform of trees.

After finishing this armlet they continued their return back the other, opposed by a strong breeze from the North West which renderd their progress slow & tedious. As it was in this Arm that one of Mr. Brown's Tenders was obligd to chastise the treacherous behaviour of the Natives by cannonading their Village, our party was from that circumstance more than usual upon their guard, as they were in expectation of meeting here a numerous & audacious tribe, but were no wise displeasd at not seeing a single Native during the whole time, though in coming back they lookd into the Bay where the fray happend, & instead of a large Village, they only found the remains of a deserted dwelling upon a small projecting Rock, which appeard to be well constructed for defence against common enemies as the top of the rock was overlaid with a platform of trees & could not be scaled without the aid of a Ladder; They saw in several places of the dwelling what appeard to be the perforations of Balls, but they were somewhat astonishd that the Tender should find it necessary to fire on a single habitation.

After getting out of this South east arm they returnd to the northward, rounding out the different Bays & Armlets on the eastern shore, which excepting one that went to the South east ward about four leagues were of little extent, & having finishd these without meeting with any thing else deserving of notice they returnd to the Vessels with a favorable breeze up the Channel & arrivd on the evening of the 30th.

All the time the Vessels lay here the wind was generally between South & South east but mostly blew right up the Channel & was frequently squally with thick rainy weather.

The situation of the Observatory was determind by Mr. Whidbey in Latitude 55° 26' N & in Longitude 230° 13' E of Greenwich & the variation of the compass was found to be about 24 degrees East, but in this the mean result of different compasses varied. The vertical rise of spring tide was about 15 feet & it was high water on the days of full & change about noon.

17th The Marquee Tents & Observatory together with the Astronomical Instruments & Time-keepers & every thing else we had on shore being brought on board, on the arrival of the Boats on the preceeding day both Vessels weighd & made Sail early on the morning of the 17th of Augt. & began working back the Arm against a fresh southerly breeze with dark gloomy weather in the forenoon, but the afternoon & night was thick & rainy, in the evening we anchord on the western shore in 85 fathoms & steadied with a hawser to the Trees, we felt little influence from either the ebb or flood tides in this days working in which we did not gain above three leagues from the Cove we quitted in the morning.

18th Early next day we weighd & began plying against a fresh breeze from the South eastward which often provd squally with a contiuation of the hazy rainy weather we experienced on the preceeding day; We soon however passed the entrance of the opening called Nass on the eastern side & the North West opening we had examined on the Western side, having afterwards at times but little wind & being so baffled with an under tow that the Helm lost in a great measure its due influence on the Vessel we were obligd to come to an anchor early in the afternoon in 45 fathoms near a rocky islet on the eastern shore about ten Miles to the Southward of Nass.

This under tow or counter current was here very remarkable for it carried the Vessel against a Tide that ran two or three knots at the surface.

19th We had thick weather & heavy rain on the morning of the 19th but the tide of ebb serving about eight we hove up the Anchor & plyd against a light southerly breeze with slow progress down the Channel; in the evening we could get no Sounding with upwards of a hundred fathoms of line so that we were obligd to keep under way all night under easy sail which by two next morning carried us out of the Channel when we stood to the westward with a light breeze.[57] At noon the observd Latitude was 55° 44' & soon after we stood to the Northwestward by a wide channel formd on the western side by numerous large Islands & the whole surrounding Country appeard much broken & intersected with openings & inlets in every direction. - In the afternoon the weather became hazy with small rain & having but little wind we again anchord for the night. - We were now in what the Spaniards consider as the Streights of De Fonta.

21st After weighing next morning we stood to the Northward steering for the opening where we had the skirmish with the Natives with a light southerly breeze & dark gloomy weather; At noon we were in Latitude 55° 25' North within two leagues of Cape Camaño which bore N 50 W by compass, we continued afterwards standing to the Northward tell we passed Skirmish Point[58] on our right hand, & soon after observing an opening on the western shore likely to afford shelter about ten Miles to the Northward of Cape Camaño,[59] the Chatham was directed by signal to stand in for it, which she did & soon anchord in a Bay within some Islands, but the wind failing we were obligd to come to on the outside for the night which continued Calm with heavy rain; Next morning we weighed & ran into the harbour where we anchord by the Chatham in 16 fathoms over a soft bottom within half a cable's length of the shore to which we steadied by a hawser fastend to a tree. We had little or no wind but excessive heavy rain most part of the day.

---

57. At the entrance of Portland Inlet, Vancouver (1798(1984):1030) mentions that he named the northern point of land in honor of William Wales, a noted astronomer. Proceeding northward up Clarence Strait, he named Moira's Sound to honor the Earl of Moira, and Wedge Island and Cholmondeley's Sound after the Earl of Cholmondeley.

58. Escape Point.

59. Although the Spanish explorer had not traveled this far north, he had placed the name "Punta Caamaño" on his map in this vicinity (Vancouver, 1798(1984):1032 footnote).

23rd The Crews of four boats having prepard themselves on the preceeding day, Mr. Whidbey set out early on the morning of the 23d in the Cutter accompanied with Mr. Swaine in the Launch with orders to go to the openings which Capt Vancouver left unexamind in the last boats cruize & after finishing them trace the continental shore to the Vessels; At the same time Mr. Johnstone set out to the Southward with two boats provided with ten days provision to begin at Cape Camaño & from thence trace the Starboard shore to the north west ward while his provision lasted, on the presumption that it was the continental shore. The weather being thick & rainy was very unfavorable for these expeditions, but from the prevailing state of it during the whole summer there was little expectation of its becoming at this time of the year otherwise.

In the afternoon we were visited by a single Canoe but the Natives in it seemd to be quite ignorant of the fray which happend on the opposite shore, & this was the case too with two Canoes which visited us two days before near Cape Camaño.

Parties were landed from both Vessels to cut fire wood collect broom stuff & brew spruce beer from the pine tops & on these duties they continued employd the following day which was fair & moderate & afforded me an opportunity of examining the Woods round the Harbour for Plants but in this excursion I met with nothing different from what I had frequently seen on other parts of the Coast. The season was now so far advancd that there were very few plants of any kind in flower & the only fruits were the black & red Whortle berries already mentiond & which we constantly used in Tarts & Pies whenever we could get them, there was also a kind of wild apple a little bigger than Haws but they were very scarce, their usual place of growth was near the Water side & upon the small Islands.

25th The 25th being Sunday & a fair pleasant day, the people enjoyd the recreation of the shore & it afforded a good opportunity for ascertaining our present situation which was found to be in Latitude 55° 38 North & by the Time-keepers in Longitude 228° 24' East.

We were suddenly disturbed in the middle of the night by a party of the Natives in a large Canoe who came into the Harbour singing dancing & making great noise, which impressd every one with an idea before they came in sight that they were very numerous & in this manner they greatly alarmd a small party we had on shore guarding the brewing Vessels linnen & other articles; but they made directly for the Vessels & performd two circuits round them before they stopped, singing all the while a vociferous plaintive song in perfect concert with their paddling, when they were informd that they would not be admitted along side either of the Vessels at so unseasonable an hour they went towards the shore abreast of us where our small party endeavourd to oppose them by pointing their Muskets with menacing threats at the Canoe, on which they instantly laid hold of their Spears with a determination to make their way good, the party then thought it necessary to receive them with a little more apparent civility, & pointing out another place to them at a little distance they there landed & remaind quiet till day light giving no further trouble to our party than sending a deputation to them for a fire brand to kindle a fire, round which they lay the remainder of the night without the least shelter from the inclemency of the Weather.

26th These Natives continued about us the two following days & behavd them selves very peaceably; During that time we had for the most part rainy Weather.[60]

28th One of these Natives was during this time very anxious in his solicitations to go with us to England & Capt Vancouver seemd inclind to indulge him as it was it own voluntary request, but on the 28th punishments were inflicted on board the Discovery of a

---

60. Vancouver (1798(1984):1035) mentions that the chief of the party was *Kanaut* and that he spoke very highly of *Ononnistoy* "who they acknowledged as their chief, and the head of a very numerous tribe." Frederica de Laguna (Emmons, 1991:263, 299) says that the name is probably "Klanott" or "Clanott," which in Tlingit means "They never die." She goes on to add that there had been a prehistoric Tongass shaman by the name of Klanott and that in the 19th century there was a Raven leader among the Chilkat Tlingit by the same name.

very unpleasant nature,[61] on seeing which all of the Natives left the Bay, & he that was before so solicitous to go with us now went away without taking leave of us & never afterwards returnd to the Vessels.

In the evening Mr. Whidbey & Mr. Swaine returnd with the two Boats having finishd the different openings we had passed in the last boats cruize & brought the presumptive continental shore to our present situation;[62] None of these openings went to any great distance from the main channel we had examind, so that it would have taken us but little time to have explord them in the last boats cruize had our provisions not been so far gone; Thus terminated however as we expected the delusive hopes of the Spaniards in considering this Channel as the Streights of *De Fonta*.

In one place they met with what they considerd as the remains of the party that had attackd the Pinnace, on their approaching them they were at first very timorous & submissive, till finding that no further revenge was likely to be taken for their treacherous conduct, they then became remarkably civil & friendly, & were very assiduous in offering every thing they had as presents to atone for their past behaviour; this being the case some consiliatory presents were given them & they were left to the remorse of their own consciences for the sufferings which their rashness had occasion'd.

For the following three days I employ'd myself in collecting live plants of any that were new & curious in the Woods & planting them in the frame on the quarter deck, with an intention of carrying them with us to the Southward to enure them to the Sea Air & tropical climates, & by this means I should be better able to ascertain the plants that were most likely to withstand our long Voyage to England & lay them in accordingly on our final departure from the Coast.

---

61. The most common punishment was whipping, and evidently when the Indian saw this, he decided that he preferred not to remain on the *Discovery*.

62. They had examined Walker Cove, Chichamin River, Anchor Pass, Bell Arm, Bailey Bay, Yes Bay and Spacious Bay. Walker Cove was named after William Walker, surgeon of the *Chatham*. Bell Island in Behm Canal was named for Edward Bell, native of Dublin and clerk of the *Chatham*. One of the finest journals of the voyage has been ascribed to Bell (Vancouver, 1798 (1984):1035,1036 footnotes).

Mr. John Stewart was employd with some of the Gentlemen in Surveying & Sounding the Harbour in consequence of which it was namd after him *Port Stewart.*[63]

During our stay here the wind was mostly from the South East quarter accompanied with rain & dark gloomy weather, but when it changd to any other quarter we had the weather generally fair & pleasant.

While the Natives remaind with us they daily supplied us with plenty of good Salmon which they very dextrously speard in shallow water along shore, for this kind was very seldom met with in the fresh water runs; When this source of supply faild us we had no difficulty in taking any quantity we pleasd of the hump backd & hawks bill Salmon, two new species with which the Channels & every rillet now swarmd & though they were coarse & not so well flavord as the common kind, yet they were generally preferd to salt beef.

In addition to these we had some ducks & wild geese from a swampy track at the head of the Harbour, which at this time afforded them a place of resort & from which our Sportsmen seldom returnd empty handed. A few Herons too were shot, which were found to be very delicate eating & preferd by some to any other game.

September 1st In the morning of the first September 1793 two Canoes came into the Harbour with Natives that were entire Strangers to us, they were under the direction of two Chiefs one of whom was at least six feet high & exceeded by far in stature any of the Natives we had yet met with on the coast;[64]

---

63. He was the Master's Mate and his chart of the harbor was published by Vancouver (1798 (1984):1043 footnote).

64. These were probably Haida Indians from a settlement about 25 miles south and west. They maintained the Tlingit name for their settlement, calling it "Kasaan" meaning "beautiful land." The Haida had been migrating into Southeastern Alaska from the Queen Charlotte Islands during the 18th century. No doubt there had been warfare between them and the Tlingit, whose lands they were invading. This explains why they prepared for battle when Tlingit approached from the opposite shore. Vancouver (1798(1984):1045) mentions that he named the southern tip of Kasaan Peninsula Grindall Point to honor a navy captain.

Another small Canoe joind them soon after, & they all remaind peaceably about the Vessels till five in the evening, when a very large Canoe full of Natives[65] was seen approaching the Harbour from the Southward on which the three Canoes who were then alongside of the Chatham instantly prepard to oppose them, by putting on their war dresses, brandishing their Spears & advancing with a wild clamorous noise of defiance to meet them; Those in the large Canoe made no preparations, but paddled into the Harbour seemingly regardless of their menaces, till they came pretty near to one another, when a conversation ensued, the Spears droppd & matters were amicably settled at the moment we expected to see a fierce attack.[66]

The large Canoe came directly along side of the Discovery with a Chief whose name was *Unanestee*[67] & who by his appearance &

---

65. From what follows, the newcomers appear to be Tlingit from the Stikine River with their leader. The present name of the southern shore of the entrance to Boca de Quadra is "Kaa Shakes Point."

66. Vancouver (1798(1984):1040-41) gives a much longer explanation of the events. "… yet those who had now entered the harbor, did not appear to be so hostilely inclined as those who had already occupied the port; as the lances of the former, though in readiness for action, were not disposed in a way so menacing. On a nearer approach they rested on their paddles, and entered into a parley; and we could then observe, that all those who stood up in the large canoe were armed with pistols or blunderbusses, very bright, and in good order. Their conversation seeming to have ended in a pacific way, the opposing party returned with the newcomers, who, on passing by the Chatham, laid down their arms; but just as they came alongside the Discovery, one of the chiefs who had been on board, drew, with much haste, from within the breast of his war garment, a large iron dagger, and appeared to be extremely irritated by something that had been said by those in the large canoe, who again with great coolness took up their pistols and blunderbusses; but on an explanation appearing to be made, their arms were again returned to their proper places; their pistols and ammunition were carefully wrapped up…"

In a footnote to this event, Dr. Lamb indicates that Puget's journal points out that they had obtained their firearms from Mr. Magee of the American ship *Margaret*. This event illustrates the suspicious and belligerent attitude so often described by explorers when speaking of the Indians of the Northwest Coast. It also shows that Tlingit and Haida were able to communicate even though their languages were entirely distinct.

67. Vancouver (1798 (1984):1032) transcribes the name as *O-non-nis-toy*, the *U-en-smoket*, of *U-en-Stikin*." This is an interesting encounter because it shows

the attention paid to him seemd to be a powerful man, he was introducd on board as the Chief of *Stekin*[68] which we understood to be a large Village somewhere to the North West of us: This Canoe containd about 24 people well equipped with Spears Daggers & some fire arms.[69]

For the entertainment of these Natives some fire works were exhibited in the evening with which they were highly delighted.

2nd Next day having got every thing off from the shore we weighd anchor in the forenoon & warped out to the South point of the Harbour by a narrow Channel on the inside of a small Island & there we anchord again to wait in readiness for the return of Mr.

---

that the people were probably using a combination of three entirely different languages.

As explained earlier, this *U-en* (Vancouver's *Ewen*) is more than likely Haida, meaning "great, important." A linguist, Jeff Leer, (personal communication) suggests that the *smoket* portion may be their pronunciation of the Tshimshian word *sim'oogyat* meaning "chief, rich man." It is possible the name *O-non-nis-toy*, *Unanestee*, had a Tsimshian origin as well. Frederica de Laguna (Emmons,1991:262-263), says that the name Ononnistoy has also been transcribed as *Gunanesti* and was of the Kiks'adi clan in the Raven moeity of the Tlingit society. The name means "Wandering in a Strange Country." In 1867, the possessor of the name Gunaneste was described as *Con-mis-ta* son of Chief Shakes. The name, later written as *Kananisty* was still in use in Wrangell in 1880. de Laguna goes on to say (Emmons, 1991:299) that the leader *Kanaut* mentioned earlier, may have been the son of *Ononnistoy*. As the son, *Kanaut* would be in the Wolf moiety and perhaps of the Nanya'ayi clan which was the family of the famous Stikine leader "Chief Shakes."

For the most part, Tsimshian and Tlingit did not get along well. In fact, in the Tsimshian language, the plural term for slaves is "LLingit," pronounced nearly the same way the Tlingit pronounce their own name. On the other hand, there seems to have been some marriages and alliances between the Tsimshian of Nass and the Tlingit of the Stikine River and Klukwan, farther north. Since these visitors were from the Stikine, they may have been friends of some Tsimshian and were familiar with their terms.

68. The Stikine River was the homeland of a large, powerful group of Tlingit.

69. Vancouver (1798(1984):1042-43) describes in detail one individual among the Indians who appeared to be a "native of New Spain." He was dressed in European style clothing, smoked cigars, was familiar with the foods aboard the ship. When they questioned him in Spanish, he acted as though he did not understand anything they said. Vancouver suspected that he was a deserter who preferred to remain among the Tlingit.

Johnstone & the two Boats. When the Natives observd us chang-
ing our situation they went away & we saw no more of them, they
had only one or two women amongst the whole of them.

3rd On the 3d we had light Southerly wind with intervening calms
& thick rainy weather, we were now eagerly looking out every
momen[t] with the utmost anxiety for our Boats, as the treacherous behaviour we had already experienced from the Natives on
this part of the Coast made us the more apprehensive & uneasy
for their safety. While in this state of suspense I made a little
excursion on shore opposite to the Vessels & in the Wood near the
Point I found a small Plant with blue berries growing pretty
plentifully which at first I took for the *Dracoena borealis*, but on
examining it found it to be a new species of the same genus tho'
neither of them agree well with that of *Dracoena*, & on that
account probably ought to be made a new genus by themselves; I
took a Drawing of this species & put some live Plants of it in the
Frame on the quarter deck.

4th In the forenoon of the 4th Mr. Johnstone returnd with the two
Boats & all his People safe & well, but the day continuing mostly
calm we could not stir, though it was intended to move on to meet
him had he not joind us.

From Mr. Johnstone we learnd that they had reachd Cape
Camaño on the first evening after leaving the Vessels, though not
without difficulties, for besides heavy rain & thick weather, they
had to beat against a fresh breeze from the Southward & a rough
swell that wetted every thing in the Boats on account of their being
so deeply loaded, they had also the misfortune to carry away the
foremast of one of the Boats at this early part of their expedition,
but having substituted a spar in its place they next morning
enterd a spacious Channel[70] & proceeded along its Starboard
shore for about seven leagues when they came to a large opening

---

70. They entered Ernest Sound, named for his Highness Prince Ernest. The
southern point of the entrance was named for William LeMesurier, master's
mate of the *Chatham* while the northern point was named Onslow, probably in
honor of George, the first Earl of Onslow (Vancouver, 1798(1984):1044-45,
footnotes).

branching off to the North East & soon after winding to the Northward:[71] this they pursued & found it interspersd with a number of small Islands & deep Bays rendering its breadth very irregular. On the evening of the 3d day they stoppd at the entrance of an Armlet going off to the Eastward a few miles to the northward of the Latitude of 56 degrees North, & about the middle of the night they were suddenly disturbd by the approach of some Natives who landed on the opposite shore & whose jabbering voices & noisy paddles at such a still & gloomy hour, impress'd them with an idea of their number being considerable, on which account it was deemd necessary to watch their movments with vigilance the remainder of the night; In the morning they were joind by this formidable party & to their surprize they found them to be only a single Canoe with three Natives in, who accompanied them a little way up the eastern Armlet & endeavourd by the most positive signs to convince them that it was clos'd up, which after going three or four leagues they found to be the case, & returnd back again to the entrance of it in the evening where they found the Natives waiting them, & next forenoon they accompanied them to the Northward by a narrow Channel,[72] which about the Latitude of 56 degrees 20 minutes North turnd to the North west ward by a narrow pass scarcely a quarter of a mile wide, this soon led them into a wider channel which continued nearly in the same direction for about 3 or 4 leagues further;[73] the Weather being all this while thick & hazy with almost incessant rain was very unfavorable for their pursuits, especially as they soon after came to a very intricate situation where they found themselves in shallow water amongst a number of small Islands, & seeing two or three deep bays or openings leading to the Northward, they sounded across their entrances in little more than a fathom water,

---

71. Vancouver (1798(1984):1045-46) named this waterway Bradfield Channel, and the eastern point of land at the junction, Point Warde.

72. Blake Channel, which leads into the Narrows. Vancouver named a point in the narrows to honor Bishop Spencer Madan. Today, the name Madan Point appears on another neck of land in Eastern Channel. The northern tip of Wrangell Island he named Point Highfield (Vancouver, 1798(1984):1046 foot-note).

73. Eastern Channel.

for which reason it was deemd unnecessary in such shallow water to explore further these doubtful openings.[74] They were here joind by three Canoes with 3 or 4 Natives in each who behavd themselves very peaceably. After getting from amongst these Islands they found the Channel very spacious & winding to the Westward[75] about the Latitude of 56 ½° North, they followd the Starboard shore of it for two or three leagues & then came to another opening branching off to the Northward,[76] they enterd this by a narrow Channel on the East side of a large Island 8 or 9 miles long, after passing which they found the Arm wider & here & there interspers'd with small Islands; they followd it under the disadvantage of incessant hard rain & thick fog till it ended in a long sandy flat about the Latitude of 56° 55' North & about a degree & half of Longitude to the Westward of Port Stewart where they left the Vessels; This being the northermost extent they could penetrate in this direction they returned back by the same Arm till they came again to the Western channel which was afterwards found to incline to the south westward & from its spacious appearance in that direction they had little doubt of its communicating with the Ocean from which they did not estimate themselves above 15 leagues, but the Weather was so unfavorable & their provisions were so nearly expended that they could not put off time to pursue it further; they therefore left the presumptive continental shore in the Latitude of 56° 30' North on the last day of August & directed their course by the nearest way to the Vessels; in this they had another very important object in view, which was to find a more eligible Channel for bringing the Vessels thither than the intricate & circuitous one they had pursued in the Boats; for this purpose they enterd next day a pretty extensive

---

74. They were now just north of the present city of Wrangell, going towards the Stikine River. Vancouver named the southern point of land Point Rothsay (Vancouver, 1798(1984):1047). Here they discovered a very large, shallow delta at the mouth of the Stikine.

75. Sumner Strait.

76. They passed Point Howe, named after Admiral Lord Howe, and then came to the entrance to the Wrangell Narrows. Vancouver named the point on the southern shore Point Craig (Vancouver, 1798(1984):1048 footnote).

opening going to the South eastward,[77] & pursued it in that direction against a fresh breeze heavy rain & thick fog till towards evening, when they came to some large Islands that occupied mid-channel, yet they found a passage through between them & the eastern shore of nearly a mile wide & apparently clear of any danger. After passing these Islands the Channel continued in the same direction & was from two to three miles wide;[78] Next day they found out that they were in the same Channel they quitted on the second day after they set out from the Vessels as they reachd in the evening the opening where they first turnd off to the North eastward by which a very important object was accomplishd in finding such a strait & eligible passage for the Vessels to the place where they had quitted the continental shore.[79] In coming round Cape Camaño about sun-set the evening before they joind us, they were somewhat alarmd at the sudden appearance of about 20 large Canoes putting off from the shore & paddling towards them, these Canoes they supposd containd no less than 250 Natives, & not knowing what their designs might be, they were unwilling to suffer such a formidable concourse to surround the Boats, & therefore made signs to them to keep off, to which however they seemd to pay little regard, till a Musket or two & a Swivel were fired over them, which made them stop, & finding that the Boats kept rowing on they crossed over to the opposite shore & relinquishd

77. As they started down Snow Passage, the point on the western shore was named after Admiral Colpoys and the point on the eastern shore they named in honor of Captain Macnamara of the Navy. Going from Snow Passage to Clarence Strait, they passed two islands, to which they gave only one name, Bushy Island. Johnstone may have thought that the two islands, Bushy and Shrubby, were one (Vancouver, 1798(1984):1050 footnote).

78. As Clarence Strait divides into Snow Passage and Stikine Strait, the southern tip of Zarembo Island, the northern tip of land, was named Point Nesbitt, while the southern shore, the northwestern tip of Etolin Island was named Point Harrington. Ten miles south of here, at the end of a small island, they gave the name Point Stanhope probably in honor of the Stanhope family who were related to William Pitt (Vancouver, 1798(1984):1050 footnote).

79. Vancouver (1798(1984):1051 footnote) named the islands they had circumnavigated York's Islands to honor His Royal Highness the Duke of York. Today, these islands are named Etolin, Wrangell and Zarembo.

their pursuit. Whatever the intentions of these Natives were it was certainly a prudent step to ward off any intercourse with them so late in the evening as a recent instance of their treachery fully evincd.

After this our party took the advantage of a light favorable breeze & stood up the Channel under an easy Sail all night by which they were enabled to join us this forenoon as already mentiond.

5th The morning of the 5th was rather cold but calm & serene & set in with all the flattering prospects of fine Weather; about eight a light breeze sprung up with which both Vessels got under way & proceeded to the Southward, but the wind being fluctuating & inconstant with counter currents & undertow renderd our progress for some time slow & tedious. We kept working to the Southward all day, sometimes towing with our boats a head & towards midnight the wind became fresh & squally from the South East with rain & thick Weather, which with the darkness of the night & narrowness of the Channel renderd our situation very hazardous.[80]

6th Early on the morning of the 6th we carried a press of Sail on the Vessel & got round Cape Camaño into the North West Channel which Mr. Johnstone had returnd from in the Boats & as the gale still continued to blow pretty strong from the South East with thick weather & rain, it was deemd imprudent to run in such weather, we therefore brought to, till about 10 in the forenoon when the gale subsided, the weather in some measure cleard up & we were enabled to make Sail again after consulting Mr. Johnstone with respect to our proper route & requesting that he

---

80. Vancouver's comments indicate that he was aware of the dangers: "Under the unfavorable circumstances of such weather, in this intricate navigation, where anchorage is so precarious and difficult to be found, and where innumerable steep lurking rocks as well beneath as rising to different heights above the surface of the sea, were constantly presenting themselves, it must ever be regarded as a very happy circumstance that we had to leeward of us the great north-west branch, of which some information had been gained by Mr. Johnstone" (Vancouver, 1798(1984):1052).

might lead on with the Chatham; This gale was the most violent we had yet experienced in our interior Navigation. Our course lay to the North Westward in a spacious channel of 3 or 4 Miles wide, we had not a very clear prospect of the Country, but what we saw on both sides appeard of a moderate height with a good deal of low land intervening between the Hills the ascents to which were even & gradual without much of that ruggedness we had been accustomd to view in the more interior parts of the Country.

In the afternoon we continued standing on with moderate wind & hazy till the dusk of the evening when we anchord near the Starboard shore[81] under the lee of some Islands about the Latitude of 56° 10' North.

7th We weighd again early next morning with light variable airs, & about noon passed through the narrows which is in the Latitude of 56° 16' North & though it is here little more than a Mile across yet we had from 20 to 30 fathoms in mid-channel; All the afternoon we had a light breeze but as the ebb tide ran pretty strong in our favor we made tolerable good progress & soon came into a wide spacious Sound leading to the Westward, just opposite to the point on the north side of it, where Mr. Johnstone left off tracing the continental Shore in his last cruize: We continued standing to the Westward, but in the evening finding we were making but slow progress even with the assistance of the boats towing a head, we anchord close to the South Shore for the night in deep water; from which a naked rock in mid channel bore N 8° E by compass. Though this Channel was 4 or 5 miles wide, yet from the irregular soundings we experienced this afternoon it did not appear to be altogether free of danger, we passed through several ripplings & at a considerable distance from the shore had soundings in 10, 15 & 20 fathoms & at other times had no ground with upwards of a hundred fathoms of line; The North shore appeard much broken with Islands & Inlets & several Rocks were seen at low Water laying a considerable distance from it.

In the afternoon we were joind by five Canoes who followd us till we brought to & slept on the Beach opposite to us all night.

---

81. The southern shore of Sumner Strait.

8th Next morning these were joind by three more & the first that came off to us were two filled with Women, who made a circuit round each Vessel singing all the while & beating time with their paddles against the edge of their Canoes as they movd round us; all these Women were disfigurd with that unnatural practice of perforating their under lips & wearing oval pieces of wood in them; We were soon after joind by the whole party consisting of upwards of 60 Natives, they offerd for sale a number of fine Sea Otter Skins & some fur Seal Skins & preferrd in exchange blue cloth to any thing else, though they sometimes took Tin & Copper Kettles Pewter Basons & Spoons &c. They also had plenty of fine Salmon of which we bought a sufficiency for all hands. In these Canoes we observd several Muskets which were kept in very good order. The Chief of this Tribe who name was *Whoagua* came on board, he was a very stout man & seemingly of a mild disposition, he was dressd in a long Cloak made of Martin Skins, on which he placd a great value, as he would not part with it for considerable offers; the rest of the Natives were mostly cloathed in woollen dresses of European Manufactory, some in Jackets & Trowsers, others in square pieces thrown over their shoulders.

9th When we weighd in the forenoon & made Sail out from the Shore the Natives all left us, it was intended to stand across the Channel & pursue the continental shore on the North side of it, but the appearance of the Weather strongly threatening another gale from the Southward, the design was given up & we hauld back to the South side keeping that on board that we might be ready to take shelter should the state of the Weather render it necessary; We continued standing to the Westward in this doubtful state until the evening, when we enterd a Bay about 2 or 3 Miles deep in which both Vessels anchord pretty well up & were tolerably well shelterd from the Southern Gales which from the advancd state of the season we had reason now to expect;[82] As we hauld into the Bay we passed a rocky reef on our left hand which

---

82. They had passed around Point Baker, named after the first Lieutenant of the *Discovery,* and entered the sheltered harbor which Vancouver (1798(1984):1056) named Port Protection.

could only been seen at low water & consequently renderd it more dangerous; We had scarcely anchord when it began to blow fresh from the South east & by midnight encreasd to a violent gale, so that we conceivd ourselves very fortunate in being so snugly secure anchord before it came on.

10th The gale continued to blow strong with torrents of rain & thick hazy weather till eight next morning when the wind changd to the Southwestward & became more moderate & by noon it was pretty fair & clear which afforded an opportunity of observing the Suns meridional altitude for ascertaining the Latitude which was found to be 56° 20' North, & we were about the same time about 20 leagues to the Westward of Port Stewart the Station we had last quitted. Capt Vancouver & some of the Officers row'd round the harbour in a boat to look if there was any situation more commodius for the Vessels, but having found none, they were both moor'd in the place where we had brought to on the preceeding evening.[83] - From the Western point of entrance a clear Channel was seen out to Sea which did not appear to be above nine or ten leagues off.

It was now resolv'd to send off two parties in different directions on surveying expeditions, for this purpose four Boats were orderd to be got in readiness with ten days provisions each.

10th Early on the morning of the 10th Mr. Johnstone set out with two Boats & went back about 6 or 7 leagues to being where he left off in his last surveying expedition,[84] & from thence he was orderd to trace the continental shore to a place pointed out to him on the opposite to where we lay & where Mr. Whidbey who also sett out with two Boats at the same time was orderd to begin & continue his examination out to Sea; he was likewise directed to ascertain an eligible passage for the Vessels to move that way should it be

---

83. In his journal, Sheriff (n.d.) has an excellent chart of Port Protection.

84. This point was named Point Barrie, in honor of Robert Barrie, midshipman who accompanied Johnstone. It is the southern entrance to Keku Strait and Rocky Pass which leads to the present village of Kake (Vancouver, 1798(1984):1057).

deemd necessary.- In the forenoon we had frequent showers of rain & hail but the wind continued moderate.

11thI landed on the 11th near the Watering place in company with one of the Gentlemen, & on a sandy Beach we found a number of small fish of the Salmon kind left by the Tide, which as they appeard fresh we carefully collected & brought them on board & found them to be very delicate eating, they resembled what are called Caplins[85] by the Newfoundland fishermen, but appeard to be a new species which inducd me to take a Drawing & description of them. - We availd ourselves of this discovery in sending daily at the retreat of the Tide to the same place during our stay & seldom faild in picking up a quantity of them for our table.

After this I took a stroll into the woods but found nothing new, nor indeed scarcely any Plant in flower, for the season was now so far spent that cold boisterous weather set in & check'd the progress of vegetation, so that I made but a short excursion; the Woods were mostly composd of four different kinds of Pines & the same variety of Underwood which has been already frequently mentiond.

In the evening Mr. Johnstone return'd with the two Boats having yesterday noon reachd the point where he formerly left off, he from thence continued his examination to the westward along the northern shore of the Channel till by this day noon he reachd the place where Mr. Whidbey commencd & so compleated his task & brought the continental shore within our view opposite to the entrance of the Harbour. No Natives were seen during the excursion excepting two men in a small Canoe, & only one Canoe had yet visited the Vessels in the Harbour with five or six Natives in her who made but a short stay.

12th The 12th & two following days we had strong gales from East & South East & thick squally weather with almost constant heavy

---

85. Dr. Ole Mathiesen of the University of Alaska School of Fisheries (personal communication) suggests that the fish is smelt. In southeastern Alaska there are several varieties of smelt including the Euclachon (*Thaleichtys pacificus*), sometimes called "candlefish" and which in Tlingit are named *saak*. These fish were prized for the oil which could be rendered from them. Other species of smelt (*Mallotus villosus*) and Rainbow smelt (*Osemius moidax dentex*) are also found in this area.

rain & at times dark fog, & from thence to the 18th though the wind was more moderate & variable yet the weather continued dark gloomy & very unsettled with frequent showers of rain; high & distant mountains which were seen to the north westward of us over the low land on the opposite side of the Channel, were during this boisterous & stormy weather coverd pretty low down with fresh snow, so that we had every reason to think that the winter was already set in on this part of the Coast.

As intervals of fair weather permitted parties went to the head of the Harbour for the purpose of shooting wild Geese Ducks & Herons which afforded a temporary supply of refreshment for the Officers tables, but the men were able to procure here little else than their usual sea victualling, which indeed had been their lot a great part of the summer.

18th On the 18th the weather was very changeable & squally with frequent strong gusts of wind from the southward & south east attended with heavy rain & foggy weather.

In the afternoon a Canoe came from the Westward into the Harbour & paddled directly past the Vessels to a small Island close by us, on which some linnen belonging to the Chatham was exposd to dry, & as there were only two men left on shore to attend it, it was not deemd proper to suffer these Natives to remain there all night, & a Boat from the Chatham was instantly sent to warn them off, when they very peaceably departed out of the Harbour & we saw no more of them.

19th Next day we had a continuation of the same boisterous weather which occasiond no little anxiety for our absent boats, from this however we were soon releivd by seeing them make their appearance about three in the afternoon round the western point of the harbour after an absence of ten days, during which they were not able to carry their operations above as many leagues from the Vessels on account of the fogginess of the weather attended with incessant storms & heavy rains, in one place they were obligd to remain for three days without stirring, exposd to the inclemency of the weather & its cold rigorous blasts. Mr. Whidbey examind the Shore to the westward from where he began opposite to us[86] & tracd the continental shore out to the Sea in the Latitude of 56 degrees North, & the unsettled appearance of the weather together with the exhausted state of his stock of provisions obligd him then to relinquish his pursuit, but in coming back he examin'd the Channel & found it an eligible passage for the Vessels out to sea. The whole of this excursion might be compleated in three or four days had the weather provd at all favorable but the season was now too far advancd to expect that advantage, it was therefore determind to quit this part of the Coast & remove to the Southward to more hospitable regions for the winter & all our operations were now directed in preparing for our departure with the first favorable wind, but the night & next day provd boisterous with strong gales from the South east & thick rainy weather so that we could not stir. The last party that returnd had seen but one Canoe with a few Natives the whole time they were absent & we had been visited only by two Canoes at separate times since we came into this Harbour, from which we may conclude that this part of the Coast is but thinly inhabited, or what may be more probable is that the inclemency of the Weather obligd the Natives to remove from the exterior edge of the Coast to the interior Channels for the winter.

21st Being in readiness for departure both Vessels on the morning of the 21st unmoord & about ten in the forenoon weighd & made Sail with a light breeze from South East which by noon carried us clear of the entrance of the harbour where the observd Latitude was 56° 21' North about a mile & half from each of the outer points, the one bearing N 50° E & the other S 55° E by compass, & the Channel out to sea which we were now going to pursue was at the same time open & ran about South half East for about nine or ten leagues.

In the afternoon having but light airs with intervals of calm, we made but slow progress in working out of the Sound, but as the Channel was nearly two leagues wide & apparently free of any

---

86. The opening on the other side was named Port Beauclerc. It may have been named after Amelius Beauclerc who served under Commander Gardner. When Vancouver also served under Gardner, he probably met Beauclerc (Vancouver, 1798(1984):1059 footnote).

obstruction we kept underway all night, during which we were favord with a light breeze from the North westward: We tried more than once for Soundings but could not reach the bottom with upwards of a hundred fathoms of Line.

22nd Next morning we had light fluctuating wind from the Northward with dark foggy Weather till towards noon when it cleard up & afforded an opportunity of observing the Latitude which was 56° North within two Miles of the outer continental point which was named *Cape Decision* & which bore S 78° W of us by Compass;[87] This is the point where Mr. Whidbey left off his pursuit of the continental shore in the last boat excursion, on the outside of it is a round Island of a moderate height with some small ones intevening which Mr. Johnstone in his Chart of this part of the Coast is a former Voyage namd Charles's Isles, these from the South East extreme of the entrance of his Christian's Sound,[88] & Cape Ommaney which forms the other point of it was seen to the North west ward. The flood tide making strong against us, we made but slow progress as the wind continued light & fluctuating till the dusk of the evening, when it began to blow pretty strong from the South east ward & continued fresh & squally with rain from that quarter all night. The Signal was made denoting Nootka the place of rendevouz in case of separation.

23rd When we got out to Sea next morning we experienced so much head swell from the boisterous Weather that the Vessels pitchd a good deal & occasiond our carrying away the sprit sail yard in a squall & nearly about the same time the Chatham carried away about eight feet of her main boom. In the afternoon the thick rainy weather continued but the wind became more moderate & gradualy veerd round to the Westward where it

---

87. As they moved out to sea, on the eastern shore, they named a large island Warren's Island in honor of Captain Sir John Borlase Warren. On the western shore, they passed a rocky point which they named Point St. Alban's. It is near the opening to a waterway which Vancouver named in honor of Admiral Affleck, Affleck's Channel (Vancouver, 1798(1984):1059-60).

88. This name is no longer in use. Today it is the southern entrance of Chatham Strait.

continued all night & blew a steady breeze with which we stood along the Coast to the South East.

24th A fine fresh Westerly breeze continued to favor our progress on the 24th & as the Weather was fair & clear we stood in for the land which by ten in the forenoon we made about the North end of Queen Charlotte's Isles & by noon got pretty well in with it, when our Latitude was 54° 14' North & the North extreme of these Isles bore N 37° E by compass distant about — leagues.

[End of 1793 season in Alaska]

Menzies' Journal 1794

Synopsis

After leaving Port Protection, Vancouver's next stop was Nootka where he remained but a few days before departing for New Spain. Along the way, they explored the outer coasts of the Queen Charlotte Islands. They remained in California until December of 1793 and then sailed for Hawaii, arriving January of 1794 (Anderson, 1960:170). For the next few weeks, the ships were repaired, restocked and the crew relaxed. Menzies carried out botanical research and climbed Mount Hualalai and Mauna Loa, one of the highest mountains in Hawaii (Anderson, 1960:174). All of this time, Vancouver was involved in political negotiations to have Hawaii ceded to Great Britain.

In early March of 1794, both the *Discovery* and *Chatham* set sail from Niihau Island. The *Chatham*, under the command of Puget, dropped anchor in a small harbor on the Kenai peninsula, where they were storm bound for the next two weeks. Meanwhile, the *Discovery*, with Menzies aboard, worked its way up Cook's Inlet, Cook's Gulf or River, as it was known at that time. Menzies' Journal now resumes in March of 1794, as the *Discovery* approaches the Alaska coast east of Kodiak Island. (See Map 3.)

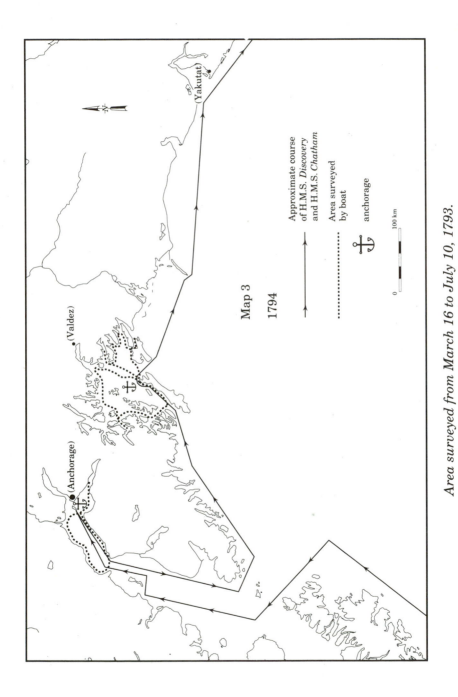

(Yakutat)

(Valdez)

(Anchorage)

Map 3
1794

Approximate course
of H.M.S. *Discovery*
and H.M.S. *Chatham*

Area surveyed
by boat

anchorage

0   100 km

Area surveyed from March 16 to July 10, 1793.

[March 1794]

16th At day light on the 16th the Chatham was not to be seen any where within our horizon from the Mast head, She had been observd following us round the little Island at some distance on the preceeding evening, & as we had shapd our course about dusk to N & W, it is probable they did not notice it, but immediately hauld close upon a wind, which was East North East instead of going a point or two free as we did, by which means we separated. A false fire was burnt as a signal to denote our situation at ten on the preceeding night but was not answerd.[1]

We perseverd in our North by West course for some days without meeting with any incident deserving of notice. The weather was dark & cloudy & the wind blew from the North East quarter, sometimes fresh & squally. We had about us several of the Birds already mentiond but their number lessend as we increased our distance from the little Island.

22d By the 22d we found the wind became fluctuating & inconstant in its direction, but the weather continued lowering & cloudy & the temperature of the air particularly in the evenings was become much cooler, so that we were obligd to throw aside our light tropical dresses & have recourse to warmer cloathing.

25th On the 25th we had a fresh breeze of wind from the Southward & South west quarter accompanied with softer & milder weather than we had for some days past, but the sky was overcast with a thick gloomy haze this & the preceeding day, that we had no sight of the sun the whole time. We had a number of Oceanic Birds about us, such as Albatrosses, Sheerwaters, & some other smaller birds of the Petrel tribe; amongst them I observd one kind of bird which I had not before seen, it was about the size of a sea gull, white about the head & under the body, the back wings & tail of a greyish colour, with a white spot in the middle of each

1. According to Manby's journal (Vancouver, 1798(1984):1206) once they parted company with the *Discovery*, they opened their Rendezvous No. 6 instructions designating Cooks River as the place they were to meet.

Wing & their tips black. As the number of birds were increasing towards evening, & the weather being exceedingly hazy, it was not thought prudent to run on all night, we therefore shortend sail & hauld our wind till day light.

We were probably inducd to take this precaution from our being now nearly in the same parallel of Latitude where Capt Cook, Mr Portlock Mr Dickson[2] & others had fallen in with those indications which strongly countenance the probability of some land existing near this situation, & as our track lay a few degrees to the West of the former tracks, it was so far favorable, by extending the search for it, had the weather not provd so very hazy that we could see but a very short distance round us.

26th After we made sail next morning the Man that watchd at the Mast head calld out that there were weeds or something floating a head of the Ship, & as we approached nearer, he suddenly calld out it was a Rock, but before he had the word well out of his mouth, the Vessel passd close to it, when it was discoverd to be the root part of a large tree wholly covered with Barnacles, & the stumps of it being above water, made it appear very much like a picked[3] Rock. Another piece of drift wood was seen about mid-day with an abundant crop of Barnacles attachd to it, but we had fewer birds about us to day than yesterday. The wind was westerly with moderate & clear weather, so that we had more sunshine this day than we had for some time past.

27th Next day the wind continued westerly & blew very fresh & squally the whole day, with some showers of rain. The different Oceanic Birds already mentioned were this day about us, nearly as numerous as on the 25th. This westerly wind coming probably from the Mountains of Siberia provd so exceeding cold at night that several Turtle we brought from the Sandwich Islands in a tub of water were all found dead next morning, & by dipping a Thermometer into the Water in which they were it was found to

---

2. Captains Nathaniel Portlock and George Dixon had explored Cook Inlet in 1786.

3. "peaked."

be so low as 40° whilst that in the open air did not fall lower than 45° from which it would seem that this amphibious animal is unable to bear so low a temperature at least in water, though I believe they are known to bear much lower in the open air.

29th On the morning of the 29th we had a very fresh breeze with rain & sleet from North West which towards noon became westerly but fair, & in the evening it veerd to the South west quarter blowing still fresh, with cloudy weather & with snow at night.

The wind continued from S W for the following day with some snow in the morning but fair & clear in the afternoon. We passd some floating sea weeds at two different times, & saw two Divers & some sand pipers or small plovers.

31st On the 31st the wind was Westerly most part of the day, in the morning it was fresh & squally with snow, when we passd some more sea weeds, but in the afternoon it was in light airs with a long interval of calm & snow again at night, & for the two following days we had variable & fluctuating wind but chiefly from between northeast & northwest with cloudy weather & some snow.

[April]

3rd In the afternoon of the 3d of April we saw land bearing North by East of us & stood for it till about 8 in the evening when we hauld off to the Southward till two next morning & then stood again towards it, by noon we passed within three miles on the east side of it, when it provd to be an Island of about eight or ten leagues in circumference, formd by elevated hilly land covered with snow, & off the South West point of it we observd some detachd rocks. At noon when we were nearly due East of it about three Miles our Latitude by a meridian altitude was 55° 48' N the extremes of the Island were from N 55° W to S 30° W & our own soundings were 23 fathoms black sand, so that the centre of the Island is about the Latitude of 55° 50' N & Longitude 204° 42' East of Greenwich, & about 20 leagues to the SW of Trinity Island, from which we had not the least doubt of its being a new discovery, unknown at least to English Navigators.[4]

We afterwards steerd to the North Eastward & at six in the evening saw Trinity Island[5] bearing N 5° W by compass with the land behind it extending a little to the Eastward, & likewise some land at a distance to the Westward of it. We stood on towards the Island till after midnight, when we had soundings in 50 fathoms which inducd us to tack & stand for a few hours to the Southward.

5th Next forenoon we passd at the distance of about three leagues to the Eastward of Trinity Island which by a Meridian Altitude obtained when we were about 5 leagues to the North East of it, we place the centre of it in Latitude 56° 30' North & in Longitude 206° 12' East which will be found to differ a little from that of Capt Cooks, but it must be recollected that we differ from him at Nootka & other parts of the Coast, in placing the whole we have yet seen a little further to the eastward; here however the difference is greater, & must undoubtedly be attributed to the perverse winds & stormy foggy weather he met with on this part of the Coast preventing him from setting it with his usual accuracy, & this more especially as we afterwards found an error of about half a degree of Longitude in the relative situation of this Island to his Cape Greville, which are not above 27 leagues apart from each other. Cape Trinity[6] is a low point with rocky islets off it on the inside of Trinity Island, & is in Latitude 56° 44' N & Longitude 206° 20' East.

In the afternoon we stood in for the Coast with mild pleasant weather & light variable winds but chiefly from the Southwest quarter & as we were proceeding to the Northeastward along shore in the evening one of those skin canoes describd by Capt Cook came off to us with two men in her from a deep bay to the eastward of two headed point. These men gave us to understand

4. Vancouver (1798(1984):1209) named the island in honor of Bering's companion, *Tscherikov* (Chirikov).

5. Now Sitkinak and Tugidak Island, known as the Trinity Islands (Vancouver, 1798 (1984):1210).

6. Cape Trinity is the southern tip of Kodiak Island.

that the part of the Coast abreast of us was called Cadiak. I got
them to count their numerals which I found to agree exactly with
those of Prince William Sound,[7] so that it is probable the same
language & the same Nation extends thus far along the Coast.
They could also count by the numerals of Oonalaska.[8] but these
they might have learnd from the Visitors that usually accompany
the Russian Traders from thence along this part of the Coast,
especially as they made us understand there were Russians on
shore at this time to the Northeast of us.

After an interval of calm in the evening a breeze sprung up from
the northeastward right against us, & in the night time we had
thick hazy weather with snow, but next day we had sleet & rain
with the same perverse wind, which blew strong & squally
accompanied with thick weather; towards evening the weather
becoming more moderate & favorable we stood in for the Land, &
made it near Cape Barnabas namd in Mr Meares chart Cape
Hollings, for what reason he thought proper to alter Capt. Cook's
name we know not.[9] We tackd & stood off again for the night.

7th The wind continued still against us on the day following but
blew light & moderate with thick rainy weather & a few hours of
calm in the afternoon, so that our progress along the Coast was
slow & tedious, & as we had but imperfect glimpses of the land, we
could form no just idea of its general appearance.

8th We persevered in plying against the perverse wind & early on
the morning of the 8th was close in with the land a little to the
Southward of Cape Greville,[10] where the Shore appeard indented

7. When Menzies had been in Prince William Sound with Colnett he had
learned to count to ten in the Alutiiq Eskimo language which is spoken on the
Alaskan Peninsula, Kodiak Island and in Prince William Sound.

8. This would be the Aleut language which is distinct from, but related to
Eskimo.

9. The eastern extremity of Sitkalidak Island, off of the east coast of Kodiak
Island. According to Lamb (Vancouver, 1798(1984):1213 footnote), Cook had
named the cape on June 12, 1788 in honor of Saint Barnabas, whose feast day
had been the previous day. The same year, William Douglas had named it Cape
Hollings, but Cook's name has survived on the charts.

10. Now Cape Chiniak.

& broken with Bays & Inlets; the inland country is elevated broken & hilly, & at this time was wholly coverd with snow, but the projecting points & reefs near the shore were bare in consequence of the late thaw & appeard dreary & barren without either trees or bushes of any kind to enliven the prospect.

A little to the Southward of Cape Greville we observd a small elevated Island at this time mostly covered with snow, it is of a roundish form, about a league in circumference & about 2 or 3 miles removd from the land abreast of it, which is a remarkable low point in Latitude 57° 25' north. Capt Cook takes no notice of this little Island either in his description of this part of the Coast or in his Chart, which we were surprisd at, as such an omission, is seldom to be met with, in tracing the footsteps of this very accurate & celebrated Navigator.[11] During the night the wind was light but more favorable for weathering Cape Greville.

9th On the 9th we had dark hazy weather & light winds the whole day with some sleet & small rain. At noon our Latitude was 57° 19' north about four leagues to the eastward of the little round Island which was the only land in sight & bore of 06° W by compass. In the afternoon we had a glimpse of the land about Cape Greville which is low & rugged & backed by elevated hills coverd with snow. In the evening it was calm with a fall of snow & in the night time we frequently sounded & had from 35 to 50 fathoms over a bottom of sand and broken shells.

10th Next forenoon we had light airs mostly from the northwest quarter & intervals of calm in the middle of the day. Our Latitude at noon was 57° 28' North at nearly the same distance from land we were yesterday, so that we had since made very little progress. We observd in the Morning that the little island & the skirts of the shore were covered pretty low down with the fall of snow we had on the preceeding evening, but it soon disappeard again with the influence of the meridional sun. A breeze sprung up in the afternoon from Northwest, with which we stood pretty close in to the shore, & observd that from abreast of the little round Island

11. Lamb (Vancouver, 1798(1984):1213, footnote) lists this as Ugak Island.

to Cape Greville, the shore is skirted with low land, & the Cape itself is low & rugged with some scatterd rocks laying off it, but we could perceive no trees or bushes any where.

11th On the morning of the 11th the breeze became fresher & more favorable with a fine clear day, so that we made considerable progress to the northward. At noon we were abreast of the Island of St. Hermogenes[12] about four leagues due East of it in Latitude 58° 14' North, where we had sight of two high snowy mountains near Cape Douglas,[13] but we had a very indistinct view of the land about Whitsuntide Bay, as we passed it at so great a distance that we could see no part of the shore.

The south side of the Island of St. Hermogenes is formed by steep elevated Cliffs, but the East and North East sides rise with more gradual acclivity to a moderate height.

In the afternoon we continued standing to the northward across the entrance of Cook's River & at six in the evening saw Cape Elizabeth[14] bearing N 45 W while that of St. Hermogones bore S 20 W by compass. At eight in the evening we put our head to the Southward till midnight & then stood again for the Northward the remaining part of the night, with a fresh breeze.

We here observed no discoloration of the water nor no casual signs or indications that would leave us to suppose we were even in the vicinity of land, had we not previously known it, far less in the entrance of a great River; in short it differd in no other respect from the entrances of those inlets we had already examind on the Coast but by its spacious appearance.

12th We stood to the Northward on the 12th towards Cape Elizabeth, passing to the Eastward of the barren isles, about noon it fell calm for a few hours when our Latitude was 59° North, about four or five leagues to the Eastward of the Cape & about the same distance from the barren isles, nearly abreast of two round Islands

12. Marmot Island.

13. According to Lamb (Vancouver, 1798(1984):1214, footnote) these would be Mount Douglas and Fourpeaked Mountain.

14. The west end of Elizabeth Island. They were now entering Cook Inlet.

laying a little off the Coast, but not noticed in Cooks Chart. From Cape Elizabeth the shore trended Eastward & rose into rugged elevated Mountains many of which were of a peaked form & coverd with Snow down to the sea beach, on their sides however we could discover patches of pine trees shewing their dark verdant tops through the snow & adding some variety to the dreary landscape before us. Of the barren isles some are of a conic form, others rugged & elevated with their summits at this time entirely coverd with snow.

In the afternoon a light breeze came on with which we stood in between the barren isles & Cape Elizabeth[15] & observed about 5 or 6 miles to the southeast of the latter, a cluster of rocks shewing their black tops above water. We passd the Cape about six in the evening & stood to the northwestward along shore across a deep bay in the Southeast part of which we saw a passage through making the land of Cape Elizabeth an Island. We pursu'd our course along shore till near midnight, when the wind heading us from the Northward we were obligd to stand over for the western shore, & had thick weather with snow all night, & with soundings from 25 to 35 fathoms.

13th Finding about day light next morning that our soundings were decreasing & that the Weather continud thick & snowy with both wind & tide against us, we anchord in 20 fathoms, & when it cleard up a little, we found we were within 4 or 5 miles of the western shore, with Mount St Augustine S 7° W & Cape Douglas S 20° E. The former is a remarkable high conic mountain, which from the view we had of it appeard to be an Island, & its form would strongly indicate its being of a volcanic origin.[16]

The weather continuing unfavorable, we remained here all day & from some glimpses we had of the land to the westward of us, it appeard very mountainous, coverd with snow to the waters edge & interspersd here & there with trees shewing their heads

---

15. In 1963, this passageway was named Kennedy Entrance in honor of President John F. Kennedy (Orth, 1971:510).

16. Mount St. Augustine, named by Captain Cook on May 26, 1778 (Vancouver, 1798(1984):1217, footnote).

through the snow, but there were considerable tracts without any. Nearly abreast of us there appeard an opening or harbour.

14th Next day assisted by the flood tide we got a little higher up the River, but when it made against us in the afternoon we were obligd to anchor again on the Western shore, where we remaind all night & had fluctuating wind with thick weather & a light fall of snow, which continued nearly the same on the following day, so that we did not move from our station during these three days. The weather was so thick that we saw none of the land on the opposite side of the River.

It was observd that the snow fell here in the form of flat small starlike flakes, some had regularly six beautiful ramified rays issuing from the centre, other had more, but these were not near so handsomely ramified. The cause of this peculiar formation of the snow flakes I am at a loss to account for, as I never noticd the like before; unless the Volcano[17] which was at this time a little to the Westward of us, might impregnate the atmosphere with some peculiar vapour that may be allowd to occasion it in the process of congalation.

16th We proceeded to the Northward on the forenoon of the 16th with slow progress having but little wind. At noon our Latitude was 60° 11' North about two leagues to the southward of the south end of Channel Island.[18] We steerd for the passage between it & the western shore as it appeared a wide channel & had soundings from 12 to 18 fathoms. Soon after we enterd it, we were met by the ebb tide, which obligd us to come to an anchor. From hence the Volcano was seen for the first time bearing S 25 W. The smoke it emitted was so pale that it was difficultly discoverd, & as we saw no appearance of fire issuing from it, even at night, it was conjecturd to be only steam, which issued from two places contiguous to one another on the southeast side a little below the summit of the Mountain.

---

17. Lamb (Vancouver 1798(1984):1220, footnote) indicates that "the Volcano" is Iliamna Volcano. To the north is Redoubt Volcano. The volcanoes in this area have continued to generate steam and some have erupted in modern times.

18. Kalgin Island, directly west of the town of Kenai, Alaska.

In the afternoon three Canoes came to us from the Western shore with one Man in each, who with the utmost confidence made their canoes fast along side of the Vessel & came on board, & finding that they met with a friendly reception & good quarters, they a little afterwards begd that their canoes might be hauld up upon the booms, which was complied with, & they remain on board to take their passage with us up the river: Their language differd from that of Prince Williams Sound, so that we understood only very little of what they said, excepting by signs, which are at best but vague interpreters between strangers. They were well cloathd from head to foot with long frocks of Racoon Skins;[19] their hand were coverd with fur mittens, & their legs with leather boots, so that they were well equipped to withstand the rigor of the climate. They had broad flat visages & wore their hair cropped short round the Nape of the neck. We questioned them the best manner we could, to know if they had seen or heard of the Chatham, but we could not learn that they had.[20]

17th After breakfast next morning I landed with Capt. Vancouver & some of the Gentlemen on the south point of a small Bay abreast of us on the Island, but we could not prevail on the Indians to accompany us. We walkd round to the other point of the Bay where the Boat was sent to meet us, & observd some drift ice on the edge of the shore, & deep snow down to the very beach, so that we could not penetrate far into the wood, which was chiefly composd of the

---

19. According to biologists, raccoons (*Procyon lotor*) were not found in Alaska in historic times; some have been introduced in more recent times. One member of this family of animals is found on Vancouver Island. Jonathan Dean (personal communication) quotes a letter from the Russian Governor Kupreanov to Lieutenant Zarembo in which the Governor says that "The Main Office above all must know where the English predominantly procure the fur of the Inot, called by them Rakun (Raccoon)." It seems unlikely that the people in Cook Inlet would have obtained skins from a type of raccoon from as far away as Vancouver Island. It is more likely that the Natives made cloaks from animals such as the hoary marmot (*Marmota calligata*) which the British thought were made from raccoon skins. Several Native groups made clothing from small animals such as the hoary marmot.

20. In earlier times, Eskimos had occupied the east side of Cook Inlet, but by this time, Athabaskan Indians had pushed southward from the interior and controlled the western side of the Kenai Peninsula. These Indians, now known

Norway Spruce,[21] intermixd on the Bank along shore with a good deal of Alder bushes whose buds shewd no signs as yet of expansion or returning vegetation. We saw the tracks of some Animals but could not make out what they were. The bottom of the Bay was a sandy flat, dry at low water & strewd over with large stones.

The Commanding Officer on board had orders to get under way with the return of the flood tide, which he did about eleven, & began working up the Channel against a light breeze from the Northward attended with clear pleasant weather. We got on board by noon, & soon after as the ship was making a tack from the western shore towards the Island, the water gradually shoald till at last she grounded on a soft sandy bank, but was soon drove off by the force of the Tide, & we immediately deepend our water to 15 fathoms, where we came to an anchor. An officer was sent in a boat to sound all round us, & on his report, it was determind to return back again out of this Channel the way we came into it & go up the other side of the Island. Accordingly in the evening we weighd & made Sail to the Southward with light fluctuating airs & the assistance of the ebb tide, & as we got well out of the Channel we deepend our water to 30 fathoms, but as we were edging to the eastward round the south end of the Island we found a bank running out a considerable way from it,[22] on which after midnight we gradually shoald over water to four fathoms, & we could not for some time extricate ourselves off it, it was suspected that the Tide from the southward set us more & more upon it. At two in the morning the ship touchd & continued now & then touching & thumping pretty hard for near two hours, though during that time we had not by the lead line less than four & a half & five fathoms,

---

as the Tanaina, spoke an Athabaskan language which is entirely distinct from the Eskimo languages. In their adaptation to this region the Tanaina borrowed many things from the Eskimo, and so it becomes very difficult to determine whether the explorers were visited by Indians or Eskimos. Generally speaking, the Athabaskan Indians did not wear the lip plug or labret, nor made skin boats like the Eskimo. However, some Tanaina did wear the labret and make skin boats (Osgood, 1937). Menzies and Vancouver refer to all of the inhabitants of this area as Indians, and did not distinguish between Indians and Eskimos.

21. See Appendix.

22. A shoal extends for several miles off the south end of Kalgin Island.

from which was conjecturd that this Bank like the flat bay we saw in the morning, was strewd over with large stones, on which the ship now & then thumpd as she was passing over them. We had a breeze of wind & kept under Sail, but we did not know how far the tide counteracted our motion, as the night was very dark We anxiously lookd forward for the day light to extricate ourselves from so unpleasant a situation where we were kept in continual dread of the consequences. At last about the dawn of day we got off the Bank on the eastern side, & to our great joy gradually deepend our water. At four we stood to the northward again with a light breeze & cloudy weather & by eight we were at an Anchor within three miles of Channel Island nearly opposite to where we started from the preceeding evening.

Being slack tide about eleven we weighd & plyd to the Northward against an adverse breeze of wind, but the tide being in our favor we made good passage & in the evening reached the narrows[23] where we anchord within three miles of the west foreland in 17 fathoms & veerd out to a whole Cable. A canoe & two men came to us from the western shore & with the others staid on board all night.

19th Early on the morning of the 19th the Tides made so strong from the southward that our best bower Cable parted & we lost it & the anchor irrecoverably. We made Sail but soon after came to again & with the afternoon's flood which made at half past one, we weighd & plyd to the Northward against a fresh breeze with cloudy weather between the Bank in mid channel on which Capt Cook's Vessel grounded & the western shore, where we found good working room without having occasion to stand into less on either side than from ten to 15 fathoms. At seven in the evening we anchord near the North foreland about a mile & a half from the western shore & at midnight the Thermometer was so low as 19° & the Tide passd the Vessel at the rate of four knots.[24]

---

23. Vancouver named the lands on each side of the narrows as the East Foreland and West Foreland.

24. Vancouver (1798(1984):1224) mentions that the Indians on board indicated that their settlement was nearby which suggests that they were Tanaina Athabaskans.

20th At two next morning a quantity of drift Ice passd the Ship & at four we weighd & stood to the Northward, but had not gone far, when about sun rise, the appearance of a sandy shoal a head with driftwood & stones scatterd upon it inducd us to anchor again. A boat was hoisted out, & Mr. Whidbey was sent to examine & sound round it, but before he left the ship the appearance vanished & it was then supposd to be overflown with the tide; he however proceeded to the northward about two leagues without perceiving any thing like a shoal; he had all the way he went nearly the same depth of water as at the ship, hence it was concluded that it must be the floating ice carried up with the Tide that had been seen, & towards noon we were convincd in this opinion by a quantity of floating ice passing the ship & at a little distance putting on the same appearance. Being thus satisfied that there was no obstruction we weighd about two in the afternoon & with the assistance of the flood tide & a light breeze proceeded to the northward & in the evening as we were standing on for the north river,[25] a little beyond where Capt Cook turnd back with his Vessels, we gradually shoald our water to about six fathoms, & perceiving at the same time some Ice aground a little distance from us it was thought prudent to come to an anchor, & it was well we did, for at low water the Shoal was quite dry to within a mile of us, & strechd out from the northern shore both to the Eastward and Westward of us, strewd over with large pieces of ice that had grounded upon it.

Our sudden transition from the tropical regions to which our constitutions had been in some measure inurd, but ill fitted us to withstand such harrassing duty in this cold bleak & dreary country we were therefore anxious to find some port, where we might take refuge & and remain comfortably till the season broke up & the rigor of the Climate so far abated that we could commence our operations, for the frost was now so very intense, that a little before we got under way this morning the Thermometer was so low as 7°, at eight it was 13° & at noon it was no higher than 18° the effect of which was that several of our people were frost bit in performing their duty on this & the preceeding day.

---

25. Knik Arm of Cook Inlet.

21st Next forenoon we had dark snowy weather with strong wind from N N W, so that we remaind at anchor till about two in the afternoon when we weighd & stood to the Eastward along the edge of the Shoal, but as we were plying to the North Eastward for the entrance of the North River we again got into shallow water which obligd us to come to an anchor about two miles to the Northwestward of the Island[26] near the entrance of River Turnagain.[27] The tide of flood ran here about three knots an hour & we had a strong northerly breeze all night.

22nd Early on the following day Mr. Whidbey was sent with two boats to examine the Channel into the North River, he returnd about noon & reported that after he left the ship, he gradually deepend his water till he approachd the entrance of it, where he had 18 fathoms, & which he considerd about 3 leagues from the ship. We got under way in the afternoon & as we were working up, we got aground on a sandy shoal, but the tide soon floated us again & as we drifted into deeper water we anchord in 7 fathoms. At 11 at night it was high water, & the vertical rise was here about 20 feet. The temperature this day was from 22 to 35°.

23rd In the forenoon of the 23d Mr. Whidbey was again employd with two Boats in sounding the Channel, & after his return to the Vessel in the afternoon we weighd & stood into the North River, which is about two miles wide at the entrance, & we had Soundings from 10 to 25 fathoms. A gun was fird as a signal to the Chatham in case she might be laying hereabout waiting for us, but we heard no reply, nor could we learn from some Natives that visited us in several Canoes, that they had either heard or seen any thing of her, from which it was concluded she had not yet arrivd. After running up the North River about two leagues we shoald our water considerably & in the evening came to in seven

---

26. Fire Island, which Cook had named Turnagain Island (Vancouver, 1798(1984):1226, footnote).

27. Turnagain Arm which had been named by Cook in 1778 (Vancouver, 1798(1984):1226, footnote).

fathoms over a black sandy bottom.[28] A vast quantity of loose floating ice passd by the ship in the night time with the return of the ebb tide & the temperature this day was from 34° to 39° so that the weather was getting milder.

24th We were pretty certain that we had now reached with the Vessel as high up this River as Capt. Cook's boats penetrated, & on the morning of the 24th I landed on the eastern shore with Capt Vancouver & some of the officers, whose objects were to look for a convenient watering place, & a snug situation for the Vessel.[29] For this purpose we examined a Bay which appeared on that shore a little to the northward of us, but found it too shallow & indeed what we sounded of the River above us provd so shallow water, that it was the opinion the Vessel could not well go higher up; it was therefore determined to remove her a little lower down & nearer the eastern shore abreast of a small stream of fresh water & there to Moor & remain till the weather broke up & the Chatham joind us, but in doing this at slack water the ship ran aground on a sandy shoal in three fathoms where she remaind fast for about an hour & half till the tide floated her, when she was hove off into deeper water, where we dropped anchor for the night. Today the temperature was from 36° to 41°.

25th Next day after sounding round the shoal & finding a proper situation for the Vessel, she was removd in the evening near the eastern shore & moord in five fathoms. In the forenoon a party was sent on shore in the Launch to clear away the place where we were to wood & water at, & in the same Boat Mr. Orchard & some others landed with their fowling pieces to take the diversion of shooting; They walked along shore to a flat marsh at the bottom of the Bay to the Northward of us, where they met with pretty good sport, & found in the skirts of the wood a habitation containing several natives both men & women who behavd very docile & friendly, & presented them with some furs.

---

28. They had gone up the Knik Arm, apparently as far as the mouth of Eagle River.

29. In his journal, Vancouver (1798(1984):1229) briefly describes an abandoned Native settlement which they encountered here.

26th On the following day parties were landed on the duties of wooding & watering, & in the forenoon a large skin Canoe[30] came along side of the ship with about 20 Men in her all of them well clothed like those we had already seen lower down the river; They all came on board without any kind of hesitation or distrust when each of them separately made a present of some furs to the Commander, & then requested that their Canoe might be hauld up upon the Booms, which being complied with, they staid with us all night.

At noon a meridian altitude was obtaind by an artificial horizon on shore abreast of us which gave us our Latitude 61° 17' North.

I this day had a stroll on shore near the watering place, & though we had pretty mild weather for a few days past, yet I could not discover the least signs of returning vegetation in any plant whatever. The snow had in some measure dissolved near the edge of the wood, but when I attempted to penetrate but a short way into it I found the snow knee deep. The woods here were thick, but the trees were in general very small & consisted mostly of Birch, Poplar, Alder willow & a few scattering stinted trees of the Norway spruce. Amongst the underwood I could distinguish the following evergreens - Ledum palustre, Arbutus vitis idea et uva ursi -Cornus canadensis Pyrola rotundifolia et secunda. I started some of the grouse kind which were so wild that I could not come within shot of them, & took them to be the Tetrado canadensis.[31]

27th On the morning of the 27th our numerous Visitors had their canoe launchd & took their departure for the shore, giving us a song as they were going away which was of the plaintive cast & accompanied with actions differing very little from what we had seen on other parts of the Coast, each of the had in his hand as he went away a small piece of Iron & an ear shell or two, which poor

---

30. Vancouver (1798(1984):1231-2) gives an extended description of the visitors, and mentions another group which had been encountered by the shore party. Those on shore spoke a different language, which seems to indicate that they were meeting both Indians and Eskimos.

31. Tetrado canadensis is an obsolete classification. Most probably what Menzies saw was the Spruce Grouse (*Canachites canadensis*) which is sometimes locally called a Spruce Hen.

fellows were all the return they had for their generosity. They behavd themselves very quiet & peaceable, & though they were numerous & allowd to range through every part of the ship, yet they shewd no inclination to a pilfering disposition.

An Indian came down to the watering place in the forenoon who sollicited of the Officer on shore attending that duty to be brought on board the ship in one of our boats; he was the tallest & stoutest of any we had yet seen of the tribe, & had not like most of them his underlip either cut or perforated;[32] this at first sight led us to suspect that he was of some other nation, but nothing afterwards turnd out to countenance this opinion; he staid with us on board all night without the least fear or timidity in trusting himself among so many strangers.

28th[33] As the weather was now become much milder it was thought fit to commence our operations, though the snowy bleakness & dreary aspect of the country was by no means favorable for

---

32. Here again, it is not clear whether visitor was Eskimo or Indian.

33. In his entry of April 28, 1794, Sheriff (n.d.: folio 146) provides additional descriptions of the people. "Port Chatham is situate about 3 Leagues to the East of Point Bede. It is a most excellent harbour to refit in, being perfectly shelter'd from every wind that blows….There was a village in our neighbourhood, but I never visited it, though the Natives were with us whenever the weather would permit. They are of a middling size, much cleaner than the Natives to the South. Their Dress consists of a long Garment made of skins of the different animals, Fox, Bear or Racoon &ec; w which if it is fine weather in the Day time, they wear the Hair outwards, but at night turn it for warmth, in Rainy or Snowy weather, a frock of thin Gut very neatly sewn, with a Hood is worn over this, the Bottom edge with a thin strip of seal skin, which when in their canoes they fix in a groove round the Hole in which they sit, which keeps all weath from them, & it may be said their Canoes & themselves are of one pair; the Ornaments they wear are Beads in different shapes & sizes, the division in the Nose is, likewise perforated but I seldom observ'd any ornament there. All I can say of the Canoes, is they are like those of the Esquimaux which is well known, only, rather broader & I saw none with more than two holes except what the Russians make use of & but few of one hole. They must certainly be a very honest people among themselves, if I may judge from their behaviour to us; every man generally brought a little bag of the different curiosities of this country, & without hesitation, when being asked to look at it, it was immediately handed up & the owner would either follow or not as he found it convenient, so that they left it entirely to us to do as we pleas'd with it; what comparison between these & the more Southern savages, but I am much afraid

Men undergoing hardship & fatigue to sleep out at nights. Two boats mannd armd & equippd with ten days provision left the Ship early on the morning of the 28th under the command of Mr. Whidbey & proceeded on a surveying expedition to the southward with orders to explore River Turnagain as far as he was able. The Indian who came on board yesterday being suspected of pilfering was sent on shore in disgrace & we saw no more of him. We had low water this day at eleven in the forenoon & with the flood tide vast quantities of loose ice came from the southward & passing us with such rapidity, that we were kept in continual alarm least the ship should be cut adrift by the Ice. At a quarter past five we had high water, so that the flood tide had run about seven hours, & it rose 34 feet in vertical height. Two Indians visited us this day from the Northward in an open Canoe covered with Birchbark similar to those usd by the Canadian Indians, which was a thing we had not before met with on this Coast; this canoe was hauld up upon the Booms to prevent its being damaged by the Ice, & the two Natives took up their quarters with us all night.[34]

29th Next morning after the launch had landed the wooders & sporting party, as they were pulling along shore with her to the watering place in order to bring off some water, they were surrounded by a batch of loose ice that took the ground on the outside of them in twelve feet water & obligd them to remain fast lockd up till it floated again with the afternoon tide. The sporting

---

they were not always treated with equal candour, as, when we were about leaving this river, they appear'd to be more suspicious & not so ready to hand up their goods unless they would come on board themselves. There are a number of curiosities among them, such as a Line, Darts, Bows, Arrows, Bags, &ec: The line is made of the gut of different marine animlas neatly plaited & some very curious work of red feathers in the plaits, the Bags are made of the large gut of marine animals likewise edg'd with neat plating of different colours. The Darts are headed with Bone in which is fix'd the line made of gut it is thrown by hand, out of a piece of wood made for that purpose. I did not see a woman while we were here, but I understand all the lines, Bags, &ec: are made by them. The Lat. & Longitude of Port Chatham is [missing]"

34. The use of the birch bark canoe is a strong indication that these visitors were Tanaina Indians, not Eskimos, because in this area it was usually the Indians who made birch bark canoes.

party walkd to the Marshy Bay to the northward of us, where they met with very good sport among wild geese Ducks & plovers, for as the weather had now broke up, game of every kind became daily more plenty.

The Birch Canoe was put into the water in the afternoon & our two Visitors left us seemingly well pleasd with the indulgence they received; their dress manners & language were the same with the other Indians who visited us in the large Canoe, but the language here seemd to be very different from that spoken in Prince Williams Sound.

We had high water in the evening at a quarter past six & the vertical rise was 38 feet, the first part of the flood ran over five knots an hour & brought in with it an immense quantity of ice which struck the ship in passing us with such force & rapidity that it carried away one of our cables.

30th On the following morning it was high water twenty minutes after six, which was nearly about the time the moon changed. As access to the shore was now become so difficult on account of the ice & the rapidity of the tide, all the parties were brought on board to attend the Vessel, which in our present situation was of infinite more consequence, & likewise to assist in our endeavours to recover the lost Anchor, the want of which would greatly distress us on account of our late losses in that way. A little past noon when the tide somewhat slackd Lt. Baker was sent in a boat with some men to seek for the Cable we had parted yesterday, & after a good deal of perseverance we were happy to find that their endeavours were successfull; the end of the cable was brought on board, by making a hawser fast to it & both it & the anchor were recoverd to our great satisfaction.

In the forenoon our old friends in the large Canoe paid us a another visit, equally numerous as before, together with a small Birch Canoe, but neither of them brought any thing to dispose of; They staid on board till the flood tide brought the ice back again from the Southward, & their Canoe being then in some danger alongside they all jumped into her, & together with the Birch Canoe went off to the Northward.

About four in the afternoon a large whale boat was seen coming towards the Ship from the Southward & on her approaching near to us, those in her fird a Musket, on which we hoisted our colours, & they then fird another Musket, but the tide ran so strong, that they were hustled past the Ship & would have missed her, had we not veerd a bouy a stern, of which they got hold, & we hauld them along side, when they provd to be nine or ten Russians in a large whale Boat made of Firplank, & rowd by 14 of the Natives who sat double banked & rowd seven oars of a side; We were so unfortunate as not to have any one on board who could speak the Russian language, they however made us understand that they had seen our two boats to the southward of Point Possession, & that they came from a Settlement on the east side a little below the narrows, & they assurd us that this great Inlet terminated a few leagues above us; that River Turnagain also terminated without going far, & was intercepted from a western branch of Prince Williams Sound only by a small hilly ridge, where they frequently cross over from one branch to the other on their commercial pursuits.[35] The were very desirous of spiritous liquor & tobacco, of both which they had a small supply, & in the dusk of evening when the ebb tide made strong in their favor they set off again to the Southward.

[May]

1st On the 1st & 2d of May a vast quantity of ice floated up & down with the tide & kept us in continual alarm, the reason of its harassing us so much at the time was that the Spring tides had floated all the loose ice which at the nipe[36] tides grounds upon the flats about the head of the inlet, & to our great annoyance was now carried up & down with such rapidity that we were under apprehensions of being carried adrift with it. On the afternoon of the

---

35. This is the portage between Portage and Whittier. At this time, there were two Russian companies engaged in the fur trade in this region. On the east shore, near the Forelands was an establishment of the Lebedev-Lastochkin Company, and farther south, on the east shore, at English Bay, was a post of the Shelikov-Golikov Company. These visitors were workers from the Lebedev-Lastockin firm.

36. Neap tides. These are the tides which occur at the end of the first and third quarter of the lunar month, and are the smallest tides.

latter day as they were heaving in the slack of the Cable at low water, the ship grounded on a rock or large Stone, but luckily the flood tide having soon made she was hove off again, & at high water was removd further into mid channel.

3d On the 3rd & 4th we had thick hazy weather with a good deal of rain & thaw, & as the tides decreased in vertical height, we were troubled with much less ice, which shewd that it was grounding again on the banks & flats. In the afternoon of the latter day Mr.Whidbey returnd from the Southward with the two boats having explored what had been calld River Turnagain, for about six leagues from its entrance, & found it so shallow that it was not conceived necessary to pursue it to the very end, indeed it was scarcely navigable for Vessels, above four or five miles from where Capt Cook anchord. After this he proceeded down the eastern shore as far as the narrows & found the navigation on that side very intricate on account of a number of picked[37] & sunken rocks with which the shore was in general lind; It was there they met the Russians who visited the Ship & who on seeing the two boats immediately armd themselves & loaded their Muskets. On the East foreland Mr.Whidbey observd for the Latitude & found it to be 60° 43' North. From thence they crossed over to the opposite point & returnd to the Vessels along the western side without meeting any opening or inlet deserving of examination. They found a Russian settlement on the north foreland,[38] where they were obligd to encamp for two days on account of the haziness of the weather. These Russians in their clothing food & manner of living, differd very little from the Natives of the Country, they made use of dryd fish for bread, & a Mess of cranberries fish & oil mixd up together formd a favourite dish with them, which they devourd with uncommon relish.

5th Next day we had variable light airs & calms alternately, & the ice being now less troublesome, the boats were again employd in wooding & watering. Two Canoes visited us from the Southward,

---

37. "peaked."

38. West Foreland.

in one of which was an old man we had left at the narrow on our way up the inlet.

6th Two boats previously prepared & victualld with four days provision, set out at four in the morning of the 6th of May, in order to examine the head of the inlet; On this expedition I accompanied Capt Vancouver & some of the Officers in the Pinnace; we first proceeded along the western shore & on coming abreast of a small elevated hammock we landed & climbd up to its summit, from whence (it being about low water) we had a good view of the Banks & sandy shoals which seemd to extend across the inlet about 3 or 4 miles above the ship, & backd one another to the very head of the arm: Our station at this time was little more than a league above where Capt Cooks boats returnd, & had they come up thus far what a satisfactory view they would have had of the termination of this great inlet, where they could behold the impossibility of navigating it higher up, & consequently prevented the indulging of those chimerical speculations concerning its spacious & unbounded extent.[39]

After leaving this station & going a little further on, we were necessitated to cross over to the eastern side where we found deeper water & where the shore was in general bolder, for the western side appeared in extensive sandy flats strewd over with vast quantities of broken ice; on approaching near the head of the Arm where it takes a little turn to the North East, we found an extensive flat meadow on which we landed with our guns to take the diversion of shooting, whilst the boats pulld on along shore, as the place was mostly clear of snow, & ducks & geese were now become very numerous on the marshy situations. We strolld across this plain till we came to the verge of the wood, where we found some huts inhabited by several families of the Natives, who shewd no kind of fear or timidity at our approach, but receivd us with a degree of frankness that we seldom experiencd amongst the Natives on this Coast, though we had every reason to believe that the Russian Traders were the only foreigner strangers who had

---

39. Menzies is critical of the Cook expedition for not having made the effort to ascertain whether or not this body of water was a river or an inlet.

previously visited them in this interior region. [Most of the men had their under lips slit across, in which they wore a piece of flat oblong ivory, but the women had their underlips perforated with a row of holes, from which appended thongs & other ornaments over their chin, & some of them were clothed in a kind of white strong fur, which we had not before seen any where on the coast, & from the size of the pelts I had little doubt but they were the skins of the Mountain sheep which are said to inhabit this Country, though I could not collect any satisfactory information concerning them, as I knew so little of the language of these Natives.]

After distributing some Beads Buttons & other small articles amongst the women & children, we reimbarkd in the boats on our return to the Vessels having now finished the examination of this great Arm, which in future we must call from the size it by the name of *Cook's Gulph* as it no more resembles a *river* than any other great Inlet on the coast. The head of it is surrounded by a ridge of high snowy mountains from which some small rillets fall into it, & both sides of it are here environd by extensive tracts of low land, mostly wooded with small Birch Trees & straggling pines of the Norway spruce. We got back to the Vessel at four in the afternoon without landing any where else; In the dusk of the evening we heard the report of a gun to the southward of us, which was answerd by firing one from the Discovery, & a little afterwards repeating it, as we fondly hopd that it was the Chatham coming towards us, but the evening being dark we could see nothing of her.

The land to the westward of the Arm in which we were now situated, is low flat & wooded for about nine or ten leagues, & extends to the northward & northwestward between the range of Mountains at the head of the Arm & those to the Westward of the great Inlet, without any intervening hills or mountains as far as the eye could perceive. It was through this low land that Capt Cook supposd the principal branch of the river to run, which we have this day determind does not exist, & indeed we cannot well reconcile Capt Cook's account of this part of the Coast to his usual precision & accuracy, as he states that they tracd the river as high as the Latitude of 61° 30' North, without seeing the least appearance of its source, yet we found its termination a few miles short of that Latitude. On the eastern side of the Arm there is also a tract of three or four leagues of low woody land between it & the range of snowy mountains.

With respect to the freshness of the water which Capt Cook observd & which principally inducd him to suppose this to be a great river, that might proceed from his being here about a month later in the season when the great quantity of Ice & Snow on the Banks & round the swampy bays about the heads of the inlet, would in a great measure be dissolvd, & cause the particular freshness which he takes notice of at low water, & this has no doubt been the case, as we now found the water saltish at every stage of the tide to the very head of the Arm.

In several places where deep water is marked in Capt Cook's Chart, we now found to be shallow & in some places dry at low water, whether these shallows have originated since his time or are owing to the inaccuracy of the survey, cannot be ascertained, though the former is not at all unlikely when we consider the rapidity of the tides, & the vast quantity of mud & rubbish they are carrying from the banks of the inlets in their continual motion up & down.[40]

7th At day light on the 7th we had sight of the Chatham at anchor about 4 or 5 miles to the southward of us near the entrance of this small Arm & soon after an Officer was sent in a boat on board her, on his return we learnd that she had arrivd in the inlet the same day we did, but enterd it between Point Banks & the Barren Isles, while we enterd it between Cape Elizabeth & the barren isles, by which means we missed seeing one another, & as the weather was then so unfavorable, she went into a harbour behind Cape Elizabeth,[41] where she waterd & refitted, after which she began her operations at Cape Douglas & examind the western side of the Inlet in her way up.

---

40. Menzies seems to be trying to reconcile his respect for Captain Cook as a navigator with the weaknesses and discrepancies in Cook's journal.

41. Vancouver named this anchorage Port Chatham (1798(1984):1250).

Having now perfectly satisfied ourselves with respect to the termination of this great inlet, we weighed about one in the afternoon,[42] & with the ebb tide in our favor made sail, & began working against a southerly breeze out of this Arm. On coming abreast of the Chatham she joind us, & we both plyd to the Southward till about five in the afternoon, when we lost the wind, & the flood tide meeting us, obligd us to come to an anchor in 15 fathoms within a mile of the Island near the entrance of Turnagain arm. From this station (the evening being remarkably clear) we had a view of the Volcano Mountain, though it was near forty leagues from us, & we also saw over the low land a range of high mountains at a great distance to the N W of us, which we had not before perceivd.

While we lay at the head of this inlet we had light variable winds or calms & fair clear frosty weather till about the beginning of May, when the weather began to soften considerably, & we then had some days of rain & thick misty weather, which with the influence of the sun in the day time, made a rappid progress in thawing the snow on the lower & ground on both sides of the inlet, and though the Mercury in the Thermometer now seldom sunk below 40° & was in the day time frequently up to 48° yet the chilly rawness of this weather was more sensibly felt by our constitutions than the preceeding frosty weather, & the consequence of it was that many complaind of lassitude & languid inactivity for some days.

In the evening two Russians came to us in a large Canoe from the Settlement which Mr Whidbey had visited on the North Foreland & they both staid with us all night.

8th Early next morning we took the advantage of the first of the ebb tide & weighd tho we had but little wind, & as we were coming over what I conceivd to be a Bar nearly abreast of the Island we regularly shallowd our water to three & half fathoms & again

42. While in Cook Inlet, Vancouver named Point Woronzof in honor of the Russian Ambassador; Point Mackenzie in honor of the Honorable James Stuart Mackenzie and Point Campbell in honor of Sir Archibald Campbell, who was Governor of Jamaica in 1785 when Vancouver was serving in the West Indies (Orth, 1971).

deepend our Soundings upwards of ten fathoms. The weather was remarkably serene & pleasant, & as we had but light variable airs & calms by turns, we were obligd to come to, & got under way as the tide suited. In the evening we anchord near the north foreland, when a boat was sent to search for a grapnell which Mr. Whidbey lost at the time he was here in the boats, & had now the good luck to recover it.

9th Early next morning we both weighd again with the first of the ebb, which with the assistance of a light air from the Northward, brought us by noon to the narrows between the Forelands, where we stopd during the next tide, & where we did not find the stream near so strong as when we went to the northward. Our Sounding in the channel to the westward of the Shoal on which Capt. Cook's Vessel grounded, was from seven to 26 fathoms.

10th On the 10th we droppd down with the morning ebb along the eastern shore till we came abreast of the Russian settlement, which is about four leagues below the narrows, & there we anchord at seven in shallow water.[43] Soon after some Russians came along side the Discovery in a whale boat, with an invitation to the Commander to visit the Settlement, & as the Pinnace was preparing for the purpose, I accompanied Capt Vancouver in her together with a Russian that came down with us from the other Settlement. As we came near the shore the Gentleman wanted us to fire off a Musket, but as this was refusd, from a motive of not disturbing some Game we saw on shore till we came sufficiently near to them, he instantly took his own pistol, & fird it in the Air, this was immediately answerd by firing a small swivel from the settlement & the same ceremony was again repeated on both sides. Whether this was intended as a compliment, or was an established signal of friendship between themselves we did not know.

We enterd a small creek with very shallow water, which did not appear to be above a quarter of a mile wide & ran into the land in an easterly direction about a mile. The settlement is situated on

---

43. Off the mouth of the Kenai River.

the summit of a bank on the north side of the entrance, under which we observd a two masted Vessel of between 60 & 70 tons burthen hauld on shore above high water mark, in which situation they told us she had been laid up two years, & was still to remain a year longer, & then she could be fitted out & sent back with a cargo of Furs to Kamschatka.

On our landing two Russians came down to the water side to receive us, & to conduct us to the settlement, which we found enclosd with high poles. On entering we observd several men drawn up under arms, which they immediately laid down on our approach, & we were then conducted into a large log house by a narrow passage guarded by a Sentinel, after passing which, we enterd a long area in the middle of the house, & were desird to walk to the further end of it, where we were seated on a bench by a small table. This house was about 25 yards long & 8 or 9 wide, wholly floord with planks, & the two sides of it were divided off from one end to the other like so many open stalls in a stable, for sleeping places; in each of these there was a broad bench, raisd a little from the floor, & divided in the middle by a small partition, so as to serve for two people, & the only bed furniture was a deer skin or a bear skin spread on the naked boards. They set upon the table before us, some cold dryd Halibut & narrow stripes of dried raw Salmon as a substitute for bread, but we could not make use of it, for the stench which assailed our Nostrils on entring the settlement made us loathe everything, it was really suffocating & such as we could not long endure - it arose from the putrid filth & garbage of animals that had been strewd about the place during the winter time, which being now thawd, & the effluvia set in motion by the suns eschalation, producd such a penetrative & putrid stench round the place that we were much astonished how any human beings could exist in such a tainted & pestiferous atmosphere,[44] & yet these people had all a very healthy appearance, though they have neither bread nor flour nor liquor but live entirely on the produce of the Country like the Natives.

---

44. Vancouver (1798(1984):1256) describes the odor as "a most intolerable stench, the worst, excepting that of the skunk, I had ever the inconvenience of experiencing."

We understood that this Settlement was established about 12 years ago & at this time it had about 40 Russians besides a number of Indians belonging to it. The present Commander Mr.Stephen Zyhoff[45] who they said bore the rank of a Lieutenant in the Russian service, had gone off about five or six days before by the way of Turnagain arm to visit the Settlements in Prince Williams Sound. The person who was at this time left in trust of the settlement, told us that he had been already eight years on this station. They were all clothd without any distinction in long frocks of dressd skins lind with the common furs of the country, engirdled by a belt round their waist & with breeches & boots of the same materials.

About one in the afternoon we returned to the Vessels & about an hour after both got under way & steerd to the Southward, but were obligd to come to again at 8 in the evening. Our Soundings this Tide were from nine to 22 fathoms.

11th Early in the morning of the 11th we again weighd & continued our slow progress to the Southward. In the forenoon we hoisted in the Launch & made other preparations for going out to sea, as it was now determined to stop no where else in this gulph, but to make the best of our way round to Prince Williams Sound, the scantiness of the wind however obligd us to come to again in the evening, to prevent our being carried back by the tide. Our station was five six miles from Anchor point & nearly abreast of it, & our Soundings this day was from 15 to 21 fathoms.

12th The following day we tided it with slow progress to the Southward & in the evening anchord nearly abreast of Coal Harbour, having between this station & Anchor point, crossd the entrance of a large deep Bay[46] running several leagues to the

---

45. Lamb (Vancouver, 1798(1984):1257, footnote) gives his name as Stepan Kasmovitch Zaikof, presumably the same person referred to as Potap Zaikov. Dr. Lydia Black (personal communication) says that the individual was Stepan Zaikov of the Lebedev-Lastochkin Company.

46. Kachemak Bay.

Eastward, with several apparent openings on the south side of it & at the bottom.

From this Bay an extensive flat woody Country environs the whole East side of the gulph to the very head of it, & at a little distance from the bottom of this Bay, a ridge of high snow mountains ran in a north easterly direction towards the bottom of Turnagain Arm, & from thence continued round the head of the North Arm, where it terminated.

Soon after we came to an Anchor, some canoes came off to us from Coal Harbour,[47] & some Russians who were on the shore sent us some fish with a message that they would come on board next day to pay their respects, & though the forenoon provd calm & favorable for their intended visit, yet none of them came near us till after we weighd about noon when they observd we were going away, though we had rousd their attention in the morning by firing a gun & shewing our colours, from thence it would appear that they were a little timorous of putting themselves in our power, whatever the cause might be, for a number of the Natives were about us in their Canoes dispensing of little articles of curiosity all the forenoon, & after we weighd as I have already observd two Russians came on board who staid about two hours, when finding the wind freshen, & that we were likely to get out to sea, they hastend into their Canoes & left us in great hurry without taking leave. These Russians told us that their Commanding Officer whom they calld Alexd[r] Barenoff[48] resided at Kodiac a little to the Southward of Point Banks where they generally had one or two Vessels in what they considered an excellent harbour, & they were very desirous that we should stay a few days longer that he might have an opportunity to visit us, as they promisd to send for him for that purpose.

---

47. Now Coal Cove in Port Graham.

48. In 1790, Aleksandr Baranov was hired as the manager of the Shelikov-Golikov Company in Alaska. Three years later, he moved the headquarters of the company to St. Paul Harbor at Chiniak Bay, the site of present day Kodiak. With the establishment of the Russian-American Company in 1799, Baranov functioned as the governor or chief Russian official in Alaska until his departure in 1817.

In the evening we passd Cape Elizabeth & soon after found the wind become light & baffling with long intervals of calm during the night, yet we kept under way in the channel between the Cape & the Barren Isles & had soundings between 40 & 55 fathoms.

14th Early on the morning of the 14th two Russians came on board & orderd a large quantity of Halibut to be hauld in from a number of canoes along side, after which finding that it was likely to come on blowing weather, as we were standing over for the eastermost of the barren isles, they went into their canoes & landed on these Islands. The wind was now fresh from N E right in our teeth, with dark gloomy & hazy weather & a short disagreeable swell, which with a strong flood tide drove us back as we stood over to the Cape Elizabeth side of the channel. This together with the unsettled appearance of the weather inducd us about noon to bear up & run into the Inlet & after passing Point Bede[49] we anchord within two miles of the small flat island abreast of Coal Harbour, where we were soon visited by several of the Natives & a brisk trade was kept up between them & our people in bartering for curiosities the whole afternoon.

15th We had light variable wind with intervals of calm most part of the 15th canoes were along side traficing as on the preceeding day, but none of the Russians who livd on shore opposite to us came near us, though they sent us some fish as before which was not accepted, as we had procurd a plentiful supply of Halibut from the Natives.

In the afternoon one of the Russians who went with us yesterday morning to the Barren Isles, came on board & told us that he had been all night on these Islands & also assurd us, that their Commander Mr. Alex^dr Barenoff was on his way thither from Kodiac to pay us a visit. After a short stay this man went on shore to Coal Harbour & about two in the afternoon we both weighd our anchors & having but light baffling wind, we drifted out with the tide which ran here about three knots an hour. After passing Cape

49. A point about thirteen miles south of the town of Seldovia, near Port Graham.

Elizabeth in the evening we experienced a fine breeze from the SW quarter, with which we stood along shore to the northwestward all night, & finally quitted this great Inlet which has occupied our remarks for upwards of a Month, & added not a little to the anxieties perplexities & hardships incidental to Voyages of this nature.

The Natives of this great Inlet or Gulph are of a low stature, but thick & stout made with fat broad visages black eyes & straight black hair, their mouth & nose are generally small. In their disposition they seem to be good naturd friendly & peaceable, & during our stay amongst them, they gave us very little reason even to suspect either their fidelity or honesty. Most of their implements exhibit a degree of neatness in the execution, that far surpassd all other rude nations we met with, for if we examind their clothing & see with what care they form & sow them, so as not to admit the least drop of rain; & their canoes are equally neat having their Seams sowd so tight as not to admit any water. Their Harpoons darts cordage & little leather bags shew a degree of art that would do credit even to the most civilized nations.

16th Early in the morning of the 16th we were visited by a vast group of Canoes, & as we had but a light breeze they easily kept way with us along shore, I dare say the number that surrounded both Vessels could not be less than 150 canoes most part of the forenoon, with generally two men in each, for we observd no women or children amongst them, & their object seemd to be to dispose of their little articles of curiosity, such as Bows Arrows Darts Lines Nets & small leather bags, together with their lip & ear ornaments, all of which were executed with a wonderful degree of neatness & ingenuity that far surpassd the handicrafts of most other indian tribes we have met with, but they had no kind of furs whatever to dispose of, which is a proof of the vigilance of the Russian Traders, as well as their honesty & upright conduct towards these new Masters. Some of these canoes joind us from sea, where they had been out fishing, & from them we procurd a supply of very good Halibut, for Beads, Looking glasses & Pewter Spoons, the white stone ware Beads were preferrd & next to them the red glass Beads.

In our little dealings with this Tribe we could not but be struck with their candour & implicit confidence for as few of them were admitted on board & the Canoes were too numerous to get all close along side, they would frequently hand on board their little bags containing the articles to be disposed of from the farthest off canoe & sufferd as many of us as pleased to overhauls them, & to fix upon what we likd, whilst the Owner sat composedly in their canoes without shewing the least uneasiness or apparent suspicion. When the Purchasers made choice of any article, it was shewn to the owner, who fixed a price upon it, & if his demand was agreed to, he was pleasd, but if otherwise he received his bag & articles again without shewing the least dissatisfaction. Most of these Natives took snuff & chewed Tobacco, a custom they have no doubt learnd from the Russians, & they frequently begd us very earnestly for both or either of these articles of artificial luxury.

This large party appeard from their having no women or children with them to be upon some occupation the object of which we could not learn. They appeard to subsist by their own industry in fishing & hunting, & were very expert darters, seldom missing their aim, as they shewd us an instance or two of their dexterity in this way by killing some gulls that lighted upon the water at a little distance from the Ship. They accompanied us till near noon, when they went into a very extensive Bay a little to the Westward of what we conceived to be Point Gore[50] of Mr. Portlock, which we make about 12 leagues to the Eastward of Cape Elizabeth. The Latitude observed was 59° 10' north within two miles of this point which has a steep perpendicular appearance towards the sea & joins the main by a low narrow neck of land.

We continued our progress to the Eastward along shore with a fine breeze from the Southwest & pleasant weather the whole afternoon. The coast here is very rugged & mountainous, with intevening deep Valleys that were at this time coverd with snow in many places, even down to the sea side & wooded with Trees here & there shewing their tops above the Snow.

In the evening the wind became variable & about midnight veerd to the northeast quarter, blowing fresh & squally with rain

---

50. On the southern end of the Kenai Peninsula.

& thick weather, which obligd us to stand off from the land most part of the night.

17th Next day the wind continued from the same quarter & blew in strong gales with heavy rain & thick misty weather. At ten we hove to, to secure our bowsprit which was found complaining & the Vessel was afterwards put under a snug sail with which we stood off & on all day without venturing to make the land in such unsettled & boisterous weather. It was some consolation to us that not withstanding our Vessel had taken the ground so often & been so much thumpd in Cook's Inlet yet it was not found now that she made any more water than usual. The Thermometer at noon was at 42°.

18th On the forenoon of the 18th the weather was much the same as on the preceeding day, but towards noon the wind veerd easterly & became more moderate which encouragd us to stand to the northward to Make the land, tho the weather was so hazy that we no observation on this or the preceeding day. We soon after saw a cluster of Islands to the N W of us, which we took to be what Mr. Portlock calld the Chiswell Islands[51] & at six in the evening, we tackd close to the outermost of these Islands but our view was very indistinct on account of the haze. During the night we plyd to windward & had soundings from 65 to 75 fathoms.

19th On the 19th the wind was moderate from E N E with showers of rain & sunshine alternately which afforded an opportunity at noon to ascertain our situation to be in Latitude 59° 16'N & as we stood afterwards to the Northward till about six in the evening, when we tackd a little to the Eastward of the outermost of the Chiswell Islands, we had a better opportunity of settling their situation than we hitherto had, but as the weather was still thick & hazy, we could not distinctly discern any other part of the coast or the Land within these islands.

We plyd to windward under an easy sail all night & next day, & had moderate wind from the N E quarter with thick hazy

---

51. Vancouver (1798(1984):1266) says that these islands had been named by Portlock (1787). They are off the southeast coast of the Kenai Peninsula.

weather & a good deal of rain. On the following evening the wind veerd to the southward with which we steerd North North East with crouded sail all night.

21st Next morning we made the South end of Montague Island,[52] which at noon bore W N W of us at the distance of ten miles, when our Latitude was 59° 38' North which will place it in Latitude 59° 46'. We stood to the Northward with a design to enter Prince Williams Sound by the passage on the East side of Montague Island but finding the wind become light & unfavourable, we bore up for the South West point of the Island, & rounded it at the distance of about two miles with soundings from 15 to 25 fathoms.

This end of the Island is very narrow & presents a bold shore facd here & there with perpendicular cliffs, backd by high & steep snowy mountains, wooded with Pines thinly scattered for a considerable way up their sides. We went up the Western side of the Island for about four miles, when at eleven the wind dying away after some heavy showers of rain we anchord within a mile of the shore in 20 fathoms.

22nd Next morning we were visited by two Natives in a canoe from a small Bay to the South East of us & as we had but light airs from the Northward, with which we could not attempt to move, the Chatham sent her Launch into Clouds Bay[53] which was about a league to the Northward of us, for some wood & water, as she was short of these articles. At ten both Vessels weighd & began working up the Channel on the inside of Montague Island, which is here about two leagues wide with the wind baffling & change-able in the forenoon, but in the afternoon it blew from the North East fresh and squally attended with frequent showers of hail & rain; as the water was smooth we however continued plying

---

52. This island had been named in honor of John Montagu, Earl of Sandwiche, the son of Viscount Hinchinbroke (Orth, 1971:651). They were entering Prince William Sound, which at that time was known as Prince William's Sound.

53. In 1789 Portlock named this small bay where he had anchored in 1787, to honor one of the mates of the *King George* by the name of William McLeod (Orth, 1971;612). Menzies must have heard the name of the harbor mentioned

against it with as much sail as we could carry to it. These squalls were at times very heavy, in one of them the Chatham carried away her jib boom, & in the Evening the we carried away the head of our bowsprit, & as we were afterwards standing in for the shore of Montague Island in order to secure it, a furious squall came off the land, which laid the Vessel down on her side very much, & in a short space of time made great havoc amongst our rigging, carrying away the fore yard in the slings & splitting to pieces several of our Sails. The Chatham being at this time some way astern of us had timely notice of the Squall by seeing our situation & was therefore better prepared to withstand its violence & she received no damage. Our people immediately set about clearing away the yard & sails that had been damaged, whilst in the best manner we could we edged in towards the shore & came to an anchor about ten in 15 fathoms, soft bottom. During the night the gale continued to blow without the least diminution attended with incessant heavy rain & thick weather.

23rd Early on the following morning, an Officer was sent on shore abreast of the Vessel with the Carpenter & a party of men to cut a spar for a fore-yard, with which they returnd about six in the evening, having fashiond it in the rough, so as to be able immediately on its coming on board to have it rigged, swayd in & bent the sails to it.[54] We had strong gales with very heavy & frequent squalls, accompanied with either haze or rain & exceeding thick weather throughout the day, but the wind being over the land of Montague Island, we were well shelterd & in a favorable situation with very little sea. The shore abreast of us appeard to be a fine beach, skirted with low land coverd with trees & backd by a high snowy ridge that rangd along the centre of the Island its whole extent.

---

but without getting the full pronunciation, hence he called it "Clouds Bay" rather than McLeod's Bay. His mistake is rather surprising since he was with Captain Colnett when they anchored and charted harbor in 1788 (Colnett, n.d. folio 199).

54. That is, the yard arm was hoisted into place and the sails attached to it.

24th Next day the weather continued thick & rainy but the wind was more moderate. A little past noon we weighd & plyd against a northerly breeze till about nine in the evening, when we again anchord under the shore of Montague Island, having this day past a solitary elevated rock in mid channel which is at least 4 or 5 miles from any of the surrounding islands.

In working up this passage there seemd to be no difficulty in getting good anchorage along the shore of Montague Island as we generally had soundings at a moderate distance from the land & the bottom was found soft and muddy.

25th On the morning of the 25th we both weighd again & began working against a moderate northerly breeze. The Chatham who seemd to have the advantage of us in sailing in this smooth water, got about noon abreast of Port Chalmers[55] & was directed by signal to lead into it & anchor, which she soon after accomplished, but we were not able to get into it, till about six in the evening, when we moord with the stream anchor in a snug situation. The Thermometer at noon was at 45°. In mid channel nearly abreast of the south point of Port Chalmers we met with a small bank or shoal, on which there was found only three fathoms water, from this & other appearances, that part of the passage between Montague Island & Green Island, ought to be navigated with the utmost caution especially at high water.

26th In the forenoon of the 26th the Carpenters were sent on shore abreast of the ship with the spar that had been cut three days ago for a fore yard in order to finish it, & the empty casks were landed at a rillet close to us on the northern shore of the harbour where the supply of water was not (at this time) very abundant.

On my landing near the watering place, the first thing that attractd my notice & indeed with some degree of astonishment, was observing the Stumps of Trees standing erect in the manner

---

55. Port Chalmers had been named by Captain Portlock. Captain Dixon called it Careening Harbor because it was here that he had his vessels heeled over on their sides (careened) for scraping and repairs (Orth, 1971:197-98).

which they grew near a low point, & far within high water mark, some of them even pretty near low water mark, when they must have formerly grown & flourishd till destroyed by the progressive invasion of that restless element which now overwhelmd them every successive tide, & coverd some of them 10 or 12 feet perpendicular height at high water, hence it would appear that the sea is here gaining on the land with a very rapid progress of late years, & the further I went along the shore, the more I found this observation verified, for where the land rose with a steep aclivity from the waterside, its banks were undermind, & the trees that had grown on it lay slantwise on the beach,[56] which made it very difficult to travel to any distance along shore, & the woods were still covered with snow down to the water side, so that I had yet no opportunity of commencing my botanical pursuits. I saw here only two kinds of Pine, the Canadian or Hemlock & Norway Spruce of which the woods were chiefly composed. One species of Vaccinium was beginning to shew bloom, but had yet put forth no leaves, nor did I observe any other signs of returning vegetation in my excursions though it was now the latter end of the Month of May.

27th Next day Mr Johnstone set out early in the morning with two boats well mannd & armd & victualld for 10 days, with orders to begin at Snug Corner Cove,[57] & proceed exploring & surveying the eastern side of the Sound from thence out to sea. Mr Whidbey was also dispatchd at the same time with our pinnace & cutter, equipped in the same manner to examine the western side of the Sound, he was desird to begin opposite to the south end of Montague Island, & from thence explore to the Northward round the head of the Sound till he came to Snug Corner Cove; and as the

---

56. This region is subject to severe earthquakes at which times the earth may rise or fall several feet. Menzies may have been seeing the effect of a major shift in the land.

57. This is on the northeastern end of Prince William Sound at the mouth of Port Fidalgo. Lamb (Vancouver, 1798(1984):1272) says that Captain Cook visited the harbor and named it in 1778. Orth (1971) does not give the source of the name.

weather was now temperate fair & pleasant, we had the most sanguine hopes of their being able to accomplish both their objects before their provisions were expended, though we knew their tasks were very intricate & requird uncommon perseverance at this inclement season of the year. Those of the people who remaind with the Vessels were now differently occupied, some in cutting down & splitting of fire wood, others in filling of water & some in brewing of spruce beer from the branches of the Canadian spruce, which was found to make very good & wholesome beverage;[58] and the Carpenters were employed on the yard which in the evening of next day they finished, when it was brought on board & rigged. The Seine was also hauld, but with very little success.

29th On the 29th & two following days we had nothing but incessant heavy rains with strong gales & frequent hard squalls of wind from the Eastward, so very tempestuous that we were hardly able to stir or have any communication with the shore the whole time. On the forenoon of the latter day our stream cable parted at the clinch in one of these squalls. During this boisterous weather we were under continual anxiety & alarm for the safety & comfort of our absent boats & their crew. This weather though stormy was of a soft & mild temperature, & it thawd vast quantities of snow, on the lower ground & the projecting cliffs, so that it might be considerd as the breaking up of the winter season in this country, for soon after, very fine weather set in, & Vegetation made a rapid progress.

[June]

1st In the morning of the 1st of June the ship grounded at low water when we had 15 feet under the main chain but she was soon floated again by the returning flood. We had continual rain

---

58. Captain Cook believed that rum and beer had antiscorbutic properties, i.e., they would prevent scurvy. Many times, the fresh water, carried in wooden barrels became stale and "stinking." One of Cook's practices, adopted by Vancouver, was to carry malt, hops and yeast to make beer. On the Northwest Coast the men were often times sent ashore to gather and cook green spruce boughs, using the resulting green water to make beer.

throughout the whole day, though not so heavy as on the preceeding days & the wind was become moderate.

One of the Gentlemen & four of the ships Company were this day after they had dind suddenly taken ill with head ach giddiness a slight pain at their stomach accompanied with reaching & vomiting which at first causd some alarm. They had pease Soup & pork for dinner, which were dressed in the ships boilers, but these were made of iron & kept exceeding clean so that nothing could be apprehended from that quarter; some said that the pease soup had tasted very strong of Tobacco, & on enquiry I found that none of those who were taken ill had ever been in the habit of using Tobacco in any shape, hence it is probable that some of it falling accidentally into the Soup might cause the above symptoms. An emetic was immediately given to each, & a copious perspiration kept up during the night, next morning a brisk cathartic compleated the cure of two, & the rest were able to attend their duty in a day or two after. In a voyage of this nature every thing that affects a number of men at once becomes doubly interesting & alarming, as the success of the enterprise wholly depends upon their health & activity, every accidental ailment of this sort cannot therefore be too early or too particularly attended to.[59]

2nd On the 2nd of June the weather was still dark & cloudy but moderate & fair. The ship was again moord & the stream anchor recoverd. At ten in the forenoon the Pinnace & Cutter returnd to the ship with one of their men severely wounded, which happend as he was quarreling with one of his ship mates, by one of the gentlemen endeavouring to separate them with the shaft of a small Indian spear, one of them unfortunately coming too near behind him, had his forearm rippd up in a slanting direction to the very bone, with part of the spear the gentleman held in his hand, which happend to be armd with iron. They carefully wrappd up his arm in rags of linnen, & brought him on board as soon as the weather permitted. When I examined the wound I found it in a very fair way & clear of all danger, yet the other man received four

---

59. At this time, Menzies was the ship's surgeon.

dozen of lashes for his quarrelsome disposition,[60] & the two boats were replenished with what provisions they had expended, & set out again in the afternoon to continue their examination of the western side of the Sound.

In the evening I took a walk with some others along shore to the head of the harbour, where we found a small bason that ebbd & filld with the tide, & reachd a lake a little beyond it, from which a stream of fresh water empties itself into the bason; we found every place we went over was wet & soakd with the late rains & the dissolvd snow that it made very unpleasant walking. The snow was still in many places down to the water side, & we saw even very large trees which were torn up by the roots in the late stormy gales. The Betula serrulata was now showing its flowering catkins, the viola canadensis was in flower & the Legusticum scoticum was shooting forth its leaves which shewd that vegetation had made some progress. Next day the Seine was hauld without any success, indeed the ground happend to be so foul with stumps of trees & large stones that it was torn in several places, so that they could not try their luck in a second haul.

4th On the 4th the Seine being repaird, it was again tryd in a different place, but still with very little success, they however got a few flat fish & some crabs.

This being our Royal Sovereign's birthday, all the Officers dind together, & the people as usual had a day of recreation & a double allowance of grog to drink his Majesties' health, which we were sure was done with a much fervency & loyalty in this remote corner of the globe as in the capitals of his dominions. The evening was afterwards spent in jollity & mirth.

5th We were expressing our surprise that none of the natives had yet visited us, when in the forenoon of the 5th four Canoes were

---

60. Historians have criticized Vancouver for the frequency and severity of his punishments. One must remember, however, that he was responsible for two vessels with nearly one hnudred and fifty men aboard. He had to maintain strict discipline and was probably no more harsh than any other sea captain of his time. As pointed out in the Introduction, Dr. Naish feels that Vancouver tended to have an obsessive personality, demanding strict attention to detail on the part of his men.

observd coming into the harbour round the north point of entrance. They landed in a small Bay near the party on shore; on seeing this I accompanied Capt Vancouver on shore to meet them & found that one of the was a Russian, another was a native of Oonamak near Oonalaska[61] & the rest were Kodiak Indians. We had nobody that could speak the Russian language, & therefore got very little information. Indeed they made but a very short stay when they launchd their Canoes again & departed. The Russian seemd to be somewhat afraid of us though we gave him no cause whatever. We askd them in the best manner we could for fish, & they brought two young Seals out of the canoes, which they offerd to Capt Vancouver, but he declind accepting such a present, & still sollicited, that they would bring us some fish, which as far as we understood them they promisd they would. They had all fire arms in their canoes & we saw some fresh cut pieces of Sea Cow, which shews that animal visits this part of the coast. When they embarkd they paddled out of the Harbour, & we walkd along the beach round the northern point of entrance into a small creek a little to the northward of the port we lay in, & on coming to the head of it, we crossd through the woods the neck of land that separates them without my being able to obtain much botanical information; the only plants I saw in flower were currants & two species of whortle berries.

In the evening two of the canoes came back to the ship after first visiting the Chatham & told us that they could get no fish.

6th In the afternoon of next day I visited the south side of the harbour, & in marshy situations in the wood I met with two plants which I had not before seen any where on the coast, one of them was a beautiful new species of *Caltha* in full bloom. The other was not in flower, but it appeard to be a *Dryas* & not much unlike in its leaves & manner of growth the D. octopetela. I brought however live plants of both on board & planted them in the garden.

We saw some Canoes crossing the entrance of the Harbour, which we supposd to be those who visited our party on shore & left the port so suddenly on the preceeding day; not knowing what we

---

61. These were Aleuts from the Aleutian Islands.

were they might probably be hovering about the entrance to prevent any Indians from coming in to trade with us conceiving perhaps that we were rivals to them in the fur trade.

7th The weather was now fine & pleasant & the sun so powerful that our gun powder was sent on shore on the 7th to be aird under the care of Mr Collet & some of his crew, which was found to be a very necessary piece of duty, as it was very damp.

Some Russians visited us in two canoes & one of them was the man who we saw on shore two days before, he brought us some eggs ducks puffins & a couple of wild geese, the latter appeard to be shot with ball, for their muskets being all rifled pieces with a rest fixd to them they can mark their object with great precision, & I believe seldom miss their aim.[62] We regretted much that we had so little knowledge of their language for though the boatswain of the Chatham could speak the Russian language tolerably well,[63] yet he had great difficulty to make out the dialect spoke by these people, & very often found it totally impracticable.

They made us understand however there was a large vessel building at a Russian Settlement between this & Cape Elizabeth under the direction of an Englishman of the name of James Shields who was assisted by three or four English seamen.[64] They spoke highly of Mr Shields abilities in his profession & seemd to respect him as a man of acute judgement & great penetration. Capt Vancouver wanted them to carry a letter to him, as they pointed out the situation of the settlement he was at on the chart to be on the inside of the Chiswell Islands not above 25 leagues off, but this they declind - alleging it was too far off. They were then askd if they had any Charts of this part of the Coast & an elderly

---

62. Vancouver (1798(1984):1275) says that the Russian was named Ammus Niconnervitch Ballusian. Dr. Lydia Black (personal communication) says that the proper name is Amos Balushin and that he was an employee of the Lebedev-Lastochkin Company at Nuchek on Hinchinbrook Island.

63. Lamb (Vancouver, 1798(1984):1275 footnote) gives the name of the boatswain as George Philliskirk.

64. This was in Resurrection Bay, which at that time was known as Port Andrews, while the Russians called it Delarov Harbor. James Shields was employed as a shipwright by the Russians to construct a 150 ton vessel named the *Phoenix* (Vancouver, 1798(1984):1262, footnote).

man answerd that they had & promisd to bring them the next time he came to the Vessels. They belongd to a settlement in Port Etches near Cape Hinchinbrook,[65] which they said has been establishd about twelve months, & is the most easterly Russian settlement they have at present on the Coast but that they traded in their boats as far to the eastward as Admiralty Bay.[66]

8th On the morning of the 8th I had a walk on shore in the woods & met with a beautiful little species of *Andromeda* in full bloom; as it provd to be a new species I namd it *Andromeda museifraga*. It was found creeping amongst the Moss on places clear of wood which are very frequent in the forests here & renders walking through them easy & pleasant. The *Pothos* lanceolata, a rare plant grows in marshy places in abundance & was now in full bloom.

In the forenoon Mr Johnstone returned to the Ship with the two boats after finishing the eastern side of the sound, & from his account of their expedition I was permitted to extract the following particulars.

After quitting the Vessels as already related, they directed their course up the Sound towards Snug Corner Cove, & slept the first evening on an Island 5 or 6 miles to the northward & westward of it,[67] & as a doubt here arose whether the opening in which Snug Corner Cove is situated was within the limits they were directed to explore, rather than it should have the chance of passing unexamind, they next day pursued it to the Northeastward for about 5 or 6 leagues, where they found it terminate, & stoppd for the second night near the head of it, after experiencing a wet & gloomy day, otherwise Mr Johnstone observes that the country here was capable of affording delightful & pleasant prospects as the shore they went along being generally low with fine pebbly beaches skirted with alder bushes, behind which the land rose with a moderate ascent & was entirely free of snow, with extensive plains varied & interspersd with woods apparently unincumberd

---

65. Port Etches is located on the southwestern end of Hinchinbrook Island.

66. Today known as Yakutat Bay (Orth, 1971;1063).

67. Which Vancouver (1798(1984):1276) named Bligh's Island and is located on the north side of Port Fidalgo.

with much brush or underwood. From their nearness to the shore this moderate rising ground intercepted from their view the distant lofty snowy mountains which would otherwise have given a bleak appearance to the landscape.[68]

It was in this arm that Mr. Meares & the Nootka's crew spent the melancholy winter of 1786 & their misfortunes will undoubtedly prove an useful lesson to others to shew the dreary situation as Mr. Meares so pathetically describes.[69] Snug Corner Cove which they quitted to go 15 miles higher up the arm, particularly the north east corner of it, Mr Johnstone thinks is an eligible a situation for a Vessel to lay in throughout all the inclemency of the year, as could be selected, & in some circumstances which contributed so much to the fatal reduction of the Nootka's crew it has superior advantages over any other place in the Arm that could be chosen, for by being nearer the Ocean, & at the mouth of the Arm, it would not have froze up so soon, or continue so long in a state of congelation as where the water is brackish from the fresh water runs higher up the Channel; and as the land on the south side of the cove is not so very lofty, it must enjoy a wider range of southern aspect, & a greater portion of sun-shine, than where the more stupendous heights higher up on the south side casts a nocturnal shadow across the channel for the greatest part of the short bleak days of winter.

By noon on the following day the party got back to Snug Corner Cove & went round the point into the next opening to the Southward of it,[70] but it soon after came on to blow so hard from the Eastward with thick rainy weather & a disagreeable swell dashing with great violence against a rocky shore, which was so much exposed as to offer no place of shelter, so that after a toilsome & fruitless attempt to get on, they were obligd to put back again

---

68. Vancouver (1798(1984):1277) says that he named the harbor Port Fidalgo in honor of Salvador Fidalgo who had visited this area in 1790 aboard the vessel *San Carlos*.

69. Captain Meares spent the winter of 1786-1787 in Port Fidalgo aboard his vessel *Nootka*. Twenty-three of his crew died of scurvy before Captains Portlock and Dixon assisted him in May of 1787 (Vancouver, 1798(1984):1270, footnote).

70. Port Gravina.

to a small Island off the point of Snug Corner Cove, where they hauld their boats up upon the Beach to prevent their being injurd by the heavy surf. There on their landing they were accosted from the verge of the wood by four Indians uttering the word *Sawley*[71] signifying friendship & advancing towards them with extended arms, this being their mode of amicable salutation, it was immediately imitated by our party, which with the addition of a few trifling presents ratified a mutual friendship.

These Indians had two Canoes hauld up in the woods & as they frequently pointed to the Northwestward, it was suppod that their residence was in that quarter of the Sound, & that they had stoppd here merely to shun the impetuosity of the storm.[72]

Our party found here an excellent place on which they pitched their Tents & after a comfortable hot meal went early to rest, as did also their Indian friends; but next morning they were not a little surprized at finding that their new companions had decampd

---

71. Vancouver (1798(1984):1277) transcribes the welcome as "lawlee, lawlee." Although Vancouver's journal (1798(1984):1276-80) also gives an account of Johnstone's survey, Sheriff's journal (n.d. folio 151, 151v) has some details not found in the other accounts which are included here. (May 29) "We reach'd the head of this arm about 8 & at 9 pitch'd the Tents, upon a spot which had been occupied before, by people possess'd of axes, whether our own countrymen or Russians it is hard to say, but many trees had been cut down with axes. (June 30) In pulling over, we observ'd smoke in that part we meant to land upon & when landed four Indians came out of the Woods with their arms extended repeating the words *Laille* frequently, which in this language is friend, we answer'd them the same, with which they were satisfied...during the remainder of the Day, the Indians remain'd with us & were treated with every civility; they appear'd to be four stragglers, alone in here, like ourselves, by stress of Weather, they frequently repeated the word *Nootka* & pointed up the Sound, whether they visited Mr. Meares when he winter'd here or meant a ship was in the Sound, we could not determine." [These were the same Indians who then stole an axe—Editor] "...In the course this Day, walking along the Beach I observ'd the remains of an old village, only one hut standing, which was built of Plank & cover'd with Turf & about 3 foot above ground & under ground, which made it 4 feet high & about the same square, the entrance was by a small hole on the North side 2 feet square, which answer'd both for Window and door. In one corner was a pile of small round stones, which I suppos'd to be the burial place of one of the family formerly residing in this Mansion, therefore I did not disturb it."

72. Lamb (Vancouver, 1798(1984):1277, footnote) says that they were probably Eskimos from Tatitlek, a nearby Chugach Eskimo village.

privately in the night time & carried with them a small axe belonging to the party, which, though not of itself an article of great value, yet was the ease with which they got off with it clearly provd how neglectful those who kept the watch had performd their duty, & as it might probably encourage these people to return again & commit further depredation by having observed the insecurity of the party at night, Mr. Johnstone thought it necessary to censure & punish the delinquent by making them do duty at watch & watch on the following night, which had the desird effect of making them more attentive & vigilant during the remainder of the expedition.

The next day provd so tempestuous & stormy that they were not able to stir from their encampment on the Island, but the day following the wind & swell was more moderate which inducd them to set out pretty early, though the weather which provd thick & hazy with heavy rains was by not means favorable for their pursuit, they however proceeded to the Eastward along the northern shore of the opening & soon found the wind increase against them, so that after 12 hours incessant hard pulling on their oars they had gaind little more than three leagues, when they were obligd again to bring up under a continued tempestuous storm of wind & rain with thick weather for the night & the whole of next day which detaind them so that they were not able to accomplish much of their object on account of tempestuous weather for the first six days of their expedition, but on the 7th day they again set out & pursued their examination for the three following days in rounding out the different branches on the eastern side of the sound with very indifferent thick & hazy weather,[73] till they came to an opening leading out to sea about nine leagues to the northeastward of Cape Hinchinbrook.[74] As they were stopping to breakfast on the latter of these days, an old & young bear were observd on the top of a pine tree close by the place where they landed, the former descended on their approach & fled into the wood, but the young one remaind in the tree till it was shot and

---

73. They examined Port Gravina, Sheep Bay, Simpson Bay and Orca Bay just west of the modern town of Cordova.

74. Hawkins Island Cutoff.

provd an excellent repast to the party. As they were proceeding afterwards to the entrance of the opening,they passd a group of small Canoes with about 20 of the Natives fishing, some of whom came along side of the Boats, but seemd very unwilling to part with any of their fish, though a very high price was offerd for them & only one Halibut could be procurd from the whole party.

On a small Island at the entrance they found a considerable village containing about 200 Natives & a party of ten Russians, who shelterd themselves by hauling their skin boat up upon the beach close to the village & turning it nearly bottom up, with one gunwale resting on the ground, & the other supported just high enough to admit their creeping underneath it. These Russians kindly invited the party to stop on the Island for the night, to which they readily consented & pitchd their Tents as it had rained very heavy the whole afternoon.

The number of natives in the Village[75] were considerably more than they would have chosen to remain with, had they not confided much in their peaceable behaviour & the good order maintaind amongst them by the Russians, of whose authority & good offices they soon experienced the beneficial effects, for the group of canoes they had passd in the forenoon returnd to the Island, & deliverd the whole success of their days labour to the Russians consisting of about two dozen of large Halibut & a very fine Salmon, the latter was very politely presented by the Russians to our party with a request that they would take whatever quantity of the other fish they pleasd.

In the dusk of the evening two large skin canoes made their appearance coming towards the Island, & after some parading ceremony of singing a slow song & paddling backwards & forwards before the Village, they landed about 20 men from each canoe. This unexpected increase of the Natives causd some little uneasiness to our party & moved them for the first time to enquire

---

75. Lamb (Vancouver, 1798(1984):1281, footnote) explains that these people were the Chugach Shallow Water People, so named because of the shallow waters they utilized in Orca Inlet. They had villages on Mummy Island, the south coast of Hawkins Island and the east end of Hinchinbrook Island. A few years earlier in this area, Captain Portlock was attacked by Natives who were after booty.

for the Officer or head of the Russian party, that they might consult with him & act jointly in case of necessity, but they had no superior amongst them, they were ten sailors of equal rank sent out from the Settlement in Port Etches[76] to collect Furs & probably Fish for their companions. They were all armd with pistols on their belts, & one or two of them had muskets, & as they shewd no kind of anxiety or alarm on the occasion, it was thought better by our party to conceal their rising apprehensions without any further observations.

One of the new comers who by his dress appeard to be a chief, came & deliverd to the Russians ten skins & a paper folded up like a letter. These appeard to be all Beaver Skins except one, which was a Sea Otter Skin, & Mr Johnstone understood that the strangers were from Groosgencloos[77] or Cook's Gulph across the Isthmus at the head of Turnagain Arm, but whether they belongd to that gulph, or were sent thither from this Sound he could not learn. The night provd tempestuous with heavy torrents of rain, yet as they were situated it was thought necessary to keep a good watch. The Russians had two sentinels who like ours challengd every half hour.

Next morning at low water the Island was found to be nearly surrounded by a dry sand bank which appeard to extend across the entrance of the Inlet, leaving a small communication for the boats with the channel to the westward of them by which they had some hopes of getting out to sea at high water & prosecute their examination along the coast to the Eastward towards Cape Suckling, but after every attempt they found it impracticable in such tempestuous weather, the whole entrance across being made up of shallow banks or foaming breakers, & a vast shoal extended along shore as far as the eye could perceive to the eastward,[78]

76. Russians from the Lebedev-Lastochkin Company had built a small garrison in Constantine Harbor in Port Etches. The Eskimo settlement of Nuchek was located further up the bay.

77. Dr. Lydia Black (personal communication) points out that this is Menzies' corruption of the Russian corruption of the German "Groses Fluss" or "Gross Fluss," that is, Cook's Great River. The term was translated into German by Magnus van Behm in Kamchatka and appears this way on many 18th century Russian charts as the head of the Cook Inlet.

78. Orca Inlet is extremely shallow and at low tide, much of the inlet is dry.

against which the sea dashd with a tremendous surf. Thus by a series of tempestuous weather which had blown from the East-ward since they left the Vessels, their further progress was entirely obstructed, so that nothing remaind for them but to return to the Vessels which they did by a new channel leading to the westward that late in the evening brought them again into the Sound.

On parting with the Russians they gave them several little articles they thought would be acceptable to them, but lamented that they could not make any returns adequate to the civilities they receivd, for as these honest fellows were extremely assiduous in rendering every service in their power to our party during their short stay on the Island, they felt the most grateful impressions at their friendly conduct at parting.[79]

From the Natives Mr. Johnstone procurd two arrows pointed with Copper which the Russians made him understand was the produce of the country, & that the Natives found it in some place to the Northeast of them, which they reachd in two days journey, & went part of the way in their Canoes by some river as was supposd from their making signs that they drank of the water of it.[80]

On the following, June the 6th the wind became westerly right against them, & as they were rowing along the southern shore of the opening to the Northward & adjoining to Port Etches they saw a cross erected in a small bay on which was inscribd Carolus IV Hispaniarum Rex An.1790 P[er] D[n] Salvador Fidalgo.[81] At noon Mr Johnstone obtaind a very good observation for ascertaining their Latitude which was the second he had since their departure, & as the day was clear it provd very satisfactory in settling their position of many of his old points which the haziness of the

---

79. Vancouver named the northeast tip of the mainland in honor of Captain Whitshed of the Navy. The northeast end of Hinchinbrook Island he named Point Bentinck to commemorate the family name of the Dukes of Portland. He named Hawkins Island as well (Vancouver, 1798(1984):1282-3 and footnote).

80. To the northeast of this point is the mouth of the Copper River. Farther inland, along this river, are outcroppings of copper and copper nuggets which the Indians learned to use to make into weapons and other items.

81. This was a claim marker erected by Salvador Fidalgo in his exploration of this area in 1790.

weather had precluded him from doing before with that precision he could have wishd, as he was often obligd to content himself with estimating the distance between them.

On their way in the Vessel they visited the Russian settlement in Port Etches called Noocheet which they found situated in a Cove in the North side of the Port; it formd an enclosd area of about eighty yards square, defended on one side by a large dwelling house about 40 yards long, strongly built with logs of timber & within divided into its whole length on each side into births for the people to sleep in, for they all livd under one roof; besides this there were two smaller houses within the square one for cooking & the other was probably a store house & a Vessel of about 70 tons burthen was hauld up upon the beach & formd part of the other side of the Area, on board of which there was one carriage gun & three others of a smaller size were mounted on carriages before the dwelling house, so that the whole appeard snug & well adapted for their convenience & afforded a sufficient security against any attack that could ever be attempted by the Natives.

On their landing they were received with great politeness by the commandant of the Settlement Mr Peter Colomnee,[82] who conducted them into the Factory & in the most friendly & hospitable manner, spread out his little table with such fare as he had before them, which consisted of a piece of boild seal with part of the hairy skin still adhering to it, some fish oil & a few boild eggs; these articles not being very inviting to people accustomed to a different diet, & as their politeness could not on this occasion overcome the delicacy of their appetite, Mr Johnstone beggd leave to add some chocolate beef & bread to the repast on the table, which was readily granted & to which their host & the next to him in command did ample justice.

Mr Johnstone was given to understand that he had about a hundred Russians belonging to this Settlement, who, with nearly the same number established in the upper parts of Cook's gulph,

---

82. Dr. Lydia Black (personal communication) says that the proper transcription of the name is Petr Kolomin. He was the foreman for the Lebedev-Lastochkin Company at Nuchek, and was in charge of the Prince William Sound operations for the Company.

under Mr. Zyhoff,[83] were in the interest of a particular company of Merchants distinct from those under the direction of Mr.Barrenoff,[84] who chiefly resided at Kadiak, & whose party extend their traffic along the exterior coast from thence towards Montague Island, while the other party occupied the interior regions of Cook's gulph & Prince Williams Sound, & carry on their intercourse by the isthmus at the head of Turnagain[85] arm but they trafic in their boats along the coast to the Eastward as far as Admiralty Bay, where they had lately had an affray with the Natives but the particulars could not be understood from their not being sufficiently versd in the Russian language, which Mr. Johnstone greatly lamented, as Mr. Colomnee appeard to be an intelligent man & extremely liberal & anxious to communicate.

It was not understood however that the Russians had yet establishd any settlement to the eastward of this station, & the next to the Westward is the one under the authority of Mr.Barrenoff in Blying's Sound[86] on the inside of the Chiswell Islands, where a considerable party were employd in building a Vessel under the direction of an Englishman of the name of Shields. Mr Johnstone earnestly requested for a sight of any chart they might have of this part of the coast, or of any of their new discoveries, but he was told that they had none, except Mr. Smyloff[87] who commanded the Galliot,& who was then absent on an excursion might probably have a Russian chart of this side of America.

Mr Johnstone further observes that the Russians retain in their service a considerable number of women as well as men of the Natives of Cook's Gulph, of whose fidelity & attachment they speak in the highest terms of praise & employ them indiscrimi-

---

83. Dr. Black (personal communication) says that this is Stepan Zaikov Samoilov, of the Lebedev-Lastochin Company.

84. As mentioned earlier, Baranov was manager for the Shelikov-Golikov Company.

85. This is the land between Portage and Whittier, Alaska.

86. Along the southeast coast of the Kenai Peninsula.

87. Dr. Black (personal communication) says that in all probability, this is Samoilov, a mariner serving the Lebedev-Lastochkin Company.

nately with their own parties on the most confidential services,[88] but the Natives of Prince Williams Sound did not appear to share the good opinion of the Russians so favorably, which might not probably be owing so much to a difference of disposition in these tribes, as to their having come more recently amongst them & not having yet a sufficient time or intercourse to induce them to submit to a state of docile subordination, however this might be, the Russians seemd to carry on their commercial pursuits amongst them with the greatest ease & the fullest confidence, of which the party they met with at the large Indian Village, how resignd themselves completely in their power is a strong instance.[89]

How long this settlement had been established Mr. Johnstone could not rightly learn, but from knowing that the Russians had no footing here when Sen[r] Fidalgo visited the Sound in the

---

88. In his account, Sheriff (n.d. folio 152 verso), adds these comments: "There are no Russian women among them, but they are supplied by those of Cook's river...each of them have one of their Cook's river Women & they appear to several to share, who are very far from being backward at granting every request. They are in my opinion the finest Indian women I have seen, not excepting those at the Sandwich or Society Islands..."

89. Sheriff (n.d. folio 152) gives additional information regarding the Russians and the Natives. "When about leaving this place, we received a visit from two Russians in skin canoes, who directed us to a small Island opposite, where they were residing, we steer'd there according to their directions, & found ten Russians living in a village, where I suppose there might be about 150 Natives...These Russians appear'd to be only upon a Trading party, they lived under their Boat which was made of Skins, about 30 feet long, & turn'd upon one gunwale to shelter them from the weather. The Indians liv'd the same, their large boats were turn'd up in that way & different partitions made in them, where the different parts of the Family or Tribe resided; they appeared to live in a very filthy manner, though the Women in their persons clean & in general handsome, they are tatoo'd on the chin in the manner of a Beard & both sexes make use of the lip piece; Most of the men are made of one piece, & the women's in three or four, with as many holes in the under lip to let them in; the females were not backward at granting every liberty & the Men did not appear to have so much of the jealously of the southern Indian, in their cooperation. By what I could observe during our short stay at this village, the women are employ'd about nothing out of doors, in the house they were making jig lines, fishing lines & other necessaries for the use of the family, all which they perform in the neatest manner, likewise the skin frocks the men wear in rainy weather."

summer of the year of 1790 he concluded that it must have been establishd since that period.[90]

Contrary winds & the inducements of the hospitable reception they met with detaind the party at this settlement longer than they intended, but before the quitting it in the evening Mr. Johnstone took an opportunity of expressing in the best manner he could, the high sense he entertaind of Mr. Colomnee's kindness to him & his party & as a small acknowledgement for the cordial reception they met with from him & his people, he presented him with whatever articles of trafic or provisions they had remaining, amongst the latter was a Gallon & half of Rum, which appeard to be by far the most acceptable part of the present, as Mr. Colomnee joyfully expressed that he had not had such a quantity of spiritous liquor in his possession for a long time, & indeed the intemperate use he soon made of it provd it to be a fortunate circumstance for him that it had been so, for Mr. Johnstone observes that most of the Russians hitherto met with in this country were immoderately fond of spiritous liquors & whenever it was in their power, used them to the greatest excess; these however being chiefly of the lower order, it was not so surprizing, but it was distressing now to behold a man far advancd in years & whose venerable deportment & superior station had justly entitled him to their respect suddenly become the object of their pity by indulging in that obnoxious vice. It is probably owing to this depravity that the company wisely prohibits any allowance of spiritous liquors at these settlements, at least it is certain that none was found at this time amongst them, except what they in this manner obtained from us or accidently procurd from other strangers who may thus casually visit them. Before his intoxication Mr. Colomnee promisd he would visit the vessels & in that state they left him in the evening & next morning as already related they arrived in Port Chalmers.

In the afternoon we found the Russians were as good as their promise, for several small skin canoes with two or three of them in each came into the Harbour, & a large one with no less than 17 of them, it had eight oars of a side double bankd, but in other

90. According to de Laguna (1956:12) there was no permanent Eskimo village at Nychek until the Russians established their post there.

respects it was made of Laths coverd with skins exactly like the large canoe used by the Natives of this Sound. Mr. Columnee himself arrivd in a small canoe, but was so late before he came into the harbour, that he did not come on board till the following morning. In the evening all the Russians went on shore to a Bay at a little distance on the south side of the harbour, where they huddled together on the beach without any shelter for the night, like so many Indians.

June 9th As the Chatham's people were now returnd, they were able to spare us two carpenters to assist ours on the Bowsprit, in order to forward that necessary service. The Russians visited us again pretty early in the morning & continued backwards & forwards between the two Vessels all day. The Commandant Mr.Colomnee came first on board the Discovery, he appeared an eldering man of between 55 & 60 years of age, & was dressd in a long frock of white fur, edged round the bottom neck and breast with a narrow strip of Sea Otter skin; he was on this occasion accompanied by the man who first visited us, equipped in an European dress & who seemd to be next to him in command. This man whose name we found to be Ballusian,[91] brought us as he had promisd a Russian chart of this part of the coast, comprehending from Cross Sound to the westward as far as Kamptschatka with the Islands off the Coast & between the two continents, but on comparing it with Capt Cook's chart & with what we ourselves knew of the Coast it had no title to correctness & was very rudely executed. It had Patries Streights[92] & Kodiak, so very like that in Meares's Chart, as to require a nice discrimination to find out any difference, in this respect both appeard to be copies of the same survey. It had also that Island which we took for a new discovery on the 4th of April to the South West of Trinity Island, & likewise that to the southward of Cape Hinchinbrook called Middleton's

91. Dr. Black (personal communication) states that his name was Amos Balushin, an employee of the Lebedev-Lastochkin Company.

92. Lamb (Vancouver, 1798(1984):1287, footnote) says that this was Meare's term for Shelikof Strait, between Kodiak Island and the mainland.

Island[93] in Mr Johstone's Mss Chart, & first seen by us in the Prince of Wales in 1788, but both these Islands were without any names annexed to them. These gentlemen were so good as to suffer Capt Vancouver to take a copy of this Chart, but there was none on board who could either explain or copy the names & writing on it - the date of it appeared to be 1789.

We were now as much at a loss for information as ever, for they could not tell us who made this chart, or who surveyd the coast it thus delineated. The only answer we could get to all our enquiries about it was that they got it at Kamptschatka.

They all agreed with our former information that this settlement in Port Etches was established about 12 months ago, but that the settlement on Kadiak under the direction of Mr. Barrenoff had been established at least 11 or 12 year.

In the evening all the Russians went on shore to the same place they occupied on the preceeding night, except Mr. Colomnee who slept on board the Discovery, he expressed a wish of having some live stock from us, such as Poultry & Hogs which could not be spard; & it is really astonishing that these people are so inattentive to their own comforts, as not to have brought these animals with them from Kamschatka, the distance being so short that they might bring over a number of domesticated animals in their Vessels with great ease.

10th We had now fine pleasant weather with light fluctuating airs & calms alternately. In the forenoon of the 10th Mr.Colomnee went on board the Chatham, when Mr.Puget took the opportunity of acquainting him, that while his people were on board yesterday, two locks belonging to a double barrelld fowling piece were missing, & beggd he would exert his endeavours to recover them. He appeard very much hurt at this piece of intelligence & requested Mr Puget to keep it secret till he should sound his people. He accordingly went on shore & in a short time returnd with the

---

93. Orth (1971:640) reports this island was named by Vancouver, probably in honor of Sir Charles Middleton, a rear admiral and comptroller of the British navy.

two Locks. The man who had them in his possession said that he had bought them from one of the Chatham's people, & mentiond what he gave for them, but he could not point out the person that sold them, so the affair ended by Mr. Colomnee ordering the greatest part of his people away from the Vessels, & he himself was afterwards presented both by Capt Vancouver & Mr. Puget with a quantity of salted beef & Pork, Biscuit Flour Rum and Tobacco, together with some culinary utensils & such other articles as he wanted that could be spard viz Iron, Sheet Copper.

As the weather was now so favorable it was deemd a proper plan to send the Chatham forward to continue the survey of the Coast, as our bowsprit was likely to be some days in getting ready & afterwards we might be detaind in waiting for Mr Whidbeys return, or perhaps for the finishing of the Sound by a second trip, if he should not be able to accomplish it in his present expedition. Mr Puget therefore receivd orders to sail with the Chatham, & to begin at Cape Hinchinbrook, & from thence continue his examination of the Coast to the Eastward as far as Port Mulgrave,[94] where he was to wait for us till the 1st of July & then to proceed in his examination to Cross Sound, leaving a note for us on a specified spot in Port Mulgrave. In consequence of this arrangement the Chatham saild in the evening but the wind dying away soon after, she anchord again a little on the outside of us.

11th Next morning the Russian commandant took his passage in the Chatham for Port Etches & the remaining part of his people left the Harbour at the same time.

As the country to the northward of us was of a moderate height & now pretty clear of snow, Mr Baker, Mr Orchard & myself set out pretty early accompanied by two attendants carrying some provisions, as it was our intention to have a compleat days ramble in the woods. We first ascended a small hill a little distance to the North East of the ship on the summit of which we kindled a fire & breakfastd. Our view from here was more limited than we expected from its apparent elevation, as other hills more remote rose somewhat higher to the Northeast of us & prevented our

---

94. In Yakutat Bay, across from the modern village of Yakutat.

seeing up the Sound, & the lofty snowy ridge which occupies the middle of the Island from the south point terminated close to us on the eastern side, but the prospect we had of the scatterd Islands Rocks & Inlets on the western side of the sound was very extensive, whilst the woods underneath us by being chequerd with clear spots, small lakes & the waving indents of the shore appeard exceeding pleasant. The trees & shrubs were now expanding their foliage & assuming their vernal bloom, the small birds were beginning to carol their notes in the thickets. The Chatham was seen sailing with crouded canvas towards the north point of the Island with our departing friends on board, & the Discovery lay at anchor in the harbour. In short the novelty of this rural prospect, heightend by the stillness & serenity of the weather, & the picturesque appearance of the more elevated surrounding mountains, was a treat which we greatly enjoyd, more especially as it was unexpected that we should here be able to penetrate so far & with so much ease into the forest. In several places on tops of this hill we saw the dung of our goats, who had strayd some days before from the party on shore at the watering place & were now missing but we neither saw or heard anything of the animals themselves in our whole excursion. After descending from this station, we directed our course to the northward round the head of Stockdale's harbour[95] & found it delightful & easy travelling as far as we went, the tract we pursued being in a great measure clear of wood, & forming here & there extensive patches of pasture land, where the soil was light & of a spungy texture, which indeed is the general characteristic of that formd from mouldering vegetables, but on some of the low ground it had acquired a degree of firmness approaching to that of meadowland. These clear spots were cropt with *Carices* Mosses & other low vegetables amongst which I observd[96] *Andromeda carulea A. notifolia* & *A. museifraga, Empetrum nigrum, Heleborus trifoliata* a new species of *Isoporum* & some dwarf *Vaccinia* with two species of *Viola, Equisetum palustre* & *Plantago macroeaipen.* In the thickets I found the

---

95. According to Orth (1971:919) this harbor had been named by Captain Portlock in 1787 in honor of his publisher, John Stockdale.

96. See Appendix.

Rubus sarmentosus, R. Nootcagensis, Menziesia ferruginea, Sedum busifolium, with two new species of *Vaccinium*, currants, willows & alders, the latter was not found to grow here to a larger size than bushes, & indeed the wood in general, which was composd of two species of *Pines* viz the Canadian & Norway Spruce were in general much smaller than on the southern parts of the Coast. The new species of *Thuja* & of *Gaultheria* so frequent & so luxurious about Nootka, was not here at all met with. The grass on the clear spots had not yet advancd much in growth, owing to the ground being coverd so lately with snow, there is no doubt however but as summer advances, they will produce an abundant crop, that would afford good pasturage for cattle Horses Sheep & Goats, but it would require some industry to procure Hay sufficient for their support in the long winter in so high a latitude.

12th On the following day the Captain accompanied by Mr Baker began surveying & sounding the harbour, & settling the relative situations of the shoals we met with on the outside, this duty occupied them most part of the three following days, during which the weather was remarkably clear & serene, & the sun was now become very powerful in the middle of the day.

Mr Swaine & I landed with our guns on the south side of the harbour on the 13th, where we spent the day in strolling about the woods without meeting much game, between the shore & the ridge of snowy mountains we found a margin of low land which producd much larger pines than I observd on the other side of the Harbour, a large proportion of them approachd the size of that cut for our bowsprit, which the Carpenter allowd was of sufficient thickness for a lower mast to a line of battle ship. In every Valley we found torrents rushing down the hills from the melting snow, & we traversd over several clear spots of fine pasture & some rich Meadows that borderd Lakes where the grass grew with a thick bottom & was already ankle high, from the aspect being more favorable & better shelterd than on the other side of the harbour. In these Meadows the *Dodecatheon* meadea & dwarf new species of Raspberry were now in full bloom, & I collected in this days excursion several species of the genus *Jungermannia* in great perfection which I had not before met with.

The Carpenters having finishd the Bowsprit, it was brought along side in the forenoon & stept into its place with some difficulty, as it was intentionally made a little thicker than the former for strength & to allow in some measure for its shrinking. The seamen were mostly employd this & the following day about the rigging of the bowsprit & yards, & getting the ship ready for Sea by the time our absent boats returnd, which were now hourly expected.

15th And by noon on the 15th Mr.Whidbey returnd to the ship with the two boats, after having finishd his portion of the survey of the Sound.[97] He informd that they began on the western side opposite to the South end of Montague Island, & pursued their examination from thence to the northward through intricate inland channels, making what appeard to us the western boundary a sound of a number of large & small Islands; here they were at times much retarded in their progress by vast quantities of drift ice which crouded into these Channels as they supposd from the more northern inlets. They had likewise to encounter with islets of ice of considerable magnitude, some floating & others grounding about them, even of the depth of twelve fathoms & many of the heads of arms & bays were still choakd up with a firm body of solid ice & hardend snow of considerable thickness; when they reachd that branch leading towards Turnagain Arm they pursued it to the very end, & saw at the head of it the narrow break in the ridge of mountains over which the Russians carry on their intercourse between this Sound & Cook's Gulph, & though they could not perceive any road or pathway over the isthmus, yet they considerd the path as very accessable, from its being of a moderate height, destitute in a great measure of wood & snow, no wise rugged & not above 12 miles across.[98] Close by on the side of the arm, they found a small decent hut, built with logs of timber, the interstices

---

97. While Menzies had access to Johnstone's reports and gives extensive descriptions of those explorations, he usually gives only a brief summary or Whidbey's surveys. See Vancouver's Journal for a more detailed report on Whidbey's exploration of Prince William Sound.

98. It appears that they went through Wells Passage to Passage Canal, just east of Whittier Alaska.

between which were carefully stopt up with Moss & hay, & the floor was strewd over with long dryd grass. This was supposd to have been built by the Russians as a resting place as it was kept in tolerable good order & no inhabitants were observd near it.

From this Arm the party pursud their examination to the northward & northeastward & met with much intricacy in their progress, from the number of openings bays islands & rocks which were strewd along that side of the Sound, till they came to that opening which Capt Cook's boats had enterd, & which at that time occasiond a difference of opinion as to its extent, between the Officers in their reports to Capt Cook, but which the party now found to be little more than two miles wide & to terminate a little beyond the researchers of these officers, in the Latitude of 61° 7' north, this being the most northern limits of the Sound, they from thence explord to the southeastward till they finishd their task on coming to Snug Corner Cove.[99]

They met with little or no drift ice in any of the northern openings of the Sound, but several of them as well as the Bays terminated with firm fixd massy ice, under which the tide kept up a crackling & rumbling noise like distant thunder.

In some places they observd immense bodies of Ice & snow sliding down from the higher precipices with accumulated weight & velocity, carrying soil trees & every thing with a hideous & crashing plunge into the Ocean, but when these ponderous fragments fell any wise inland, a tremulous agitation like the shock of an earthquake was produced for a considerable distance round the place accompanied with a noise resembling a clap of thunder, & as the Mountains on the sides of these arms, were found in many places steep high & cliffy, these huge fragments of Ice & hardend snow may in some measure account for the formation of those Islands of Ice they met with grounding in 12 fathoms. On exposd situations the devastations of the late stormy gales were likewise

99. Vancouver's Journal (1798(1984):1288-1297) gives an extended description of this survey, with the naming of several geographical features including Cape Puget, Port Bainbridge, Point Erlington, Point Pyke, Point Waters, Point Countess, Point Culross, Point Cochrane, Passage Channel, Point Pakenham, Point Pellew and Point Freemantle. Many of these names were intended to honor friends or acquaintances.

very conspicuous by a number of the trees being fresh torn up by the roots, while others lay about shatterd & broken.

In some places the arms were skirted by low land, with fine clear sandy beaches, over which they could walk for miles together without meeting any obstruction. They saw no Birch in all their researchers which is somewhat singular, as it is so common under the same parallel in Cook's gulph. The woods were chiefly composd of small scrubby pines, bushy alder, & low brush wood, which formd here & there into thickets, leaving intevening clear spaces of considerable extent, & diversifying the country with pleasing Savannahs.

They shot three porcupines during their cruize of weight from twenty to thirty pounds each, two of these were cookd & found to be very good & palatable eating, but the third stunk so intolerably that they could make no use of it. They saw only about a dozen of the Natives the whole time they were absent, & most of them seemd to be at variance with the Russians, hence it would appear that the population of that side of the sound they examind is very inconsiderable, & indeed from the reports of both boat parties it would seem that the population of the whole Sound is far short of what it has been represented by late visitors.

This being Sunday the returnd boats crews & the rest of the Ship's company had leave to take the recreation of the shore.

And next day the sails were bent, the ship was unmoord & every preparation made for leaving this port.

In the evening, the Sheep that had been landed for the advantage of feeding near the party on shore were brought on board, but the Goats who were landed at the same time, we not to be found, nor indeed were ever seen or heard of since they first strayed away into the woods soon after their landing. The loss of these animals would be less regretted had there been a he-goat amongst them, by which there might have been some hopes of their encreasing, stocking their country & in time becoming useful to the inhabitants, but as all four were she goats, their increase rested on the vague probability of one of them being in kid of a he one which was very uncertain. If they should however chance to increase in this way, we conceive the country very favorable for rearing such hardy animals.

We were likewise this day visited by two Russians in a small canoe, who came with a present of fish & eggs from Mr. Colomnee, & as we were on the eve of departure, they staid on board all night, to go back with us in the Ship next day & had their canoes hauld up upon the booms for that purpose.

June 17th Early in the morning of the 17th our Anchor was weighd, & there being but little wind we warpd out into the fair way, at seven we made sail & stood with a light breeze into mid-channel but soon after had the misfortune to strike upon a rock on a falling tide were we remained fast. By sounding it was found that this rock occupied but a very small space as it had almost nine fathom water at a little distance all around it, & it produced neither weeds nor broken water to indicate its existence or point out the latent danger. It is situated about one mile due west by compass from the north point of the harbour, & at slack tide we found it coverd with twelve feet water close to our bow, whilst we had five fathoms under the main chains & seven fathoms under our stern.

Whilst we were thus fast upon the Rock, the Carpenters embracd the opportunity which the favorable position of the ship afforded, of repairing the sheathing & copper,[100] which had been a good deal damagd & rubbd off of the bows by the ice in Cook's Gulph. In the mean time the stream anchor was carried out, & by 11 the tide had rose so far, that we were able to heave the Vessel off the rock without receiving any apparent damage, & there being little wind, we afterwards warpd further out into deeper water, where we anchord over a muddy bottom & remaind for the night, during which some cod & Halibut were taken with Hook & line.

18th Next morning the weather was calm & gloomy with some rain, but a light breeze sprung at E N E n the forenoon, with which

---

100. At this time, the hulls of most ships were covered with sheets of copper to prevent parasites from boring through the wood. The Vancouver expedition also carried some sheets of copper for trade with the Natives. Along the Northwest Coast large pieces of copper known simply as "coppers" came to be prized family possessions and metallurgical analysis of these coppers shows that they were obtained from the Europeans.

we weighd & made Sail to the northward, & by noon reachd the north end of Montague Island, where we hauld the wind, & during the rest of the day kept plying out towards Cape Hinchinbrook. In the evening two or three canoes came along side from the settlement in Port Etches, but as we were then standing out to sea with a moderate steady breeze, there stay was short, the night however proving mostly calm, we were driftd back again into the Sound, at the mercy of the tide, & could obtain no sounding with upwards of 80 fathoms of line which renderd our situation rather precarious, as the shores were very rocky, & the sea dashd against them in violent surges, both objects of uncommon dread in a dark night & in a vessel ungovernable.

19th The weather was fair & pleasant on the 19th but the wind was still scanty & fluctuating, & as we were not likely to get out soon, rather than drift backwards & forwards with the tides, we bore up about one o'clock in the afternoon & stood into Port Etches where we came to an anchor on the north side of it near the entrance into Port Brooks[101] in 31 fathoms. Two Russians armd with Muskets passd us early in the morning in a large skin Canoe paddelled by sixteen indians going out towards the black rocks in the offing, as we supposd to kill seals or sea otters, but they returnd in the afternoon & came along side of us without any booty whatever.

Soon after we came to an anchor a number of Russians came off to us & staid on board till the evening, bartering boots made of seal skins & articles of curiosity with our people for the former, though rudely executed they found a ready market, as shoes were now from the length of the voyage become exceeding scarce amongst us. The articles they chiefly took in exchange were Shirts worsted stockings & other cloathing, but to these they would always prefer spiritous liquors or Tobacco when they could get them.

A part of the Officers went on shore after dinner with Capt Vancouver to visit the Russian Settlement, where they were received by Mr. Colomness & Mr Ballusan with every attention &

---

101. Dixon, in 1787, gave this name to the harbor now known as Constantine Harbor (Orth, 1971:235).

civility their situation could afford. These gentlemen introduced them to Mr. Smyloff the commander of the Galliot mentiond by Mr. Johnstone, it seems he had gone over to Cook's Gulph with Mr Zykoff by the Isthmus a little before our arrival in this Sound, for the purpose of learning what we were, but not finding us there, he hastend back again, & just arrivd at the settlement a little before our party landed. It is very singular that Mr. Zykoff who must certainly have known at the time of our being in Cook's Gulph, should pass over to this Sound so near to us without satisfying himself in that particular.

Mr Smyloff came off with the party & remaind on board with some others of the Russians all night, he told us that there was a small river a little to the eastward of this Sound where the Natives went up in a N N E direction to a Lake which they reachd in about 5 or 6 days, & there found in the rocks considerable veins of native or virgin Copper,[102] which they collected & manufacturd into various articles of utility & ornament. The coincidence of this information with that which Mr. Johnstone obtaind renders it very probable that this Metal might be procurd in considerable quantity in the vicinity of this Sound, & if so, what a valuable source of commerce, as the Natives on every part of the coast are so exceeding fond of it. Mr. Symloff also informd us of a river that emptied into Controller's Bay, but which yet had not been explord to its source. These streams he said were however so shallow & inconsiderable as to be only fit for boats or canoes to navigate. We also receivd information from the Russians that the Chatham had got out of the Sound the day after she left Port Chalmers, & that since that time a Brig came into the Sound & steerd towards Snug Corner Cove.[103]

20th Next morning the weather was serene & nearly calm, yet we weighd anchor pretty early, though we made but little progress till towards noon when a westerly breeze sprung up, with which we

102. See above, concerning Natives traveling up the Copper River. In the 19th Century, the Kennicott Corporation carried on extensive copper mining along the Copper River.

103. Lamb (Vancouver, 1798(1984):1302, footnote) suggests that it was the *Arthur* which Vancouver was to meet later in Cross Sound.

worked out of the harbour, & a Mile & half of Cape Hinchinbrook had a good meridian altitude, which places that Cape in Latitude 60° 16' North & according to our mensuration, it is 35 miles of Longitude to the Eastward of Port Chalmers.

At this time Mr. Smyloff took leave us, & we hoisted in our boats, bore up, & made sail to the south eastward with a favorable breeze from North West, which continued until towards evening, when it became light & fluctuating & was calm all night, during which we had soundings from 36 to 40 fathoms muddy bottom at the distance of 8 or 9 leagues to the southeastward of Cape Hinchinbrook.

The channel by which we came out of Prince Williams Sound is about seven miles wide, with bold rocky shores & steep high land on each side, & off its entrance there is a small cluster of black barren rocks about seven miles to the southwest of Cape Hinchinbrook & nearly the same distance from the shore of Montague Island, & we were not a little surprisd to find that these rocks considering their dangerous situation, should have escapd the notice of Capt Cook, both in his Charts & narratives of this part of the Coast.

21st In the morning of the 21st the Land about Cape Hinchinbrook was seen bearing west, & having then a moderate favorable breeze we continued our progress to the south eastward, till in the afternoon we reachd within about four leagues of Kay's Island[104] when the wind veerd to the North East quarter & continued mostly against us for the four following days, during which it frequently blew very fresh & squally with some showers of rain & was generally attended with thick & gloomy weather, so that with all our vigilance in taking every advantage by plying & working against this perverse wind we were not able to pass the south end of Kay's Island till the afternoon of the 26th, when with a light westerly breeze we stood in for the land a few leagues to the

---

104. Today this is known as Kayak Island. In 1778 Captain Cook had named it Kaye's Island in honor of Sir Richard Kaye, a chaplain to the King and a friend of Banks. Vancouver named the southern end of the Island in honor of Sir Andrew Snap Hamond (Vancouver, 1798(1984):1302, footnote; 1310).

eastward of Cape Suckling & then steerd along shore to the eastward all night.

The south end of Kays Island is a remarkable bluff barren head land facd with a whitish rugged precipice, much higher than the land immediately within it, & a little detachd from it is a huge rocky pinnacle, which may be seen 8 or 9 leagues off, & on which account it has been very aptly named Cape Pinnacle[105] it is in Latitude 59° 48' North & Longitude 145° 41' West

In fixing the situation of this Cape there is a disagreement of near two degrees of Longitude between Capt Cooks narratives & his chart, but as the latter gives its relative situation nearly as we found it, it may be presumd that the former is an error of the press. The rest of Kays Island forms a narrow ridge of a moderate height, coverd on both sides with wood, but the summit in many places is naked, & of a whitish rocky appearance. As we were passing about two leagues to the eastward of Cape Pinnacle at five in the evening we had a very distinct view of Mount St. Elias for the first time bearing N 38 E by compass upwards of a hundred miles off, yet it then appeard pretty high out of the water from our deck which will give some idea of its immense height.

27th On the 27th we had calms & baffling light airs alternately, with some showers of rain & thick gloomy weather, so that our progress to the eastward was very inconsiderable, & our view of the shore was but very indistinct, the higher mountains being mostly envelopd in thick fog. Our soundings were from 35 to 50 fathoms at three or four leagues from Coast.

A few leagues to the eastward of Cape Suckling the shore falls back & seemingly forms a shallow bay skirted by a track or border of low woody land extending to the eastward before a ridge of high steep snowy mountains, here the water appeard pale & muddy near the shore, & one or two small openings were observd, apparently the mouths of some considerable streams pouring forth their muddy torrents from the dissolving snow.[106]

---

105. Lamb (Vancouver, 1798(1984):1313, footnote) notes that Vancouver did not mention the remarkable Pinnacle Rock, which Captain Cook thought looked like a ruined castle.

106. They were sailing south of Cape Yagataga.

28th The 28th & two following days we had to encounter a foul and perverse wind which at times blew strong & squally with thick & rainy weather, during which we continued plying along shore taking the advantage of smooth water, till on the forenoon of the 29th we reachd abreast of a Bay[107] about 25 leagues to the eastward of Cape Suckling, which appeard remarkable from its being choaked up with massy ice & frozen snow, & on that account it obtaind the name of Icy Bay; it forms the bottom of a considerable valley gradually ascending the western side of Mount St. Elias, from which & the adjacent mountains, it seems to have accumulated in its course, by the alternate operations of frost & thaw, & the annual falls of snow an amasing & perpetual encumbrance even down to the waters edge.

To the westward of this Bay the shore is steep & rocky & indented & to the eastward a considerable tract of low land extends to Admiralty Bay,[108] backd at some distance by a very high & rugged ridge of mountains cloathd in perpetual snow, from which the conic peak of Mount St. Elias rears its lofty summit above the clouds & is situated about 14 leagues inland in Latitude 60° 25' North and Longitude [missing]

This tract of low land presented to our view a dreary naked surface strewd over with large stones or lumps of Lava & patches of snow, but apparently destitute of soil or the least vestige of vegetation, except here & there closer to the shore & where some scrubby pines & bushes were seen thinly scatterd.[109]

July 1st The morning of the 1st of July was calm & clear & the range of high mountains to the northward of us was for the first time free of clouds & distinctly seen extending in a compact ridge from Mount St.Elias which now bore N 16° W of us to the north westward behind Comptrollers Bay.

---

107. Icy Bay. Vancouver (1798(1984):1312, footnote) named the southern point of the bay to honor Edward Riou, who had been with Vancouver on Cook's third voyage.

108. Now Yakutat Bay. (See Map 4.)

109. In the past two hundred years there has been a warming trend and increased vegetation in many places.

In the forenoon we were favord with a gentle westerly breeze with which we stood to the Eastward along shore, till in the evening it was succeeded by fluctuating airs for the night, & at this time we were crossing the entrance of Admiralty Bay,[110] within 5 or 6 leagues of Port Mulgrave, the appointed place of rendezvous with our consort, & in the dusk of evening had the pleasure of hearing the report of one of her guns, which was answerd by firing another, & about 4 next morning Mr Manby the Master came to us in a skin canoe, attended by two others of the same kind conducted by seven Indians, & from him we learnd that the Chatham had arrivd in Port Mulgrave only four days before, & after having examind the coast so far, they were then waiting for us ready to sail to the southward.

The forenoon was mostly calm with small rain & thick hazy weather, at noon we were about three leagues to the south westward of Cape Phipps[111] & soon after a light breeze sprung up from North West, when two guns were fird as a signal for the Chatham to join us, & as we were creeping on to the Eastward, the canoes which brought Mr. Manby slipt off & made the best of their way for the Port, leaving him on board, not withstanding they were calld to & entreated to the contrary, we therefore made sail & stood along the coast to the eastward, with Soundings from 36 to 40 fathoms, & as Mr. Manby went with us, I collected from him the following particulars of their transactions since we separated.

The Chatham got clear out of Prince Williams Sound as has been already observd the day after she left us, & having a favourable wind, they coasted along the exterior shore of Hinchinbrook Island which is about 7 or 8 leagues long, till they

---

110. Vancouver (1798(1984):1312) named the western point of Yakutat Bay in honor of the master of the *Chatham*, Thomas Manby.

111. Now named Ocean Cape. It is the eastern point of entrance to Yakutat Bay and Port Mulgrave. According to Lamb (Vancouver, 1798(1984):1334, footnote), "Vancouver's chart indicates that what was named Cape Phipps is the present Point Carew, rather than Ocean Cape, now considered to be at the SE entrance to Yakutat Bay (Vancouver's Beering's Bay). The name is spelled Carrew on Dixon's sketch, although he named it after his first mate, John Ewen Carew. Point Turner was named after his second mate. The position of Point Carew is latitude 59° 33' 30' N. long. 139° 50' 15" W (220°09'45" E)."

came to its northeast extreme name Point Bentenek[112] where they got abreast of the shallow opening which terminated Mr. Johnstone's researches on the eastern side of the Sound, & as he had then observd they found a shoal extending from thence along shore to the eastward, & afterwards inclining to the south east, towards the north end of Kay's Island they tracd the other edge of this sandy shoal which they found to extend from one to two leagues from the coast & in many places dry at low water without observing any apparent opening, on the contrary, the land presented a high connected ridge of snowy mountains ranging to the northwest ward from Comptrollers Bay,[113] across which bay the same shoal continued to extend to Cape Suckling, leaving however a narrow passage close to the inner side of Kay's Island & the little Island to the North West of it, which they attempted to go through, but found it so intricate that they twice grounded on sandy banks & were on that account obligd to relinquish their design, & to go round the outside of these Islands rather than put off much time about a passage which promisd so little utility as it was found from their examination by a boat to be rocky & shallow at the east entrance & only fit for small Vessels, so that it should always be attempted with great caution. On the western side of Kays Island they found good anchorage & excellent shelter from the prevailing easterly gales, far within the limits which is occupied on Mr. Dixon's chart with an extensive shoal which might deter visitors to this part of the coast from taking advantage of so commodious a situation in stormy weather. They met with no Natives on either Kays or the other Island, though the remains of a pretty large Village was seen on the north and of the former which seemd to have been recently deserted, & while they lay under the latter, its rugged cliffs afforded them a considerable supply of eggs from the haunts of an infinite number of Oceanic birds.

---

112. Bentinck Point.

113. Comptroller's Bay, which Vancouver calls Controller's Bay (Vancouver, 1798(1984):1324), was named by Captain Cook in 1778 in honor of Maurice Suckling Comptroller of the Royal Navy when Cook had left on his voyage (Orth, 1971:235). In his journal, Vancouver (1798(1984):1324) says that he named Wingham Island and then Point Martin after Sir Henry Martin.

The whole of Comptrollers Bay being occupied with shoals & dry sand banks except the intricate passage close to the north end of Kay's Island as already mentiond, they proceeded round the south end of Kay's Island, & from Cape Suckling, tracd the shore to the eastward without meeting any opening deserving of notice till they came to Admiralty Bay[114] & though the distance is not above 40 leagues, yet such was the baffling adverse winds & unfavorable weather they met with, that this space occupied them nine tedious days. In rounding Admiralty Bay they sent a boat to examine an apparent opening at the bottom of it,[115] which was found to be a small Creek choakd up with a compact body of ice, with no less than seven fathoms of water close to the edge of it. In pursuing their examination from thence down the eastern side of the Bay to Port Mulgrave, it was found interspersd with Islands Rocks & Shoals, on one of which the Vessel ran aground & remaind fast till next tide, when she was got off again without any apparent injury & though they perseverd in their route on the inside of these islands to Port Mulgrave,[116] yet as the passage was found in some places very narrow intricate & shallow it is to be considerd by no means commendable, while a much more eligible entrance to the port exists near Cape Phipps.

On their arrival in the Bay they were not a little surprised at meeting a party of nine or ten Russians, with a fleet of about 450 skin canoes containing upwards of 900 Indians from Cook's Gulph & the Island of Kodiak, all hunters & warriors, for there was not a woman or child amongst them. In the commander of this numerous party they had the pleasure to recognize their old

114. As pointed out Menzies' biography, both he and James Johnstone, commander of the *Chatham*, had visited Yakutat Bay with Captain Collnett in 1788.

115. According to Vancouver's journal (1798(1984):1329), the boats went to Haenke Island and past a point which Mr. Puget named Point Latouche, and on to what they named Digges' Sound, but which is now Disenchantment Bay.

116. Puget named Knight's Island in Yakutat Bay (Vancouver, 1798(1984):1331, footnote; 1332 footnote), probably in honor of Sir John Knight. Puget also named a cove south of this island "Eleanor's Cove," but the source of the name is unknown.

acquaintance Mr. Portoff[117] who had been there constant visiter while they lay in Port Chatham, and he & some others of them were amongst those who visited the vessels near Cape Elizabeth, & part of the Indians were no doubt those we saw the day after we left that place, as Mr. Portoff stated that he had left Cook's gulph 5 or 6 weeks before with a fleet of 700 canoes, part of which were left here & there along the coast for the purpose of hunting & killing sea otters. On their way thither they had touchd at Blying's Sound, calld by them Chugashee sound behind the Chiswell Islands & from thence brought a letter from Mr. James Shields a Lieutenant in the Russian service & commandant of the settlement, adressd to both or either of the Commanders of the Discovery & Chatham, in which he laments the not knowing sooner of our arrival on that part of the coast, otherwise that nothing should have kept him from visiting the vessels whilst they were in Cook's gulph, especially as he had understood from the Russians that the Discovery stood in need of repairs, & that we wanted a fit place to lay her on shore in which case he strongly recommended the Port he was in as a very excellent situation for the purpose,& very politely offerd to assist with all his artificers in repairing any defects that might be discoverd, which he said he could easily do, either in Smiths or Carpenters work, as he had then with him a party of 50 Russian artificers & 4 English seamen employd in building a small ship for a company of Russian Merchants, & to compleat our refitment, he tendard their service in the most genrous and frank manner. After giving some general directions about entering Blyings Sound, he stated that he had no chart of it, as he had not made any surveys, having only arrivd there late the preceeding year from Kamschtka, but as his employers meant to prosecute the fur trade on this coast with great spirit & continue their progress to Nootka, in order to open a trafic between that place & Kamschatka, that would be very much to the advantage of the English, he requested as the greatest favor, to send him any

117. Dr. Black (personal communication) gives the proper transcription of the name as Egor Purtov, and says that he was Baranov's foreman for the sea otter hunting expeditions. Lamb (Vancouver, 1798(1984):1329 footnote) gives the name as George Purtov.

old chart of the Coast, any English books or old newspapers that could be spard. He further stated for our information that there was at this time two Russian companies engaged on this coast in the Fur trade, each employing about 200 men. The one to which he belongd had their principal settlement on the Islands of Kodiak under the Direction of Mr. Alex[dr] Barrenoff a respectable Russian merchant. Those belonging to the other company were dispersd between the head of Cook's gulph & Prince Williams Sound, & were very disorderly & mutinous, having not long ago sent their Director to Kamschatka in irons.

Mr. Shields also related that in the year 1789 he had seen in the city of Irkutsk the capital of Siberia a Portuguese & a Lascar,[118] who had savd themselves & were the only survivors of the crew of an English vessel commanded by a Mr. Peters that had been unfortunately cast away on an Island near Kamschatka. He said he had likewise understood from the Natives since his arrival on this coast, that about 4 or 5 years ago, two Vessels which from their description of the seemd to be English were cut off & destroyd by the Indians in Prince Williams Sound, where some of their Iron works & Nails had been seen by the Russians. These were the principal communications & civilities containd in this gentleman's letter & we could not help regretting our loss in not having seen him, not so much for any assistance we stood in need of, as for that interesting information concerning the Russian establishments in this country & their manner of subduing the Natives to that quiet & peaceable subordination we had observd, which he appeard well qualified to give us, not less so from his abilities than from his station & residence amongst them.

As the Russians had advancd along the coast on their way thither with their numerous attendants, they stopd some days on the low border of land in the shallow bay a few leagues to the Eastward of Cape Suckling, where they describd two rivers entering the Sea, the westernmost they calld Mali Unalla, & the other Bulchi Unalla,[119] & from their accounts they both have very

---

118. Person from India.

119. According to Dr. Lydia Black (personal communication), the transcription of the names of these rivers should be Malaia or Malyi (Little) Unalla and Bolshaia, or Bolshoi Unalla (Big) Unalla.

shallow entrances, but the latter was supposd to be of sufficient depth on the inside for the Chatham. Here they found between 40 & 50 native Indians, who in a very treacherous manner murderd one of the Russians, to revenge which they put six of them to death & brought away some Prisoners amongst whom were two children, whom they said they would carry home & rear up at their settlement.

Mr.Portoff sends the Kodiak hunters out to sea in parties of from 10 to 20 canoes in different directions & they never fail to return daily with fish & a number of sea otters which they skin for the Russians & use the carcasses stewd for their own feeding.

But the most material nautical information obtaind from these Russians, was an account of a dangerous rocky shoal laying about 21 leagues out from the Coast in a south by west direction by compass from a point calld Leda Uliana,[120] which was understood to be the western point of Icy Bay. Its discovery was owing to a Russian galliot, being wrecked upon it, the crew of which happily saved themselves in their boats, but from its dangerous situation, it is much to be feard that it has provd the destruction of more Vessels than one, whose crews have not been so fortunate as the Russians, especially as it is well known that Mr. Meares's consort the Sea Otter commanded by Mr Tippings has never been heard of since she left Prince Williams Sound in the year 1786.

To this Shoal which they stated to be 4 or 5 leagues long, the Russians now frequently resort for the purpose of killing sea Otters, & Mr. Portoff said that he & his party were to visit it before they returnd to Kodiak, on which occasion they would set out from the shore early in the morning & by going a direct course for it, they would be able to reach it in their canoes in the evening the same day.

---

120. Dr. Black (personal communication) says that this could mean either Ledianaia, "Wall of Ice," which was a Russian term for Glacier Bay in Southeastern Alaska, or Ledianoi Proliv, "Icy Strait." Vancouver (1798(1984):1330) mentions this place saying, "...a dangerous rocky shoal, about fifteen miles in length, lies by compass in a direction S. by W., 63 miles from a place called by them *Leda Unala*. This Mr. Puget conceived to be near the point that I had called Point Riou."

The Chatham had been here some days before they had seen above 9 or 10 of the Natives, & as the Bay had been found pretty numerously peopled by former visitors, they were led to suppose, that the greatest part of them had fled into the woods at the approach of the Russian party, especially as they found at the mouth of a small creek within the entrance of the Harbour the remains of an extensive village, which had all the appearance of being recently evacuated, as a vast number of their dogs were found still hovering about it, unwilling to quit their old abodes, and a large burying place was seen close to it where a number of dead bodies were deposited. That this was the case appeard evident from the statement of the Russians themselves, who related that a few days before, about 50 of the Natives made their appearance in two large canoes & several small ones, apparently with hostile intentions, but after reconnoitring the strength of the Russian party, they again retreated & dispersd which conduct shewd that they were not inclind to be upon friendly terms with these invaders of their natural rights, though they could not oppose them. The Russians too were not without their fears & apprehensions of their treachery & revengeful dispositions, which inducd them to concentrate their whole party & encamp on the Island abreast of the Chatham, in order to enjoy the advantage of her protection.

July 3d On the morning of the 3rd we had again to contend with foul wind. About ten in the forenoon we saw a Vessel to the eastward of us under the land, she brought to about two leagues to windward of us & sent her boat towards us, for which about noon we shortend sail to give her time to come up with us, when we were given to understand it was the Jackal[121] commanded by Mr Brown who had been on the Coast the two preceeding summers as one of the Buttersworth's tenders, which Ship Mr. Brown then commanded, but having sent her on the southern whale fishery to return to England by the way of Cape Horn & Stantonland, he

121. They had met the *Jackal* the previous year in southern southeastern Alaska.

proceeded himself last autumn with the Jackal & other Tender to China for the disposal of the Furs they had collected on the coast. They both left China the 24th of Feb^ry for Cross Sound on this coast, but experienced very tempetuous weather, which occasiond a separation, & the Jackal who now bore down & joind us made the land near Cape Fair Weather on the 1st of this month, but from their not having had any observations for sometime past to correct their reckoning, they were unacquainted with their real situation till we informd them of it, & they were not a little surprizd on hearing that they were so far to the northward of Cross Sound, as they estimatd themselves to the Southward of it. From them we had the first intelligence of the death of the King of France[122] & the state of warfare in Europe.

In the night time the weather provd squally with rain & a heavy rough swell from the Southeast, against which & foul wind we continued plying for the two following days with little advantage; but the Jackal[123] who intended to accompany us to Cross Sound parted in the night time to keep nearer in shore in smooth water & finding the wind continue perverse, she bore up for Port Mulgrave to try her luck amongst the Russians.

From the east side of Admiralty Bay a tract of low land densely coverd with wood extends to the south eastward forming an extension border before the ridge of mountains for about 15 leagues along the coast. Our station for the two last days was a few miles to the Northward of the latitude of 59° & within a few leagues of the coast so that we were nearly abreast of that part which Capt Cook distinguishd by the name of Beerings bay, but found it nearly a straight indented shore with sandy beaches, & in one or two places where there appeard to be some shallow openings & inland waters the land was naked sandy & barren. The great distance at which Capt Cook passd this part of the coast prevented his seeing the low border of land which stretches out from the bottom of the mountainous ridge & consequently led him into a mistake with respect to the true trending of the shore, but

---

122. Louis XVI was executed on January 21, 1793.

123. Vancouver (1798(1984):1338) spells the name of the vessel Jackall.

we cannot plead the same excuse for Mr Dixon who afterwards had a good opportunity of rectifying this mistake by having anchord for some time with his Vessel in Port Mulgrave, but in place of which he copied Capt Cook's error into his chart & represents an extensive bay on this part of the coast, where no such bay exists, hence it is very probable that Admiralty Bay as namd by Mr. Dixon is the place which Beering visited, & which Capt Cook meant to have distinguishd by his name, though it is situated a few leagues to the north west of where Capt Cook expected to find it.

6th On the 6th after an interval of calm we were favord with a moderate breeze from North West, which soon enabled us to regain the ground we had lost on the preceeding days, by edging in for the shore & steering close along it to the southeastward. About six in the evening we passd what I took to be Cape Fairweather, a low bluff point hardly distinguishable as a Cape, but renderd conspicuous by being the southern point of a small opening or harbour with an island in its entrance that appeard to pervade a narrow border of land before the high rugged ridge of mountains. This Cape I make in Latitude 58° 45' North & Longitude [missing]. A few leagues to the southward of this we passd another small opening or bay, which may probably afford shelter & anchorage to Vessels,[124] & the weather being clear & favorable, with the advantage of long twilight in this high Latitude, we had sight of Mount St. Elias appearing pretty high above our horizon till after 11 at night, when it became obscurd by a thick haze, & when its distance was upwards of 50 leagues from us; this will afford further proof of this amazing height of this conspicuous mountain.

7th Next morning we had light westerly wind with thick for that entirely obscurd the land from our view, except the summits of the inland mountains, we however continued on our slow progress along the coast & towards noon the fog dispersd, when our

124. Lituya Bay. La Pérouse had anchored in the bay in 1786 and named it Port de Francais. Several of his men perished when their boat capsized.

Latitude was 58° 14' & our Longitude [missing]. The northwest point of entrance into Cross Sound, which is a conspicuous promont that obtaind the name of Cape Spencer[125] after the noble Lord of that name bore N 59° E by compass about the distance of two leagues. Off this cape there are some rocky islets that extend about a mile or a mile & a half, & the shore abreast of us was steep rocky & much indented with islets & rocks scatterd along it that renderd a near approach apparently dangerous.

In the forenoon we were visited from the shore by a few of the Natives in a canoe, & notwithstanding our earnest invitations, none of them would venture on board, until one of our Seamen went into their canoe as a hostage & then one of the came into the ship & remaind some time perfectly contented. The seaman made himself so agreeable to the party in the canoes, that when he was calld on board, they shewd great reluctance at parting with him, which occasiond some menacing threats, & hostile preparations on our part that was treated by them in a jocose manner, as they came along side with our man in very good humour, & when he got on board the Chief of the party presented him with a sea otter's skin & some articles of curiosity as a testimony of their friendly intentions & they then departed for the shore singing a song, whilst we proceeded into Cross Sound[126] which we found to be a very spacious opening apparently divided into several branches notwithstanding its existence has been publicly denied by late Voyagers who visited this part of the Coast, & that even contrary to the report of Capt Cook & others who had seen it previous to their publications. In our progress up the Sound we were met by large lumps of floating ice, which appearing like dark colord rocks just level with the surface of the water & the sea breaking against them, occasiond at first considerable alarm, till the nature of the apparent danger was discoverd, when our apprehensions vanishd, on finding we could not reach bottom with 90 fathoms of line. Towards evening it became calm & foggy & as we could not reach

125. Vancouver (1798(1984):1317) named this point in honor of Earl George John Spencer, First Lord of the Admiralty (Orth, 1971:68, 906). (See Map 4.)

126. The sound had been named by Captain Cook on May 3, 1778, Holy Cross Day (Orth, 1971:248).

an anchoring place or get sounding with upwards of a hundred fathoms, we were obligd to submit ourselves during the night to the influence of the tides. In the evening we were visited by a party of the Natives in several canoes, amongst whom we recognized some of our forenoon visitors off the entrance of the Sound.

July 8th Next morning (being still foggy) the roaring noise of the Surf to the eastward of us created some alarm at our approach to the shore, & as we found ourselves in 40 fathoms we immediately anchord, & as the weather soon after cleard up, we found ourselves near a small Island on the eastern side of the sound when Mr Whidbey was sent in one of the Cutters to look for a more eligible situation for the Vessel. About noon the Chatham was seen entering the Sound, on which, two guns were fird to announce our situation, but as we were not certain that they were heard, & as she had but a light breeze & misty weather, Mr Manby was sent in a boat to conduct her to our station. About four in the afternoon Mr Whidbey returnd & reported that he found a commodious Cove fit for our purpose on the south side of the small Island close by us,[127] on which we immediately weighd & saild into it, followd soon after by the Chatham, where both moord in a moderate depth of water over a stiff muddy bottom.

The Chatham quitted Port Mulgrave on the 6th where she left Mr Browne in the Jackal trading with the Natives, together with the whole Russian party, but before their departure a small assortment of books & other articles were left with a letter in charge of the Russians for Mr. Shields as a small acknowledgment for his friendly offers. On entering the Sound they were visited as we were by a party of Indians in a Canoe from near Cape Spencer, who requird in the same way that one of their people should remain in the Canoe whilst one of them staid on board disposing of a few Halibut & perfectly at his ease till the man was calld out of the canoe & the same instant he returnd into it. As no precautions of this kind had been before requird in all our intercourse

---

127. They anchored in Port Althorp which Vancouver named in honor of the heir to Earl Spencer, Viscount Althorp. The anchorage was in Granite Cove on George Island (Vancouver, 1798(1984):1320 and footnote).

with the Natives of this Coast, it is probable that these people have been maltreated by some European visitors to this part of the Coast, which has inducd them to adopt such mistrustful conduct towards strangers.[128]

The fallacious rocky appearance of the floating ice in the sound had equally deceived them on board the Chatham, & they tackd to avoid the apparent danger till they found out their mistake, & then steerd into the Sound when they were met by Mr. Manby who conducted them into the Cove.

9th Next day I botanized on the small Island, where I found some new plants. In the course of the day several Canoes arrivd in the Cove containing men women & children, who for the advantage of being near to us, took up their abode on the Island abreast of the Vessel at the head of the Cove, where I found them busily employd in erecting temporary huts near the landing place. They appeard open & friendly in their disposition on shore, though I understood none of them had yet venturd on board either of the Vessels. They furnished us with a quantity of Salmon & Halibut for small Trinkets, & a number of Sea Otter skins & other Furs were purchasd for old cloths & square pieces of coarse, blue cloth. In all their dealings they appeard to act with the most scrupulous honesty.

July 10th On the morning of the 10th of July I set out with Mr Whidbey who with three boats under his direction were armd & victualld for a fortnight so as to proceed to explore the interior branches of the Sound. We edged over to the North West point of entrance, passing vast quantities of ice in huge lumps drifting about with the tide which greatly incommoded our progress, especially as we had rainy weather, with fog so very thick that we

---

128. The Tlingit used hostages in a variety of ways, including the holding of artifacts as hostages until payment could be made for certain crimes. To settle a long-standing feud, hostages were exchanged and later set free. Since deer were considered the most peaceful of all animals, these hostages were called "guwakaan," the Tlingit term for deer. As mentioned earlier, this term may have been the source of Menzies practice of referring to the Tlingit as "Woagan."

could see but a short distance round us, & the Noise of the Surf against the Beach first announced our approach to the opposite shore, which we made a little more to the eastward of Cape Spencer & commencd our examination by coasting along it to the northward up an arm that terminated in an icy vale[129] which made conspicuous appearance on our entering the Sound behind Mount Fairweather. The shore was found rocky & indented, with some Coves that appeard likely to afford shelter & anchorage but we had not time to sound them. In pursuing the western shore, we passd about 5 or 6 miles up the arm a small rivulet, near which we saw the ruins of an old indian village & a little further on our progress was obstructd by a vast field of drift ice, extending from shore to shore, that renderd it impracticable to proceed higher up at this time with the boats, & from a glimpse we had through the haze, it appeard to form a dense covering to the feet of the icy vale before mentiond, where the arm evidently terminated & where a continual rumbling & crashing noise was kept up by the ice. We therefore crossd over to the eastern shore, which we began to trace down till we came to a small bay near some Islands, where finding a convenient situation, we pitchd our tents for the night.[130] The land immediately behind us was low & marshy & producd a luxuriant crop of grass, but further back it became mountainous, & appeard every where coverd with pine trees.

11th The weather next morning was still gloomy but the fog had in some measure dispersd & enabled us to proceed with more certainty in our examination. Our course was directed between some rocky islands & the Main, where we had considerable difficulty to encounter, as the passage was nearly choakd up with

---

129. They went up Taylor Bay where they saw the face of Brady Glacier. (For the area surveyed, see Map 4.)

130. Vancouver (1798(1984):1344) says that "Here were erected two pillars sixteen feet high, and four feet in circumference, painted white; on the top of each was placed a large square box; on examining one of them it was found to contain many ashes, and pieces of burnt bones, which were considered to be human; these relics were carefully wrapped up in skins, and old mats, and at the base of the pillars was placed an old canoe in which were some paddles." These were Tlingit mortuary poles, one type of "totem pole."

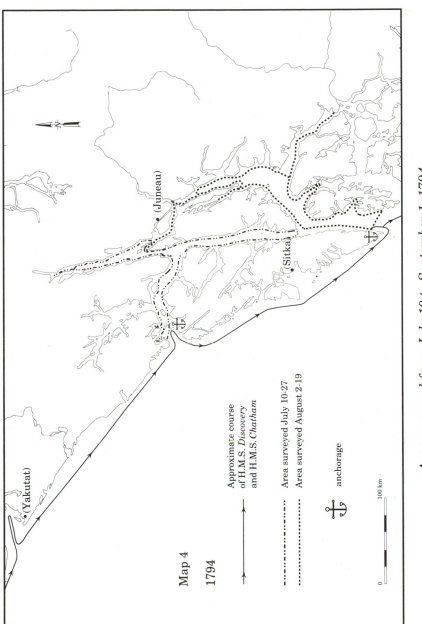

Area surveyed from July 10 to September 1, 1794.

(Yakutat)

(Juneau)

(Sitka)

Map 4
1794

Approximate course
of H.M.S. *Discovery*
and H.M.S. *Chatham*

Area surveyed July 10-27
Area surveyed August 2-19

anchorage

0   100 km

huge lumps of ice, some of which were aground in pretty deep water, where they seemd to remain stationary from year to year, as their summits were made up of different layers of ice & snow, & the surrounding ice always preserves a sufficient coolness in the atmosphere to prevent their melting wholly away even in the hottest summer. A precaution was here taken of sending the Pinnace ahead, as she was the strongest boat, & the two Cutters followd close in her wake, by which contrivance we got through without receiving any damage & proceeded to the eastward, entering soon after a spacious opening leading nearly in that direction, & steerd with a group of rocky islands about four leagues from the entrance of the Sound, between these, the Tide went through with great rapidity, forming whirlpools in which large bodies of ice movd about in all directions, so that it requird the utmost vigilance to keep ourselves clear of instant destruction, as many of these pieces of ice were of such magnitude that two of them approaching from opposite directions would crush either of our boats to pieces in a moment. We however happily got clear of this perilous situation,[131] & soon after enterd another arm winding off to the northward & northwest, which we pursued for about ten miles, till we saw it terminated backd by very high mountains.[132] A little below the head of it a small shallow branch went off to the westward in low marshy land, which may probably communicate with the icy branch we examined the day before, as the distance here between them, was not discoverd to be above 3 or 4 miles. Finding the navigation near the head of the arm renderd very intricate with a number of small Islands & sunken rocks we returnd back along the eastern shore of it, till we came

131. They were passing through North Inian Pass where at extreme flood tides, the incoming tide rushes in. They passed Point Wimbledon, which Vancouver (1798(1984):1344 and footnote) named to honor the birth place of the second Earl Spencer.

132. Vancouver (1798(1984):1344) named the point of land on the southeastern end of this bay, Point Dundas. In 1879, W. H. Dall named the bay itself, Dundas Bay. Henry Dundas was born in Edinburgh and became the Solicitor General of Scotland in 1766. He was elected to Parliament in 1744, and became Treasurer of the Navy in 1791 (Orth, 1971:289).

William Healy Dall (1845-1927) was an authority on Alaska, and became Acting Assistant of the U.S. Coast Survey in 1871. He was very well educated

to a deep bay skirted with a considerable tract of low land well wooded with pines. Here we saw the appearance of a village with some natives, but in attempting to approach it our boats grounded before we got within a mile of it, so that we were obligd to relinquish our design, & also our pursuits on this shore, which appeard to be strewd with low woody islands, we therefore crossd over to the opposite side of the arm, & put into a small Cove to dine, which gave some of the Natives from the village an opportunity to join us in two Canoes with an acceptable supply of fish. They were very inquisitive to know where we left the Vessels, from a desire no doubt of visiting them, & when we made them understand that they were not far off in a certain direction, & that plenty of fish would be very acceptable article of trafic to them, they quitted us very peaceably, apparently well pleasd with the information & the treatment they receivd. In the afternoon we got out of the Arm & pursued the northern shore of that which led to the eastward, & after rowing about two leagues, we came in the evening to a shallow bay with a fine sandy beach, skirted by a low flat tract of meadow land, which offering a very eligible situation for encampment, we landed & pitchd our tents for the night. From this station the arm appeard as far as we could see it to the eastward strewd over with vast quantities of ice floating backwards & forwards with the Tides & currents, many huge pieces of which grounded at low water in the bay, that kept us in continual anxiety & alarm for the safety of the boats, & the utmost vigilance became necessary to prevent their being damagd or carried adrift by the ice, notwithstanding which the Chatham's Cutter was actually torn from her grapnel, & owing to the darkness of the night, was some distance from adrift before she was observd, luckily however the loss of the grapnel was the only damage she sustaind, & Mr. Lemeurier[133] who commanded her, continued to supply its place tolerably well for the rest of the cruise with a wooden one fixed to

---

and in compiling the 1879 edition of the Coast Pilot he named many geographic features, often times using information from Vancouver's journal to give nearby features appropriate names (Orth, 1971:11-12).

133. Mr. William Le Mesurier, midshipman aboard the *Chatham*. In 1897, W. H. Dall named one of the islands on the west end of Icy Strait, Lemesurier Island, in honor of this young man (Orth, 1971:571).

a heavy stone; for the present she was hauld on shore till the morning. Many of the large pieces of ice that grounded about the boats as the water fell from them, became either top heavy or some part of them by their position loosing their equilibrium tumbldd off with a crashing noise that frequently awakened us in the night time & had any of the Boats happend to be near or under these falls, her fate must have been inevitable destruction; to guard therefore against these alarming dangers we passd the night with very little rest & by no means so comfortable was we expected from the eligible situation we had chosen.

12th We breakfasted next morning before we set out as the Chatham's cutter took some time before she could be got ready & launchd. This interruption afforded me an opportunity to bota-nize round our encampment, where I met with two plants I had not before observd any where else on this coast, one of them was an Alpine plant, the *Selena acaulis*, apparently brought down from the mountains by a large torrent which emptied itself into the bay close to us, & the other was the *Pulmonaria maritima*, whose trailing branches with glaucous colord leaves adornd the barren beaches; & thus, it is wisely ordained by providence, that every situation however barren or parchd should have its appropriate productions or ornaments, for this very plant removd to a good soil will generally pine away, but on the sea beach, its natural situation it thrives spontaneous luxuriously, & the same thing will happen with regard to many other plants.

We pursued our course to the eastward on the larboard shore & soon after passd the entrance of a small creek, where we saw a few temporary huts & some Natives, who were put into the greatest consternation at the sudden appearance of the three boats. Some of them began to carry their effects back into the wood, where the women & children also fled in great hurry to hide themselves, whilst a few of the men stood their ground at the water side & brandishd their spears to oppose our landing, till we convinced them by amicable signs & steering a different way that we intended them no harm, on which two Canoes put off after us with three men in each & followd us for some time very peaceably. To the eastward of this creek we opend a large bay choakd up with ice & backd by a considerable tract of country presenting a prospect the most bleak & barren that can possibly be conceivd;[134] the higher mountains were envelopd in perpetual snow, whilst the Valleys were chockd up with a huge mass of rugged ice down to the water side, not a tree or shrub could be perceivd over this lifeless & dreary tract, which with the surrounding ice diffusd a piercing chill we could scarcely endure. As we were rowing amongst the ice for a projecting pillar in the middle of the bay to satisfy our curiosity & take some bearings from the top of it, we suddenly found ourselves in a most critical situation, by perceiving that many of the huge pieces of ice about us were aground, while others of less magnitude were in rapid motion by the influence of the tide, & frequently dashing against the stationary ones with a force sufficient to crush either of our boats that might come between them to pieces, & indeed one of the boats had a very narrow escape which led to the discovery of our perilous situation. We at this time sounded & found we were in four fathoms about two miles from the shore, with a vast body of ice moving down upon us from the eastward & out of the bay.[135] This obligd us to relinquish our design & instantly steer out into the middle of the arm where in deeper water we should have only to encounter with floating ice, & as we staid across the arm along the edge of this immense moving field, which nearly extended from side to side & was so closely packd together as to be impenetrable to the boats, we expected no less than to be carried back with it a considerable distance, but continuing our exertions for a place of safety, we reached nearly the opposite shore, where the ice was observd to be less compact & a likelihood of our being able to force our way through it, we therefore made the attempt & by using the same precautions as already mentiond of the two cutters following the

---

134. Icy Strait, which is a translation of the Russian name "Proliv Ledyanoy" (Orth, 1971, 442).

135. Vancouver (1798(1984):1346) mentions that "To the north and east of this point, the shores of the continent form two large open bays, which were terminated by compact and solid mountains of ice, rising perpendicularly from the water's edge..." This was what is now the entrance to Glacier Bay. In the past 200 years, the glaciers have retreated more than sixty miles to the north; at this time, there was no Glacier Bay.

pinnaces tract closely, we happily succeeded, & found the encumbrance become less & less as we advancd to the eastward, till in the course of a few hours we got entirely beyond it & passd two or three very high pieces of a pyramidal figure that were little short we conceivd of 30 feet high above the surface of the water, from thence some idea may be formd of their size & magnitude, as ice is allowd to shew but a tenth or twelfth part of its whole bulk above water.

The arm now took a turn to the south eastward & appeard wide & spacious & clear of any ice for at least ten leagues in that direction. A little to the eastward of us was a large Island of a very moderate height & well wooded with pines, & as the shore of it appeard very inviting,[136] we landed on the south point at four in the afternoon to take some bearings & with an intention to dine, but not being able to find any water upon it, we continued our progress for the continental shore, passing a little to the southward of a group of small Islands,[137] & on coming abreast of a large rivulet in the evening we landed on its banks & pitchd our tents for the night.[138] Here we found growing plenty of wild orach, which we dressd, & as none of us had tasted greens or fresh vegetables of any kind for a long time, it made a very acceptable addition to our salt provisions, which from our long fasting too & the fatiguing adventures of the day, we ate relishd with a keen appetite. The boats were brought to a grapnel in what was conceived to be a sufficient depth of water & near enough to the tents to cooperate with the party on shore in case of any alarm, but the tide had fallen so low in the night time, that it was necessary to remove them much further out, & in doing this one of the cutters grounded on a bank where she remaind till next morning, we otherwise continued unmolested for the night.

---

136. Dall named this Pleasant Island because of its "pleasant shore" (Orth, 1971:762).

137. Porpoise Islands.

138. Locally, this area is known as Home Shore and Village Point. The Tlingit had settlements along this part of the coast. Just east of this point, at a place known locally as Groundhog Bay, archaeologists found a site which was occupied about 9,000 years ago, and many times after that.

Our station was about 14 leagues nearly due east from the entrance of the Sound, & the Arm was here about three leagues wide.

13th The launching of the Cutter & other preparations necessarily detaind us next morning till after we had breakfasted, this afforded an opportunity to several of the Natives to join us in their Canoes & along the beach from a small village a little to the northward of us, They were a promiscuous party of men women & children, & though they livd so far inland, they did not appear unaccustomd to such visitors, as they approachd us unarmd & without the least sign of fear or distrust, & on our part we endeavourd to strengthen their confidence by distributing small presents amongst them, as beads buttons hooks and bells & such other little ornamental articles as the women or children fancied. The women were all disfigurd like those in Cross Sound & to the southward with large oval pieces of wood in their lower lips. Their chief was a man of very modest & friendly behaviour & seemd to have considerable authority over his people, we therefore kept him close by us, that he might be answerable for their behaviour; at breakfast he partook of some of our fare with good relish & when he observd any of the women or children too troublesome in dunning us for presents he made them give over. He orderd his people to assist in launching our cutter off the bank, & when we were going away, in carrying ourselves & our luggage dry into the boats by means of their canoes, which they performd with the utmost cheerfulness, & to do justice to their honesty we did not miss the least article; this drew a further distribution of small presents from the different boats, to convince them of our approbation of their conduct, after which we parted in the most friendly manner.

On a commanding eminence close to our station was the remains of an old village that seemd to have been well guarded with pallisades[139] all round & naturally well situated for making

---

139. About this period of time, according to Tlingit oral tradition, there was an settlement here which played an important part in local history. It was known as Grouse Fort or "kaax' nu."

an obstinate resistance against attacks of even a superior force, yet the chief gave us to understand that its present desolate appearance was owed to the ravaging & inexorable cruelties of a tribe, who a few years back came from the opposite side of the Arm & Massacred the greatest number of its inhabitants, in which catastrophe he seemd to lament with unfeignd grief the unhappy fate of a sire & many relations.

As we now advancd to the southeastward we could not help observing that the country assumd a more pleasing appearance; the shores were every where fine sandy beaches, & the mountains which were pretty lofty rose on both sides of the arm with a gradual slant, & were coverd to their very summits with a continual forest of pine trees. The weather too seemd to have been more mild & favorable as we receded from the sea coast, & the wide spacious canal on which we were advancing scarcely ruffled by the fanning breeze added a grandeur to the scene before us which made us soon forget our late difficulties.

We had not advancd above four leagues from our resting place, when we came to a low point that divided this arm from another very extensive & wide one running N by W & S by E & no obstruction could be perceived in either of these directions as far as we could see from an elevated rocky islet[140] laying a little to the southward of the point to which we had repaird as a convenient station for taking the necessary bearings, & while Mr. Whidbey was engaged on this duty, others employd themselves in shooting Plover & Sea pies[141] about the rocks for dinner.

Whilst we were at this station we observd that the tide of flood came from the Southward & went rapidly into the arm we came from, which made it pretty evident that the southern branch

---

140. They were at the confluence of Icy Strait and Chatham Strait, by Rocky Island, just off shore. Later, they went ashore, probably on Couverden Island to fix lunch. Vancouver (1798(1984): 1347 and footnote) named this point of land "after the seat of my ancestors, Point Couverden." Vancouver's ancestors lived in Couverden in the province of Drenthe, in the Netherlands.

141. Lamb (personal communication) points out that Sea Pies was a term used for the birds we now call Oyster Catchers. When cooked into a stew, they are said to make a fine meal.

communicated with the sea,[142] & no doubt the strength of this tide over that which comes from Cross Sound has been the means of clearing these inland beaches of ice, by forcing it all out towards the Sound where we were perplexed & endangerd with such abundance of it.

It being near noon we hastend over to the low point that divided the two arms where Mr Whidbey observd for the Latitude by an artificial horizon, & made it 58°, 12' north, & our protraction about 17 leagues inland from the entrance of Cross Sound. Here we dressd our game & found no difficulty in procuring plenty of salubrious greens to relish them, for the beaches everywhere here producd abundance of wild orach, which in our situation was conceivd equal to the best spinanga. Some Natives that came in a Canoe brought us also some fish, so that with these additional luxuries, we made a very hearty meal, nor did any of us seem to regret the want of regular cooking or high seasond sauces, in short no one who has not tried it can conceive the high relish which these excursions give to the most homely fare.

After dinner we set off to the northward along the western shore of this large arm, & about two miles from the point passd on the inside of some black rocks & rocky islets laying well off in the channel[143] & after a fatiguing row against a strong breeze of wind, we were obligd to put up at dusk in a small bay about four leagues from where we dind. The arm was here about two leagues wide & the land on the opposite side was of a very moderate height & seemingly broken into Islands, whilst the shore we were pursuing is hemmd in by a compact ridge of mountains.

---

142. Later they found this to be true. Chatham Strait extends 150 miles north from Coronation Island to its junction with Icy Strait. The early traders called it "Menzies Strait," and Colnett had named the southern portion of it "Christians Sound." Lamb (Vancouver 1798(1984):1366, footnote) says that Henry Wagner, the cartographer, believed that Colnett named the sound after Rear Admiral Sir Hugh Christian. La Pérouse named the passage "Tschirikow Bay" and Don Juan de la Bodega y Quadra had called it "Enseñada del Principe" (Orth, 1971:201).

143. When one comes around Point Couverden from the west in a small boat and turns north, Couverden rock, surrounded by many smaller rocks, appears to lay far offshore.

14th The following morning we were in motion to the northward by the dawn of day & soon after passd some small Islets close to the shore & towards noon crossd a bay in which there appeard several Islands to reach a conspicuous bluff point[144] where the Latitude was observd to be 58° 35' & the shore opposite still seemd to be much broken & intersected with inlets.

In a sandy cove a little to the northward of this station, we landed to cook some refreshments which gave me an opportunity to examine round the place for plants, I walkd back into the woods in a border of low land which here intervenes between the shore & the Mountains, & soon came to an extensive clear Savanna, richly croppd with grasses & a variety of other vegetables, amongst which I spent my time till summond to dinner with much satisfaction. The *Ledum latifolium* which we frequently experienced as a useful substitute for tea was found here in great plenty & we did not fail to lay in a good store of it for that purpose.

After dinner we again resumd our northerly course with the discouraging circumstances of a strong breeze of wind, & a constant drain setting against us while the arm still continued in the same direction & appeard as wide & extensive before us as it did on our first coming into it. This put almost every one in bad humour at the extent & direction it was likely to carry us, but for my own part the little acquisitions I was able to make here & there to Botany, more than compensated for whatever I felt on the score of repining. Amongst them was a beautiful new species of *Caltha* which I named *Caltha celiarius*. I also met with the *Caltha palustria* for the first time on this coast. After a fatiguing row we advancd this day about 24 miles, & brought up in the evening in a sandy bay, where we were comforted with an uninterrupted night's repose.

15th Next day we continued our pursuit to the northward, & by noon reached some Islands that appeard in mid channel,[145] where on a remarkable sandy point nearly opposite to the southernmost

---

144. They had passed the entrance to St. James Bay. The northern point was named Point Whidbey by George Davidson of the U.S. Coast and Geodedic Survey in honor of Lt. Joseph Whidbey (Orth, 1971:1041).

145. Sullivan Rock and Sullivan Island.

of them the Latitude was found by a quicksilver horizon to be 58°
54' & our distance from the entrance of Cross sound was only
about 18 leagues in a northeast direction. Here we stopd to take
some refreshment, & whilst it was getting ready we divided into
parties in different directions with our guns in search of game, as
the land was clear & level with some Lagoons at the back of it, but
we saw very few birds of any kind, & only shot one duck. On this
low ground the soil is clayey & pretty deep, intermixed with white
sand which produced a large kind of Poplar that grew promiscuous & in abundance amongst the pine forests.

The arm was here about five miles wide & on each side bounded
by a loft ridge of mountains, whose tops were coverd with perpetual snows to the very edge of which vegetation appeard in
luxuriant verdure, though the wood which coverd the sides of
these ridges ceasd to grow a little lower down. We had now been
two days in this arm & had not yet seen the traces of a single
inhabitant.

In the afternoon we continued our progress along the western
shore, passing on our right a large Island of about four miles long
& soon after on our left a deep Valley choaked up with an immense
body of rugged ice down to the water's side; here the arm became
much narrower, & took a more westerly direction,[146] & the water
of it became pale & muddy which gave us some hopes of our
drawing near its termination this made us advance with greater
spirit in tracing the shore we were on till towards evening, when
we found it grow so shallow, that we were obligd to steer over to
the other side, where we deepend our water considerably. A little
before this we were visited by some of the natives in a small
wooden Canoe who told us that their village was a little higher up,
& as we were crossing over we plainly saw the smoke of it on the
side of the arm about ten miles off, but as it was nearly dark, & we
anxiously wished to enjoy our repose in quietness, we pitchd our
tents for the night on an open beach on the opposite shore, a little
to the northward of a naked sandy island of a conic form in the
middle of the channel.[147]

---

146. Chilkat Inlet.

147. Pyramid Island.

As we were now in the vicinity of a tribe of Indians, whose number & disposition we were unacquainted with, a strict watch became essentially necessary & after it was set, some muskets were fird off to deter them from approaching us for the night which we passd undisturbd.[148]

16th At day light next morning some of the Natives paid us a visit in a peaceable manner in several canoes, & as they approachd, they one & all of them accompanied the motions of their paddles with a plaintive song which was by no means destitute of melody nor unsuitable to that solitary gloom with which we were surrounded, stationd in the bottom of a deep narrow vale with high impending mountains confining our prospect on both sides, & nothing to diversify the dark verduous hue of the pine forests that coverd their sides, excepting the uncomfortable appearance of perpetual snow, which capt the rugged summits.

The termination of the Arm though apparently within view, was yet doubtful. At a little distance before us its breadth was indeed much contracted by a tract of low land backd with lofty mountains, but in the north side of this low land an opening appeard of rather more than half a mile wide, & from a small eminence which I ascended in quest of plants, I could plainly perceive that it afterwards widend & took a sudden turn to the northward between the ranges of mountains, & if any dependence could be place on the information of the Indians, they told us it went a considerable distance, & enumerated the names of several chiefs that livd with their Tribes on the shores of it far beyond where our view terminated.[149] This was very discouraging information for us who were already brought to an unexpected distance this way, for we were now a degree of latitude to the Northward of Cross Sound, & about a degree of Longitude to the eastward of it, there was however no other way of consoling our chagrin than

---

148. This was the homeland of the Chilkat and Chilkoot Tlingit. The Chilkat were one of the largest and most powerful groups in northern southeastern Alaska.

149. The main settlements of the Chilkat were up the river at the site of the village of Klukwan.

by pursuing it to the end, we therefore set off pretty early with the three boats, who were orderd to separate some distance from each other & sound as they went along. We did not go above a league when we all shallowd 'our water to about a fathom before we reachd within 2 miles of the opening already mentiond. This being considerd satisfactory we put back again to the place we had quitted & breakfasted. Here the party of Indians had now augmented Men Women & children to near a hundred in number & finding that we were returnd back, they earnestly entreated us to stay a few days, till the Chief higher up the arm had time to visit us, & as an inducement, they assurd us, they would bring plenty of furs. Two of these named Gincaat[150] & Ishet were according to their accounts very great chiefs.

These Natives appeard to be of a tribe of the Woagan nation, as they spoke the same language as those at Cross Sound & along that part of the exterior coast. They were chiefly dressd in the furs of land animals, but had trinkets & ornaments about them as well as cloth Muskets & other articles that evidently provd they had some communication either direct or indirect with Europeans. All the women had their lower lips pierced & stretchd round the edge with oval pieces of wood as already noticed.

All that we could learn from these people concerning the termination of this arm, was from some rude sketches of it they made on the sand, by which it appeard that after going on some distance it divided into three branches or rivers that terminated in Lakes, round which they said the inhabitants were very numerous.[151] To these lakes they could advance in their canoes, but they stated it as a Voyage of Several days; & this account is

---

150. It is difficult to determine what his name might have been. In interviews with elderly Chilkat Tlingit from Klukwan, none of them could ever recall a leader with the name "Gincaat." In modern Tlingit "Ginkaat" means "10," literally, "the hands of a man." So they may have been asking for, or offering, ten of something. It is possible that the Indians may have been talking about the leader of their settlement and were saying in Tlingit, "Jilḵaat" [Chilkat]. There is no sound in English similar to the sound transcribed by "l" in "Jilḵaat" and Menzies may have heard it as an "n."

151. They were probably trying to explain how they went over the mountains to trade with the Athabaskan Indians of interior Canada.

further corroborated by the statements of Mr. Brown & his Officers who afterwards came in the Jackal to trade amongst this very tribe & told us on meeting with them at Nootka, that they understood from these natives, their communications beyond this place by means of canoes were very extensive & took them at least eight days to reach the farthest end of them. Mr. Brown happend to have a skin Canoe over his Vessel's stern which he had purchasd of the Kodiak Indians at Port Mulgrave, & on seeing it these natives immediately describd the tribe he procurd it from by stating that the men wore ornaments in a slit in their lower lip; this observation clearly shewd that they are no strangers to that characteristic tribe which are supposd to inhabit the northern shores & extend across this great continent.[152]

We now set out on our return along the eastern shore & soon after came to a narrow point where the arm divided, & passing between it & some scatterd rocky islands to the southward of it, we crossd the entrance of another branch, which we did not pursue, as we supposd we saw its termination about 3 or 4 leagues off, at least the ridge of mountains round the head of it seemd so compact that we were pretty confident it could not go much further, as it was separated from the Arm only by a narrow slip of low land. We therefore directed our course to the southward, but did not proceed far when we were overtaken by a large canoe well mannd by about 20 Indians, who paddled round our boats in great state, with all hands singing & some dancing & capering in the strangest manner; after they had finishd their ceremonial introduction, which is very common with the Indians on this coast, they pointed out to us their Chief, whom they called Gincaat, who immediately enquired for our chief, & when Mr.Whidbey was pointed out to him, he presented him with a sea otter skin. Having done this, the canoes removd to a little distance, & the chief equipping himself in his best apparel, stood on a square box in the middle of his canoe, & whilst all kinds of people joind in a song, he dancd & caperd for some time in the most frantic manner that can

152. The Tlingit traveled long distances to trade and raid, and were fully aware of the Eskimos and their cultural differences. One Tlingit term for Eskimos translates as "walrus face" based on the fact that the men wore labrets.

possibly be conceived, with a rattle in his hand which now & then he kept twirling backwards & forwards with a quick vibrating motion. We stopt on our oars to gaze at this ludicrous entertainment with astonishment, which made him repeat it, & having finishd the second time, he came alongside, & wanted us to land, to barter with him for furs of which he had plenty in his canoe, this we declind, but made him understand that we meant to bring up for the night a little further on, on which he seemd willing to accompany us, & seeing this, we offerd him a seat in the pinnace which he declind accepting of, unless Mr Whidbey would take his place in the Canoe, & finding him thus scrupulous, one of the gentlemen jumpd in the canoe for Mr Whidbey, he then sufferd his son, a youth about the age of 17 to come into the pinnace, but would not venture himself.

This Chief was a stout robust man upwards of 50 years of age, & joind with the stiff punctilious deportment of an old warrior the most princely appearance of any chief we had met with on the Coast, particularly when apparelled in his best robes, which consisted of two coverings thrown loosely over his shoulders, one thence came down before to his knees, & the other fell behind to his heels. These were made of fine wool, the produce and manufacture of the country curiously wrought & diversified with a great variety of black emblematical figures on a white ground with a yellow border, & both were fringd round the edges with the richest furs, & decorated here & there with tufts of various colours.[153] He had at the same time on his head what bore a striking resemblance to a crown, adornd with glittering copper & brass & wreaths of the finest furs; & from the hind part of it, a loose train of pure Ermine fell down his back almost to the ground.[154]

---

153. The Indians of this area are famous for their robes, now known as Chilkat Blankets, woven of mountain goat wool and cedar bark. But at this period in time, they may have been making a transitional form, known as the Raven's Tail Blanket. From the description given, it is uncertain which type of robe was seen because both styles are large and beautifully woven.

154. High ranking Tlingit wear a headpiece known as a *Shakiyaat*. Indeed it is like a crown, with a crest on the front and usually has sea lion whiskers on the top and ermine skins hanging from the side and back. On ceremonial occasions, the top of the crown is filled with bird down, which flies out as the dancer moves his head. The falling down is a symbol of peace.

Thus enrobd he stood before us sometime, with a rattle in his hand, in a majestic attitude, in short his address & magnificent appearance, was so different from any we had seen, that he was by us instantly dubbed with the name of Emperor of the Lakes, round which we had understood his tribes & the principal part of his territory lay.

We rowd along the shore to the southward accompanied by this larger large canoe & in the dusk of the evening brought up in small Bay where we landed & kindled a fire to dress some victuals. The canoe put on shore at the same time,& we were not a little surprised to see the Chief who caperd about so frisky a little before, obligd to be carried on shore between two of his people. At first we thought this was in consequence of his great dignity, but as he was an old man, we were afterwards more inclind to attribute it to his inability to walk,[155] whether or not he might want the use of his limbs, he did not want the use of his tongue, for he chatterd incessantly with his people the whole night long. Mr Whidbey made him some presents for his sea otter skins, & we observd that they had in the Canoes 3 or 4 muskets & a blunderbuss that was in good repair & loaded, this made us be more on our guard notwithstanding their friendly appearance, & after supper we all retird to sleep in the boats, there being no suitable place for the tents, & left the chief & his party on shore.

17th At day light next morning we were quite surprised to find that three canoes had arrivd in the night time unperceived who were all well provided with long Spears & other warlike weapons, & another large canoe was seen approaching us from the northward, when the old Chief Gincaat observd us stirring, he came alongside of the Pinnace in his canoe & requested leave to be admitted on board, but as we were then in some confusion he was desird to keep off, instead of which he jumpd into the Pinnace, & was in the act of handing some Mats & other things into his canoe, when it was though high time to interfere, & turnd him out by force into his canoe which was shovd off from the boat. This only seemd to irritate & render them more daring, & as they were

---

155. It was a sign of respect and power to be carried from the canoe.

coming alongside of us again, evidently with an intention to plunder, a Musket was pointed at the canoe with threats to fire at them, if they persisted in their attempt, on which the chief soon very cooly took up his blunderbuss, & pointing it at the boat, shewd that they were equally ready to return the fire & this he did with so much adroitness as to leave us no doubt of his being perfectly acquainted with the management of it, this being the case, it was thought necessary to use our endeavours to keep them off by fairer means, as the boat was still in such confusion on account of our sleeping in her, that we could not readily get at all our firearms. In the mean time Mr. Whidbey orderd the grapnel to be weighd, & hailing the other boats, round which the other canoes were equally daring, he desird them to weigh, got their arms ready & follow his motions, by which we all droppd gradually further out into the arm, where we had more sea room to cooperate & by the time the other large canoes joind them we were in perfect readiness to resist any attack they might be inclind to make; but on observing this they declind any further attempts towards plundering us, & now sollicited in a more peaceable manner with furs & sea otter skins in their hands to come along side to barter with us, but their apparent treacherous behaviour renderd this inadmissable, & none of them were afterwards sufferd to come near any of the boats, especially as we were uncertain of their original motives, & we therefore left them without discharging a single musket & pursued our course to the southward.

For though in the large canoe they all appeard friendly disposd on the preceeding evening, & were not sufficiently armd for hostility, yet the canoes which joind in the night time had a great number of Spears & other hostile weapons. This together with the Chiefs boarding us so abruptly in the morning were the principal things on which we grounded our suspicions, for the large canoe that joind as we were coming away had in her a promiscuous party of men & women that did not appear armd, & their chief was exceedingly anxious to make the business up, & be admitted into our favor, but we remaind inflexible to his entreaties though he followd us for some time at a little distance, hailing us now & then through a brass speaking trumpet & at times looking at us through a spying glass, in a manner which shewd that he perfectly knew the use of these instruments.[156] Gincaat also, followd us in his large canoe, holding up skins & other alluring signs, but finding that we turnd a deaf ear to all their sollicitations, they both returnd back after following two or three miles, to the little Bay where they had left the armd canoes.

On the whole it is not improbable but that these people on hearing of three small boats wandering about in these interior channels at a distance from protection, might be inclind, either to take or plunder them if they thought it practicable, & the Chiefs coming so slightly armd themselves might be to prevent suspicion & create a greater confidence on our part to favor their diabolical plans, else how are we to account for those other canoes following them so well armd & for the old Chiefs conduct too in jumping into the pinnace & attempting to plunder, so different from his scrupulous behavior on the preceeding evening, than by supposing that as he found his party now so strong, he threw off the mask of friendship & conmmencd his drepedations. In short in whatever way we view their conduct, the plan adopted of getting clear of them as soon as possible, was certainly the most prudent that could be devisd, as it equally savd them from becoming objects of our revenge, & us from the painful task of punishing their aggressions with the destruction of some of their lives, should their hostile intentions become more apparent. The whole party did not amount to a hundred natives.[157]

With these pleasing reflections we pursued our course along a rocky indented shore to the southward, passing about noon a large deep bay,[158] & towards evening the wind & weather being very

---

156. The Tlingit were obtaining a variety of weapons and other equipment from the American and British traders. When the Russians expanded into southeastern Alaska, they were alarmed at the number of firearms the Tlingit possessed, and the way in which these Indians defended their territories from the encroachment of outsiders.

157. Vancouver (1798(1984):1350, 1352) named the point of land at the tip of the Chilkat Peninsula, Seduction Point, "in consequence of the artful character of the Indians who are said to reside in its neighborhood." Also, Menzies and Vancouver differ slightly on the details, Vancouver saying that "their numbers had now increased to at least two hundred."

158. At this time, Vancouver decided to name certain features in honor of his mother's side of the family. He named this passageway Lynn Canal in

unfavorable we brought up amongst the northernmost of a group of Islands nearly opposite to the point on which the Latitude was observd three days before,[159] & passd the night without any other molestation then what we experiencd from a stormy gale attended with heavy rain.

18th Next day we resumd our examination by an intricate channel with rocks & islets of about two miles wide between the group of Islands & the eastern shore, & soon after passd an immense Valley inland choaked up with rugged ice similar to those already mentiond from this Valley a large Rivulet issued forth through some low land, on which we saw several Indians, who kept beckoning to us as we passd along, but the boats could not approach them on account of the shallowness of the water which here extended some distance from the shore,[160] we therefore continued standing on, & in the afternoon passd through a narrow contracted part of the channel,[161] after which it suddenly widend again & took nearly a southeast direction, this we pursued, passing on our left some Islands bays & low broken land, where some small openings appeard that were not thought deserving of examination. From this port 3 or 4 canoes joind us, & kept following us along shore very peaceably till about the dusk of the evening, when wishing to get rid of them, we steerd across the arm

remembrance of his home in King's Lynn, Norfolk. The large bay and the southern point of land were named in honor of his mother, Bridget Berners. The northern tip of land at the mouth of the bay was named St. Mary's to commemorate his mother's birth place, St. Mary's Wiggenham (Orth, 1971:126,160, 827).

159. The northernmost of these islands is North Island, but nearby Benjamin Island has a fine cove on its north end and that may have been where they camped.

160. The Eagle River valley leads from the coast inland a few miles to the Eagle and Herbert Glaciers. The shallow beach is Eagle Beach which at low tide extends nearly a mile out into Lynn Canal. In his journal, Vancouver (1798(1984):1354) says that, "...they came to the north point of a small bay where the shoal terminated..." and that they stopped to dine. This was more than likely Eagle or Amalga Harbor, at the south end of Eagle Beach.

161. They were passing by Tee Harbor, Lena Cove and Point Lena on the mainland, and Shelter Island lies to the west.

to the opposite shore with intent to bring up for the night, this the Indians perceivd & got possession of the very beach where we intended to land before we could reach it.[162] The night was dark & a little hazy, yet it was thought the termination of this arm was now very apparent, this together with some lights that were seen on the opposite shore,[163] which made it probable that the Natives here were very numerous induced Mr. Whidbey as the breeze was favorable to turn back & run out of this arm altogether rather than run the risuqe of being again entangled with Indians, & by two next morning, we again got into the main channel,[164] by the south end of the group of Islands above mentioned, but it was afterwards found that we relinquished this part of our researches too hastily, for Mr. Whidbey in his next boats cruize from our station near Cape Ommanney, came into this channel by the very arm, which was not thought to be closd up, & Mr. Brown commander of the Jackal found a fair passage this way for his Vessel to the Southward. After we found ourselves again in the large arm,[165] we stopt to take some repose in a small cove about four leagues to the northward of the point where we first enterd it, & after breakfast we continued our southerly coast along the eastern shore of this great Arm, which we found rocky & indented, with small sandy bays & a few detached rocks & islets laying near it here & there,

---

162. Lamb (Vancouver, 1798(1984):1354 footnote) says regarding Vancouver's text that "This description is difficult to follow..." and then describes the various islands and visibility. In the summer of 1990, I cruised this area to attempt to replicate the course. It seems that they came down near Point Louisa, then turned west across the southern end of Shelter Island near the shore at Symonds point. In the haze and dim light, they probably could not see beyond Point Young where the channel continues east southeast along the west side of Douglas Island. Later, Menzies criticizes Whidbey for not continuing around Douglas Island, but from their location, that channel was not visible.

163. The Auke Tlingit had their major village just to the east of Point Louisa, and the voyagers saw some lights in the vicinity of the village.

164. Vancouver (1798(1984):1355) describes the events a little differently when he reports that, "There was now no alternative but either to force a landing by firing upon them, or to remain at their oars all night. The latter Mr. Whidbey considered to be not only the most humane, but the most prudent measure to adopt..." Vancouver named their stopping place Point Retreat.

165. Chatham Strait.

but the weather was so thick & foggy with light rain, that we could seldom see the opposite side of the arm.[166]

20th Next day however the weather became more favorable & it was the more fortunate as we had now advancd upon new ground, having passd the place where we had enterd this large channel from Cross Sound, & now continud our progress to the southward without perceiving any apparent interruption before us, in a spacious channel of at least two leagues wide, & the more we advanced the more we became convincd by meeting the flood tide regularly from the southward of its communicating with the Ocean in that direction. In the evening we pitchd our tents on a very pleasant situation, which inducd us to breakfast next day before we set out.[167]

21st Although we had now advanced upon new ground above ten leagues, the arm still preservd the same direction & spacious appearance, a little before us the Shore we were pursuing fell back to for a large bay, the bottom of which appeard skirted by a considerable tract of low broken land. We had gone but a few miles from our resting place when we perceived a small opening into this lowland,[168] & a number of Natives in several large canoes at the entrance of it. This inducd us to have our firearms in readiness, & as several of the muskets had been loaded some days, they were fird off into the air, in order to be fresh loaded, after which to our no small surprise, we heard the report of an equal number of muskets, dischargd in the same way from the canoes, we however

166. They were moving along the east shore of Chatham Strait. Vancouver (1798(1984):1356 and footnote) named Point Marsden, to honor either William Marsden or Samuel Marsden, who arrived at Parramatta, New South Wales on March 2, 1794.

167. Vancouver (1798(1984):1356 and footnote) named the islands west of Chatham Strait, the King George the Third's Archipelago. This name is no longer in use. Vancouver also named Point Parker, probably in honor of Sir Peter Parker of the British Admiralty, and this name has been preserved (Orth, 1971:739).

168. This inlet is now known as Kootsnahoo Inlet, and is derived from the Tlingit expression *Xutsnoowu* meaning "fortress of the brown bear," or grizzly bear. The village of Angoon is located at the mouth of this inlet.

stood on, fully prepared for whatever might be their intention, & as we approachd, they retreated into the opening & landed on the north side of it, apparently to watch our motions. As we rowd towards them we endeavourd by amicable signs to make them sensible of our peaceable disposition, on seeing this the chief orderd them all to lay down their weapons & crouch themselves on the beach, whilst we stopt a little short of it on our oars, till a canoe came off to us with a man who made a very conspicuous figure amongst the rest from his being cloathd in a fine scarlet coat, we soon conciliated his friendship by some presents, & askd for fish, which was immediately sent off to us, & having procurd a suffi- cient supply of that article for small trinkets, we put back again out of the opening, deeming from its size rocky appearance & the improbability of its leading far, as an object unworthy of further examination. The natives on observing our motions being unwill- ing to loose the opportunity of trading with us, followd in their canoes in great numbers of men, women & children; & soon surrounded the boats in great confusion, offering fish, furs & other articles to barter, with such eagerness, that it was found neces- sary to restrain their impetuosity by ordering them to keep off. The Chief observing our aversion to their teazing conduct, beat off several canoes himself, & with an imperious tone, orderd them all to go back, excepting one or two, which he sufferd at our own desire to follow us with him.

On the whole what little we saw of these people, they appeard to be so equitable in their dealings & so friendly in their behaviour, that we could not help lamenting the shortness of our stay amongst them. They had chosen a delightful situation for their abode, which was on a commanding eminence on the south point of the entrance,[169] where they were erecting a fortified village, & from its apparent size we were certain it could not be intended for less than 5 or 600 inhabitants. Several temporary huts were

169. This site has probably been occupied for a very long time. de Laguna (1960:172-73) says that "We are unfortunately unable to identify the settle- ment visited by Vancouver's Lieutenant Whidbey in the summer of 1794, for parts of the description would fit Thayer Creek north of Angoon, other parts Angoon itself, and still others no locality in the vicinity. Yet the account obviously refers to a settlement somewhere between Point Parker and Killisnoo

strewd here & there along shore, but their chief residence at this time was in a small Creek behind where they landed, & which no doubt they meant to defend with their whole force had they found us inclind to hostility.

On both sides of the opening we saw several little gardens neatly fencd in & apparently kept in very good order, & as these were the first signs of horticulture we had observd in any of our interior examinations on this coast, our curiosity was much excited & it was natural to regret our not being able to have a nearer view of them. I happend to be the only one of the party who had formerly seen similar little gardens near Cape Edgecumbe about eighteen leagues in a south west direction from this place, others we have been informd have seen them about the north end of Queen Charlotte's Isles & the northward of Cross Sound under Mount Fairweather on the exterior edge of the coast. The sole produce of these gardens is I believe a small species of Tobacco[170] which the Chiefs on this part of the coast are very fond of chewing intermixd with a kind of whitish powder similar to that used by the Chinese with the Betel nut.

Here then we see the first dawns of agriculture excited amongst these savages, not in rearing any article of real utility either to their comfort or support, as might naturally be expected, but in cultivating a mere drug to satisfy their cravings of a fanciful appetite, that can be no ways necessary to their existence; hence we perceived how readily man even in a state of nature improves or increasers his original wants & thereby gradually advances to luxury & refinement, & from this perhaps a good lesson might be derived for the tedious process of civilizing these inhabitants, which is first to give them a relish for those articles of luxury that are most like to succeed in their climate & soil, & by thus creating

---

Island; and Angoon, despite difficulties, seems to be the most likely place intended." She goes on to give an extended description and explanation of archaeological sites around Angoon and neighboring bays. In 1988, Drs. Madonna Moss and Jon Erlandson found remains of fish traps from the Angoon area and through carbon dating they were found to be about 3,000 years old (personal communication).

170. Menzies was absolutely correct in identifying the crop as domesticated tobacco (See Appendix). He had previously seen tobacco at Sitka while with Colnett in 1788.

artificial wants a spirit of industry & emulation favorable to civilization would not fail to be excited.

On the north side behind these gardens we saw what we conceivd to be their tombs, which were square boxes raisd some feet from the ground & supported on posts with their fronts fancifully painted & one or two long white poles stuck in the ground close to each.

Many of these natives appeard newly clothd with Jackets & Trousers of European manufactory, & they had many other articles about them that strongly indicated there having a late intercourse with some of the Traders this induced us to enquire of these where they had procurd these commodities, & they pointd to the south westward over the Mountains on the other side of the arm, saying that they had them from a vessel in that direction, which we afterwards understood was the Lady Washington in Norfolk Sound near Cape Edgecumbe commanded by Mr. Kendrick,[171] of whom they had the Jackets & Trousers & the red coat above mentiond. This shews the great distance these people go to make their markets, & also proves the connection of this arm with the Ocean by channels in that direction.

After parting with these Natives we pursued our course to the southward across the bay, passing two other small openings apparently of little import running into the low land, & on our landing to dine[172] several canoes that followd us at a distance watching our motions, came up with us, apparently with no other intention than a desire of trading with us, as they had fish furs & other articles, which they were very anxious to dispose of, for cloth

---

171. Howay (1973:6,24) describes the *Lady Washington* for the year 1788 as follows: "An American sloop of Boston, 90 tons, companion to the *Columbia Rediviva*, and owned by the same persons. Arrived on the coast in September, 1788; and in 1789 under her master, Robert Gray, traded north and south from Nootka. In July, 1789, Kendrick and Gray exchanged vessels and from that time forward the *Lady Washington* was under the command of Kendrick, until his death. His last season on the coast was 1794."

172. Just south of Angoon, Vancouver (1798(1984):1358 and footnote) named the western tip of Killisnoo Island Point Samuel, and the bay to the south of it, Hood's Bay, to commemorate Samuel Hood, Baron Hood, a Vice-Admiral, and a member of the Board of Admiralty.

wearing apparel arms or ammunition, the latter of which they sought more anxiously after, but finding that they could not get any, they readily partd with their finest furs for any kind of old wearing apparel, which was greatly preferd to either Copper or Iron. That we might not be tiezd with their importunities, during our meal time, they were requested to move a little from us, which they readily obeyd, & remaind quiet till we were done, in short they seemd to be a very peaceable tribe, & though their Chiefs were not with them, they were easily kept in good order, & as traders they were liberal & honest in their dealings. When we movd they returnd peaceably to their Village, & we rowd along shore, passing two smaller bays[173] with some rocks & islets laying a little off them, till we came to a small Cove, where we brought up for the night.[174] A little after dark some natives were approaching us, but when they were made acquainted, that their visit at that unreasonable hour would be very unpleasant to us, they quietly retird & we saw no more of them.

22nd Next morning it was observd that the arm which was still about two leagues wide, preservd nearly the same distance without any interruption as far as we could view it, we therefore perseverd in our examination to the southward, now pretty certain from the spacious appearance before us, & the apparent oceanic swell, that we should be able to get out to sea through Christian Sound,[175] near where we left off the preceeding season, & as the weather was now pretty favorable, & we had no latitude for some days past, we pushed pretty hard for a conspicuous point a head of us, on which we landed a little before noon; here Mr. Whidbey found the Latitude to be 57° 1' north which is nearly the latitude of Cape Edgecumbe but situated about 16 leagues to the eastward of it & about 100 miles in a south east direction from Cross Sound.

----

173. Chaik Bay and Whitewater Bay.

174. Wilson Cove.

175. The southern entrance to Chatham Strait where they had concluded their survey in 1793.

The prospect which here opend to our view was very interesting, for though we saw a clear & spacious opening out to sea between Cape Ommanney & Cape Decision & saw even distinctly the land over the latter, in a south by east direction, where we left off last year, yet to the eastward of us an extensive opening appeard,[176] which dampd all our expectations of finishing this cruize, as it ran among some low broken land, where it was very likely to branch in various directions, that would render the examination of it both tedious & delatory. Nor could we here help reverting in our minds on the great length of the spacious channel, which we had thus far explord, from the certainty we now had of its running nearly in a north by west direction upwards of three degrees of Latitude, that is from its entrance near the latitude of 56° to where we left it off beyond the latitude of 59° north.

The land on the western side of this channel as far as we could see it towards Cape Ommanney rose with a steep ascent from the water side to form a compact lofty ridge of mountains toppd with snow but whose sides were wooded with a continued forest of pines.

A little to the Southward of the point we were on lay a barren rocky islet & about a league to the southeastward a small round island coverd with trees.[177]

The shore which we now followd, stretchd to the Eastward & was very bold & rugged with many detatchd rocks, but we had scarcely advancd five miles when we found it trended to the northeast, which direction we pursued for about 5 miles, further & then encampd for the night.

23rd On the morning of the 23rd we had thick fog which particularly hoverd over the low land to the eastward of us, & prevented

---

176. Later on, Vancouver named this opening Frederick Sound for his Royal Highness Frederick, Duke of York, son of King George III of England (Orth, 1971:354).

177. They were at the tip of Admiralty Island which Vancouver named in honor of Sir Alan Gardner. They then turned to the east and after ten miles came to rest for the night at Point Brightman, which Vancouver (1798(1984):1359 and footnote) named Point Townshend, after J. T. Townshend, a member of the Board of Admiralty. Vancouver's name is no longer in use.

our forming any distinct idea of the extent of the opening before us, & this being the last day for which we were victualld, on examining into the state of our provisions, it was found that we had scarcely sufficient to serve us back to the Vessels, which, the nearest way we could go, were at least 120 miles from us. To accomplish this distance would take at least four days, unless assisted by favorable winds, on which we could not depend having hitherto made so little use of our Sails; this & the improbability of our finishing, should we even run the risque of remaining out a few days longer, on a stinted allowance, operated so strongly, that we immediately resolved on our return to Cross Sound, & this we did more readily as we were now certain of a clear passage out to sea by Cape Ommanney for the Vessels should the interior navigation be preferrd, which excepting close to Cross Sound appeared very eligible, with the apparent advantage of good anchorage & moderate soundings in the different bays one each side of the channel.

When we again enterd the great channel on our way back, we were favord with a fresh southerly breeze which brought with it thick rainy weather & a rough swell, that renderd our situation in the boats very uncomfortable, running at times no little risque of being swampd by the roughness of the sea; we however too the advantage of the wind, & kept before it in mid channel without landing any where till night when we brought up on the eastern shore & found ourselves about 60 miles nearer to Cross Sound than when we set out in the morning.

24th The following day we had fair clear weather with very little wind, so that we movd on as usual rowing, but the short irregular swell left by the preceeding gale greatly retarded our progress. About noon we enterd the branch leading to Cross Sound[178] &

---

178. Icy Strait. Lamb (Vancouver, 1798(1984):1360 footnotes) explains how Vancouver came to name the points on the southern shore, Point Augusta, Point Sophia and Point Adolphus. "Named in honour of Princess Augusta, daughter of George III. This was the first of seven features named after sons and daughters of the King. The previous year he had commemorated three other sons in Prince Ernest Sound, Duke of Clarence Strait and Prince of Wales Archipelago." Princess Sophia was a daughter of the King, and Adolphus, Duke of Sussex, was his son.

continued this & next day along the western shore which was found rocky with some Islets laying near it, & in some places a large opening went off to the South West,[179] but the evening of the latter day we past the point where the arm bends to the westward & encampd for the night about six leagues due east of the Vessels on the southern shore, near where we had the last encounter with the ice. Here we saw a tomb, similar to those already mentiond, in exceeding good repair it consisted of a large square box made of planks,& was supported about six feet from the ground by firm wooden posts, the side of it that facd the water which appeard to be the front, was fresh painted with different emblematicated figures & close to it a long pole of near 30 feet high, was erected, which was also fresh painted with alternate streaks of red & white; in the inside of this tomb two small square boxes were seen in which the remains of human bodies were deposited.[180]

A good deal of drift ice was now seen, but not nearly so thick on this side as we had experienced it on the opposite shore, which must undoubtedly be attributed to the strength of the flood tides coming from the southward , & forcing it mostly into the bays on the northern shore, where we met with it in such quantities.

26th On the morning of the 26th we continued our return along the southern shore, passing on our left two Bays one of which appeard to be pretty deep,[181] & on our right a pretty large Island of about two leagues long - situated nearly in mid-channel, which is here about seven miles wide,[182] & soon after we enterd Cross

---

179. Port Frederick which Vancouver named for King George III's son, Frederick, Duke of York. At the present time, the village of Hoonah is located just inside the mouth of Port Frederick. There may have been a settlement there when the expedition passed by, but it would not have been visible from the entrance.

180. This type of mortuary pole, with horizontal or diagonal bands, was also sketched by Suria with the Malaspina expedition at Yakutat in 1791. A photograph of this sketch can be found in de Laguna (1972:976) and on the following page there is a sketch by Suria of mortuary boxes.

181. The deep bay is Idaho Inlet which extends about eleven miles to the south.

182. Lemesurier Island, see above regarding W. H. Dall and his naming of this island.

Sound by a narrow navigable passage on the south side of the group of rocky islands mentiond on our outset on this expedition,[183] & which may be considerd as the eastern boundary of the Sound. The passage on the north side of these Islands is the widest, & excepting the inconvenience arising from large pieces of floating ice as already noticed, both of them appeard free of any other apparent impediment to Navigation.

In the afternoon we arrived at the Vessels after traversing in our circuitous mode of examination upwards of 600 miles in the boats in about 16 days.

In the course of the forenoon the Jackal arrivd in the Cove. This vessel after parting with us at sea, bore up for Port Mulgrave as already mentiond where she remaind some days after the Chatham left it, collecting Furs from the Natives, for though the Russian party had been there before Mr. Brown & remaind during his stay, the animosities which s ubsisted between them & the Natives, precluded their having any chances of rivalship in trade, nor had they indeed proper articles to purchase any furs were they even upon the best terms with them, their sole dependence being on the success of the Kodiak hunter as already noticed, & this perhaps may be the chief reason which irritates the Natives so much against them, as they conceive them no doubt as intruders in their territories, in draining their shores & coasts of Seals Otters & Fish on which their subsistence chiefly depends, & that too without making the least return for their depredations.[184] Before the Jackal had quitted Port Mulgrave, these animosities had come to an open rupture, for one day about fifteen Natives armd, in a canoe carried off six Kodiak Indians as prisoners, & about a hundred canoes of the latter tribe were soon after dispatchd in quest of them, but not finding them, they brought ten of the natives in

---

183. They passed through South Inian Pass, just south of the Inian Islands. At the western end of this pass, Vancouver named the southern point of land Point Lavina to commemorate Lady Lavina Spencer, wife of the second Earl Spencer (Vancouver, 1798(1984):1345 and footnote).

184. The Tlingit were very resentful of outsiders intruding into their territory. Later, when the Russians increased their hunting activities in southeastern Alaska, the Tlingit often times attacked the Russian and Aleut hunting parties.

three canoes as prisoners to the encampment, & in a second trip they capturd several more of them, to be kept as hostages till the Kodiak Indians should be returnd. One time Mr. Brown had the curiosity of accompanying Mr. Portoff[185] & a numerous fleet of Canoes up the bay in one of the Jackals boats, in expectation of seeing a battle between the contending parties but on their coming up with the adverse party a long discussion ensued, after which an exchange of some of the prisoners took place, but Mr. Portoff detaind the remainder, amounting to about a dozen men women & children until the rest of the Kodiak Indians should be restord.

About five days after our departure a Brig namd the Arthur belonging to Bengal but last from New South Wales commanded by Mr. Barbar arrived in the Sound for the purpose of collecting Furs[186] & after staying about a week she proceeded on her Voyage to the Southward.

The weather they had experienced in the Port during our absence was in general very boisterous accompanied with heavy rains & at times thick fog. The Thermometer on deck daily observd at noon rangd between 51 & 55.

The number of Natives that continued visiting the Vessels were not very numerous, ten or twelve canoes with men women & children were the utmost they had about them at any one time, & as they were backward & forward almost daily, it was supposd that their residence was not at a great distance. While they remaind at their temporary abode in the Cove, they behavd very orderly, seldom giving much trouble or intruding themselves on board either Vessels, & they generally brought a daily supply of fish, both Halibut & Salmon, so that considerable advantage was

---

185. Dr. Black (personal communication) says that the proper transcription of the name is Egor Portov, and that he was Baranov's foreman in charge of the hunting parties. Lamb (Vancouver, 1798(1984):1329, footnote) gives the transcription as George Purtov.

186. This was probably the vessel that the Russians had seen in Prince William Sound on June 12 (Vancouver, 1798(1984):1302, 1342 and footnote). Howay (1973:21,30) describes the *Arthur* as a British brig of Bengal, under Captain Barber, with a crew of twenty-two men. Charles Ley deserted the *Arthur* and was mustered into the *Discovery's* company on July 24th and deserted the *Discovery* on April 27, 1795 (Vancouver, 1798(1984):1652).

gaind from their intercourse, till their dispostion to thieving was detected in one or two flagrant instances, which in some measure interrupted the amicable trafic. The first instance happend on board the Chatham, her cabin windows being open, the natives found an opportunity by that means to reach a Hanger which they were carrying to the shore when it was observd & a musket pointed at them, finding themselves thus detected they instantly returnd back & deliverd it, without discovering the least embarrassment or apparent concern for their conduct. In another instance they were detected in stealing part of the rudder chains from the Discovery, several muskets were fird at them without effect & a boat was sent therefore in pursuit of them, which overtook them just as they were going to land, by the Canoes oversetting & consequently losing their prize & other valuables, the Canoe however with one man & two women were brought on board the Discovery, where the delinquents were confind in irons till next day, & then the man was punishd with four dozen of lashes on his bare back, after which he & the two women were sufferd to depart in their canoe. This transaction occasioned as might naturally be expected a temporary interruption to their friendly intercourse, as the Natives all quitted the cove, & none of them visited the Vessels for some days, & when they did approach them, it was with the utmost caution, but being friendly received, they soon forgot the transaction & became daily visiters again. The man who was punishd, was met a few days after by Mr. Johnstone amongst a small party who were fishing near the entrance of the Sound, & he behavd himself very friendly, being indeed the most forward in shewing little acts of civility & kindness, which provd that he harbourd no kind of resentment for the castigation he receivd, & one of the women who was a little hurt when the canoe upset, visitd the Vessel daily for surgical assistance.

The cove where the Vessels were staiond is situated about 10 miles within the entrance of the Sound in the Latitude of 58° 12' north and Longitude [missing]. The variation of the compass was found to be about 29 East, the tide near the full & change of the Moon rose 16 feet in the night & 14 feet in the day time, & was high water about the time of the Moon's passing the meridian.

July 28th Having compleated our wood & water, & got everything in readiness for sailing, we both weighd on the morning of
the 28th & made Sail out of the Cove, with light airs & the
assistance of the boats towing a head, it soon after fell calm before
we had advancd above a mile, & this with the tide of flood making
against us obligd us to anchor again till the afternoon but the
Chatham continued under sail.

The Jackal was left in the Cove preparing to proceed to visit the
inland tribes of Indians we had discoverd in our boat expedition,
with expectations from our reports of procuring a good collection
of furs amongst them, & indeed there could be little doubt of her
success, from the quantities of sea otter Skins & other Furs we saw
amongst them & which they seemd so anxious to dispose of, that
they often threw them into our boats, & took any thing for them
in return that was offerd. In the prosecution of this object we
afterwards understood that Mr Brown carried his vessel to the
northward as far as the boats had penetrated, where he was very
civilly treated by those very Indians whose conduct appeard to us
so suspicious, & in going to the Southward he discoverd a clear
navigable passage for his Vessel by the channel we had too hastily
quitted on the evening of the 18th,[187] by which he continued his
route, passing through another passage, that had escaped the
vigilance of our boat examination, upwards of 20 leagues inland
from Cape Decision, which last year was supposd to be the
Continent, but which he thus provd to the contrary. And this
instance will clearly shew, that where the examination is so
difficult & intricate however carefully performd, it can have no
pretensions to infallibility.

In the afternoon we again weighd & after hoisting in our boats
continued working out of the Sound against a flucuating breeze
from South west, but having the ebb tide in our favor we soon got
out to sea,[188] & remaind off Cross Cape all night, waiting the

---

187. This is the northern end of Stephens Passage which connects with
Frederick Sound at its southern end. Stephens Passage extends north around
the west side of Douglas Island and joins Saginaw Channel in Lynn Canal.

188. The point of land on the northwest end of Port Althorp was named Point
Lucan. Now named Cape Bingham, the northern end of Yakobi Island was
named Point Bingham by Captain Vancouver to honor Margaret Bingham,
Countess of Lucan, mother of Lady Lavina Spencer (Vancouver,
1798(1984):1361, 1362 and footnotes).

return of day to continue our examination in tracing the exterior line of shore to the southward.

29th Next day we had light baffling winds from between South & South West, with which we were allowd to make but little progress, & the weather was thick & foggy with drizzling rain, so that we could seldom see the land distinctly, we could however observe that this part of the coast is strewd with a vast number of rocks & islets & several apparent openings likely to afford shelter as harbours, amongst these it was difficult to distinguish that calld Portlock's Harbour[189] from the imperfect view we had of the Coast in this days progress.

30th On the 30th we were favord with a moderate breeze from WNW which dispersd the haze & gave us a pretty distinct view of the shore & even of the distant mountains to the north ward of Cross Sound, that which has been denominated Mount fair weather, from the different views we now had of it, we were rather inclind to consider as an assemblage of Mountains, rising from the shore of Cape Fairweather in steep cliffs & rocky precipices, & towering high above the other ridges of Mountains in irregular & broken summits.

We stood along shore with this favorable breeze towards Cape Edgecombe, in passing which at noon we had an observation for the Latitude which reducd to the Cape agreed exactly with the Latitude assignd to it by Capt. Cook, & our Longitude of it was a few miles to the Eastward of his, as has been the case on most other parts of the Coast. The land we passd this forenoon appeard much broken & indented with Bays & Inlets, & with small Islands & Rocks laying near it, which induced Capt Cook to name it the Bay of Islands.[190]

---

189. Portlock Harbor lies behind Hogan Island on the west coast of Chichagof Island. In poor weather it would be difficult to identify. Vancouver (1798(1984):1364 and footnote) named the point of land on the southern end of Portlock Harbor, Cape Edward in honor of Edward, son of King George III, who later became the Duke of Kent and the father of Queen Victoria.

190. Now Salisbury Sound. Just north of here, Vancouver (1798(1984):1365 and footnote) had named two points of land Point Mary and Point Amelia after Princess Mary the fourth daughter of King George III, and Princess Amelia, his youngest daughter.

The land near the shore is low & wooded with Pines, but soon swelld into moutains of considerable height, though not of that rugged aspect & elevation which the chain of mountains exhibit along the coast from Comptrollers Bay to Cross Sound, the summits of which are envelopt in perpetual snow, but here the summits of the mountains appeard bare & rocky & only in some places coverd with snow. Cape Edgecombe is low flat land with a steep rocky shore wooded to the very brink, the Mountain of that name is situated a few miles back & rises gradualy from a broad base to form an obtuse conic mount of no great elevation[191] when compard with those to the northward of Cross Sound, but as it stands detachd & the land round it is mostly low, it still has a very remarkable appearance from that of the adjacent country.[192]

After passing Cape Edgecombe we crossd the entrance of Norfolk Sound[193] which is about ten miles across & continued our course along a tract of low broken land intersected with inlets bounded by a rocky indented shore till late in the evening, when the breeze died away to light airs with which we stood off shore all night.

31st Next morning we had westerly wind accompanied at times by thick fog which in pursuing our course induced us to draw near or recede from the land accordingly as the weather became more or less favorable, so that we had but a very indistinct view of this part

---

191. 3,271 feet high.

192. Mount Edgecumbe was named by Captain Cook. He probably named it after Mt. Edgecumbe at the mouth of Plymouth Harbor in England, or George, the first Earl of Edgecumbe. Prior to that, the Spanish explorers had named it "Montana de San Jacinto," and later the Russians named it "Gora Svataya Lazarya" (Orth, 1971:301).

193. Now Sitka Sound. (See Map 4.) Don Juan de la Bodega y Quadra and Francisco Antonio Maurelle had named it "Enseñada del Susto" meaning "Bay of Terrors." In 1787, Captain George Dixon had named it "Norfolk Sound" after the Duke of Norfolk. The French trader, Etienne Marchand visited the sound in 1791 and 1792 and called it "Tchinkitanay Bay" (Orth, 1971:881). Marchand evidently heard the Tlingit speak of it as *Lingit aani*, which means, "Tlingit land," or "Land of the Tlingit [people]."

Vancouver (1798(1984):1366) gave the name Point Woodhouse to the western tip of Biorka Island located in the southern end of Sitka Sound.

of the Coast, which appeard to be much indentd with bays & small openings & a rocky shore. About noon the weather cleard up, when we reachd Cape Ommanney[194] & as we were hauling round it into Christian's Sound we had a meridian altitude of the Sun within a mile of the little Island laying close to the Cape which will place it in the Latitude of 56° 11' North & its Longitude is [missing]. At the same time we had sight of the hazy isles bearing S 36 E five leagues by compass. We proceeded up Christian's Sound along the western shore of it about 2 leagues when we came to a Bay of 2 or 3 miles deep, in a south west direction, into which we plyd,[195] & in the evening both Vessels anchord in four fathoms in a small cove on the north side near the head of it, where they moord head & stern, the Cove being too narrow to admit of their Swinging.

Augt 1st The vessels being now stationd I went in a boat the following forenoon to examine the Shore for any kind of fresh vegetables that might be made use of by the people to qualify their sea diet & at the head of the cove I found plenty of Marsh Sampire (Salicornia herbacea) which when boild made a good substitute for greens, & was accordingly daily usd as such by both men & officers during our stay. Capt Vancouver went with Mr Johnstone & Mr Whidbey to the entrance of the bay to view the opposite shore & fix with them upon a plan of conducting two separate boats expeditions, & on their return on board four boats were orderd to be equippd with arms & a fortnights provisions.

Augt 2nd Early next morning Mr Johnstone set off with two of these boats to the south eastward across the Sound in order to begin at Cape Decision where we left off the preceeding season,[196] & from thence proceed in his examination of the eastern side of the

---

194. Captain James Colnett had named Cape Ommaney in 1789. Since Menzies had been with Colnett, this was a familiar landmark. In fact, some referred to it as "Menzies' Cape" (Orth, 1971:724).

195. Vancouver (1798(1984): 1371) later named this Port Conclusion to mark the completion of his survey on the Northwest Coast.

196. Cape Decision is about twenty-five nautical miles southeast of Port Conclusion and is the southern tip of Kuiu Island. (For the area surveyed, see Map 4.)

Sound to the northward; whilst Mr Whidbey set off at the same time up the Sound with the other two boats, to begin at Latitude 57°[197] where he left off in his last boat expedition, & from thence continue the continental shore onwards until both parties should meet, which, as the unexplord space between them occupied only a degree of Latitude, was expected to take place before their provisions should be expended, & in that event a final termination put to our laborious examination of this Coast.

After their departure I landed on the south side of the Cove & penetrated through the forest some way up the sides of the adjacent hills, where meeting here & there with swamps & clear spots, my time was pleasantly occupied in collecting a variety of curious & rare plants that employd me the following days in arranging & examining. The salmon net was set across the entrance of the Cove, where it remaind till near our departure & though frequently examind & daily attended, yet we derivd scarcely any supply from the expedient. The Seine was likewise hauld two or three times in different places & with nearly as little success, having only got a few rock fish & some large Salmon Trout, so that our chief dependence for such refreshments was on our hooks and lines, which seldom faild in procuring for us a good supply of Halibut, by sending a boat for that purpose out to the entrance of the harbour, which was almost our daily practice.

5th Since our arrival we had light variable airs but chiefly from the South West quarter, with dark gloomy weather & slight showers of rain, on the 5th however it assumd the appearance of fair & pleasant weather which inducd a party of us to land pretty early, for the purpose of spending the whole day in the woods, in ranging the hills on the south side of the Vessels. Their object was amusement & recreation mine was examining the produce of the country & as the woods here were interspersd with small Lakes clear spots & Savannas, they afforded a fine scope for my pursuit. We ascended an eminence near the head of the cove, where we kindled a fire & breakfasted, & where we had a fine prospect of the opposite side of the Sound, which appeard to be low land, but much

---

197. At Point Gardner on the southern end of Admiralty Island.

broken & ruggd; from thence we descended into a cove that approachd within a quarter of a mile of the one we anchord in from the Southward & rangd its shores in pursuit of game with indifferent success; here we observd a few old Indian huts, but no recent traces of any Inhabitants, after this we ascended other hills, but not to any great height, & in the evening we returnd on board much fatigued, but well satisfied with our excursion. The collection of plants I made employd me on board for some days in describing & examining.

8th On the 8th Capt Vancouver began to make a survey of the Harbour, which at the entrance he found to be about a mile across, but narrowing gradually to the mouth of the Cove where we lay in, where it was a little more than a quarter of a mile wide, & continued of the same breadth to the head of it, which was about a mile further, the soundings were pretty deep even close to the shores & without any apparent danger, but the whole of it lay exposd to the north east winds & a considerable range of sea. To compensate for this disadvantage, a small snug harbour or bason of about a mile long & half a mile wide, with a narrow channel leading into it, was found a little within the north point of entrance, & as the passage into it is tolerably clear & of sufficient depth, it may be considerd as a secure retreat, & much more eligible for Vessels than the small cove we anchord in, as it abounds with fine sandy beaches, excellent runs of fresh water, & is surrounded with thick forests of stately pine trees.[198]

The shores of the outer harbour which is near three miles deep in a south west direction are in general steep & rocky, the land on the South side is of a moderate elevation, & is interspersd with clear spots or savannahs, but the land on the north side rises by a steep rugged ascent to form hills of considerable elevation, which are coverd with wood from the waters' edge to near their summits, these joining with the hills at the head of the harbour, form part of a compact rugged ridge coverd with snow running towards Cape Ommanney.

---

198. This is the site of the modern fishing settlement of Port Armstrong, and it does provide a good, safe anchorage.

9th On the 9th we experienced boisterous & squally weather with heavy rain that continued unsettled for some days, & obligd us as a further security to steady the vessel by fastening the end of the stream cable to the trees on shore.

Several days passed without any thing happening that claimd particular notice, our not being visited by any of the Natives made our time pass with greater sameness in the ordinary duties of refitting the Vessels, & procuring a daily supply of such refreshments as the place afforded, these consisted principally of Halibut & Sampire as already mentiond. The woods also producd red & black whortle berries, tho not here very abundant, & these were now ripe, & when they could be got made very good tarts that provd excellent corrections to our salt provisions.

Parties were employd on shore in compleating our wood & water, in brewing spruce beer from the fresh branches, & boiling down a quantity of the decoction of Spruce to carry with us to sea. The carpenters were cutting down Spars for different purposes, & fashioning large logs of wood by making planks; others were no less necessarily employd in caulking the water ways on the quarter deck & under the fore castle, which stood much in need of it; & as we were now drawing out our labours on this coast so near to a conclusion I made almost daily excursions on shore, for the purpose of filling the frame on the quarter deck with live plants, of such as were either new or curious, in order to carry them if possible in that state to England, to be added to his Majesties' valuable collection of Exotics at Kew.[199]

14th On the 14th two gentlemen started pretty early from the water side to ascend a considerable hill on the western side of the Harbour,[200] for a wager, which they both gaind by reaching the summit of it considerably within the time limited, where they kindled a fire & displayd a flag as a signal to those on board of their having succeeded in their attempt, & after resting some time on

199. As was mentioned in the introduction, it was this case which was left open, and many of the plants were destroyed. It was this event that caused a dispute between Menzies and Vancouver.

200. There are several peaks in the area whose elevations range from 1,500 to 2,700 feet.

the top of the hill they returnd to the Ship again to dinner. They gave a terrible description of the difficulties they had to encounter in this undertaking, from the steepness & ruggedness of the ascent, from the density of the forest & thickets, & from the dead old trees that lay in every direction & thwarted their progress in almost every step. One of them in particular was so exhausted with fatigue, that he was taken very ill & was several times on the eve of giving it up, had he not been much assisted & urgd on by a stout man that accompanied him; indeed they both declard that they would not undertake to perform the same task again for any consideration. They were favord with a most delightful day, by which they had a good prospect of the entrance of the Sound & the broken land on the opposite side as far as Cape Decision, but their view to sea ward and the hazy isles was obscurd by thick fog.

15th On the following day, the time for which the absent boats had been victualled expird, & we began to be under some apprehensions that they would not be able to finish this trip, especially as they had been already absent considerably beyond our expectations in prosecuting a task that was supposed at their departure would not occupy them much more than half the time, as we were now however in hourly expectation of their arrival, both Vessels were removd in the forenoon from the Cove to the opposite side of the harbour, where they lay at single anchor steadied by a hawser fastend to the trees on shore, in order to be in readiness to proceed as circumstances might require with the first favorable breeze after the return of the boats, for which we now kept a constant & anxious eye.

Though we were so moord in the Cove as scarcely to have any perceptible motion, yet one of our lines was so damagd with the rocky bottom, that about 20 fathoms of it was obligd to be cut off, from thence the Cove we lay in is by no means to be considerd as an eligible anchorage.

Nothing but a tedious state of suspense occupied our minds for the three following days with increasing anxiety & the utmost solicitude for the rest of our absent friends in safety. The weather in general was moderate & favorable until the 19th when it became squally & blew very fresh from the South East with continual heavy rain, this greatly augmented our uneasiness & apprehensions for the welfare of our friends, especially as they had staid so long beyond the time for which they were provided, & we were not without the most serious alarms least some accident might have befallen them from the treacherous disposition of the Natives, when in the forenoon the four boats made their appearance round the north point of the Harbour & instantly changd our alarms & gloomy reflections to a sudden glow of joy that brightend every countenance for as they returnd altogether, it was to our minds a presumptive proof that they had finishd the laborious & intricate examination of this coast & when they reachd the Vessels & confirmd our conjectures of this desirable event, our feelings may be more easily conceivd than describd, a mutual exchange of three congratulating cheers from the crews of each Vessel expressd the cordial satisfaction they all felt on this joyous occasion, in having thus put an end so successfully to a tedious & laborious enterprise for the completion of which an uncommon zeal had activated every individual to the most unwearied & persevering exertions, under all the circumstances of hardships & laborious toils of dangers & difficulties to which the nature of the service unavoidably exposd them they on all occasions performd their duty with alacrity, & cheerfulness, & with a manly perseverance that contributed in the highest degree to attain the great object in view. Every one was elated with the most pleasing sensations & the fondest hopes of returning home to enjoy repose in the bosom of their country & amongst their dearest connections. All work was suspended & the rest of the day was devoted to festivity & convivial mirth, enlivend by an additional allowance of grog,[201] whilst the social pleasure of recounting past dangers & future expectations alternately beguild the happy hour over the flowing cup.[202]

Notwithstanding our readiness for departure, the weather provd so boisterous with heavy rain thick fog & a continued gale from South east that we were detaind in port for the two following

201. A mixture of rum and water.

202. This concluded their search for the mythical Northwest Passage, and they were now free to return home, having been gone three years and four months.

days. This delay afforded me an opportunity to collect from the reports of the Officers the following particulars of the last boat expedition, which happily terminated our laborious investigations on this coast.[203]

Mr. Whidbey & his party reachd the place where we left off in the last boat expedition from Cross Sound about noon on the day after their departure, & from thence they pursued the same shore which took a direction northeastward for about 10 or 12 leagues & which was found very rugged & indented with coves & small bays, strewd with a vast number of Islands Islets & Rocks,[204] through these intricacies the party advancd with very unfavorable weather being so thick & hazy, that they had no distinct view of either the extent or appearance of the arm before them, till they came to the entrance of a branch leading in a north westerly direction & the weather then clearing up, they perceived the arm they were in to be very spacious & at least 3 or 4 leagues in breadth, & strewd with many Islands.[205] They first examined the north westerly branch which was found to be 9 or 10 leagues long & from two to three & in some places four miles wide, bounded by rugged rocky shores, with some large & a number of small Islands & Rocks near the head of it.[206] There they saw a small party of

203. Lamb (Vancouver, 1798(1984):1367, footnote) reports that "No first-hand account of these expeditions is available. The latter part of Johnstone's journal, and the logs or journal kept by Whidbey and Barrie, have disappeared, and Swaine gives no details in his log. The only descriptions are those given by Vancouver and Menzies, neither of whom participated in the expedition." Mr. Whidbey and Mr. Swaine took the *Discovery's* yawl and large cutter while Mr. Johnstone and Mr. Barrie used the *Chatham's* cutter and the *Discovery's* small cutter.

204. Vancouver (1798(1984):1372 and footnotes) named Point Nepean to commemorate Evan Nepean, secretary of the Admiralty; Point Pybus; Point Gambier, to honor Vice Admiral James Gambier. He is the same Baron James Gambier, who participated in the capture of Charleston, South Carolina in 1780 (Orth, 1971;359).

205. They were turning up Stephens Passage which Vancouver (1798(1984):1376) named for Sir Philip Stephens, secretary of the Admiralty.

206. This was Seymour's Canal which Henry Wagner, the cartographer, suggests was named after Vice Admiral Hugh Seymour (Vancouver (1798(1984):1372 footnote). The eastern point of the entrance was named Point Hugh.

Indians who provd so shy that the party had no intercourse with them. In quitting this branch they rounded its north point of entrance which is a high rocky promont in about the Latitude of 57 ½° & on the 6th day after their departure proceeded up this former arm, which was soon after found to contract in its width to about 3 or 4 miles & to run in a north westerly direction, separated from the branch they had last examined only by a narrow hilly ridge,[207] & for about 15 leagues pursuing a course nearly parallel with the great channel explord in the last boat cruize from Cross Sound, but situated about ten leagues to the eastward of it. The western shore of it was found nearly straight & compact, environd by hills of a moderate height which were covered with a continued forest of pine trees, whilst the opposite side presented a stupendous range of lofty barren mountains with perpetual snow. At the end of this long reach which is about the Latitude of 58° 10' they found the arm divide into three branches, one went to the northward,[208] a small one to the north westward[209] & the largest which was about a league wide took a westerly direction.[210] The latter they pursued & found it gradually winding to the north westward & decreasing considerably in its width. In this branch the party had not advancd above 6 or 7 leagues, when it was discoverd to be the same which had been too hastily relinquishd as already noticd in the account of our former excursions on the evening of the 18th of July last,[211] but the mistake of supposing it then closed up was now fully detected by the party reaching the place of its communication with the large channel & thus compleatly circumnavigating in this & their former trip a large Island of upwards of two hundred miles in circumference, which till then was considerd as part of the continent.[212]

---

207. Glass Peninsula.

208. Taku Inlet, the mouth of the Taku River.

209. Gastineau Channel.

210. This is a continuation of Stephens Passage which goes around the western side of Douglas Island.

211. They rowed back to Point Retreat.

212. Admiralty Island. The point of land on the eastern edge of a bay was named Point Young, probably in honor of Admiral Sir George Young (Vancouver, 1798(1984):1374 and footnote).

The north side of this branch was found to be an Island of about 6 or 7 leagues long,[213] formd by the narrow north west branch, which was so choakd up with ice that the boats could not penetrate their way through it,[214] they therefore returnd back to the junction of the three branches by the same channel as they went. They saw two Indian Villages, one on each side of the arm near the place where it was formerly thought to be closed.[215] As they went first past these villages they were followd by several canoes with a number of Natives, but as they did not wish to be troubled, or have any intercourse with them so late in the evening, a musket was at first fird over them as a warning to intimidate them & to make them keep off, but instead of which, it seemd to incite in them a redoubled exertion to get up with the boats. On observing this another musket was then levelld & dischargd at the headmost canoe which was supposd to have hit her, all her Crew instantly squatted down to screen themselves, at the same time managd by paddling so as to retreat in great haste followd by all the other canoes back to the villages, whilst our party continud their pursuit onward, but next evening as they were returning back the same way, they past pretty close to one of these Villages & heard the most hideous lamentations & yellings that can possibly be conceivd, in this dirge the Natives were all so intensely occupied, that none of the attemptd to come near the party or were even seen out of their huts; from this it was much feard that some of them had been either killd or badly wounded by the shot fird at the Canoes on the preceeding evening, & it was equally regretted

---

213. The island was named Douglas Island to commemorate Reverend John Douglas, Bishop of Salisbury, who had edited the journal of Cook's third voyage (Vancouver, 1798(1984):1376 and footnote). In the 1883 Coast Pilot, Dall named the small island off the tip of Douglas Island, Marmion Island to commemorate a narrative poem by Sir Walter Scott. He also named the point of land, Tantallon Point, to commemorate Tantallon Castle, North Berwick, Scotland, home of the Douglas Clan (Orth, 1971: 948). Originally a point in Taku Inlet was named Point Salisbury, but it was misplaced on the early charts, so the name was given to the point opposite Marmion Island, and the point further to the east was called Point Bishop (Orth, 1971:138,830).

214. At that time, Gastineau Channel on which the city of Juneau is located was filled with ice, probably from the Mendenhall or Taku Glaciers.

215. These two villages were the main village of the Auke people on the eastern side, and a smaller settlement, perhaps a summer fish camp of the Auke people, on the west side in Young's Bay.

that such a measure was then necessary in order to get rid of them, when probably their object in pursuing the boats might only be a desire of trafic or to satisfy mere curiosity.

The party now proceeded to examine the third branch leading to the northward,[216] which was found to run nearly in that direction for about four leagues through most dreary regions in which they had to encounter strong winds, cold showers of sleet & a quantity of floating ice, that greatly incommoded & retarded their progress. They however perseverd against these difficulties & reachd its termination, which formd a bason of near two leagues across, surrounded by a range of high steep rugged mountains coverd with perpetual snow almost down to the waters edge exhibiting a prospect the most chilly barren & inhospitable that can possibly be conceivd; scarcely any of the vegetable tribe was to be seen, excepting a stinted pine tree here & there upon the lower cliffs.

The shores were so steep & rugged with rocky precipices & the gullies were so choakd up with massy ice, that no landing could be effect any where, they therefore on the 10th day of their excursion quitted this bleak & dismal situation which was the most northern of their pursuit[217] & is about 30 leagues nearly due east from the entrance of Cross Sound, & as they returnd to the southward along the eastern shore of the long reach which has been already stated to be about 15 leagues in length, they here also had to contend with strong contrary winds, boisterous weather, heavy rain & a rough swell, that greatly retarded them & renderd their situation in the boats cold wet & uncomfortable. The shore they were thus pursuing was found to be much indented with Coves & Bays, & bounded by a steep rugged ridge of barren snowy mountains. When they got again into the spacious part of the Arm, they found the shore of it to run nearly in the same southerly direction

216. Taku Inlet.

217. It was at this time, August 12, 1794, that Whidbey more than likely realized that there was no Northwest Passage. They had looked at every passage leading north or east from Puget Sound to Cook Inlet, and the Taku Inlet, just ten miles south of Juneau, Alaska, was the last possible entrance to any Northwest Passage.

as the long reach, for about 6 or 7 leagues further,[218] to a low
projecting pint in about the Latitude of 57° 10' which is nearly due
East about seven leagues, from where they commencd their
examination, & the intervening space is occupied by a wide sea,
strewd with a number of large & small Islands. Here they enterd
a wide spacious arm leading first to the eastward for a few
leagues,[219] & then winding to the southeast, & also becoming
considerably contracted in its width & spacious appearance. As
they pursued their examination in this Arm against strong gales
& unfavorable wet weather, its shore was found much indented
with remarkable projecting points - bays & coves environd by a
tract of low land forming a border of small extent, before a range
of very lofty snowy mountains, which in one or two places approachd
the arm in overhanging precipices of vast height, & when viewd
from underneath of a singluarly awful & terrifc appearance, from
the great quantity of ice & snow with which they were encumberd
& which seemd to threaten instant destruction on those who
approachd the base of either of these precipices.[220] After the party
advancd in this arm about 10 or 11 leagues, they conceivd it from
all appearances to be closd up, at least so much so as not to merit

218. Vancouver (1798(1984):1377-78 and footnotes) later commemorated his
native county of Norfolk by naming several places. Point Styleman was named
for Henry Styleman of Snettisham, Norfolk. Port Snettisham was named for
the town of Snettisham, a few miles from King's Lynn where Vancouver had
been born. Point Anmer was also named after a town near King's Lynn. Point
Coke was named to honor Thomas Coke, Earl of Leicester, who built a large
mansion at Holkham, Norfolk. He named the bay south of Point Coke,
Holkham Bay. Although Vancouver named Astley Point, there is no indication
why the name was given. Windham Bay was named for William Windham, a
statesman who had been associated with Norfolk. Point Hobart was probably
named after Lord Robert Hobart. Point Walpole and Port Houghton were
named to commemorate Houghton Hall, a mansion built for Sir Robert
Walpole, near Harpley, Norfolk. Or, the point may have been named for Robert
Walpole's famous son, Horace. Finally, in Stephens Passage, at its juncture
with Frederick Sound, Vancouver named Cape Fanshaw (perhaps after Sir
Richard Fanshawe, an important 17th Century English diplomat).

219. This was the eastern end of Frederick Sound.

220. Probably the Horn Cliffs, on the east side of Frederick Sound, across from
the present-day town of Petersburg, the northern entrance to the Wrangell
Narrows.

any further examination;[221] they therefore returnd back along the opposite shore anxious now to make the best of their way for the Vessels, from which they were upwards of a hundred miles distant, & their provisions almost wholly expended, being already absent beyond the time for which they were victualled. It afterwards however came to our knowledge, that the examination of this Arm, like the one to the Northward had been too hastily relinquishd as we were informd by Mr Brown commander of the Jackal at Nootka, that at this very place he found a shallow passage through,[222] which he went with his vessel to the southward upwards of 20 leagues to north east or inland from Cape Decision, by which he thus insulated a considerable tract of broken land that had been considerd until we met him as part of the Continent.

This being the case it renders the laborious & fatiguing examination of Mr Johnstone & his party from Cape Decision, though not less intricate & toilsome, though not less strewd with dangers & difficulties, yet far less important to the object of our researches, I shall therefore only state a general outline of their proceedings, whilst I leave the present party pursuing their way back in this arm to meet them, in which they were followd by a large Canoe full of Indians, whose general behaviour after a short intercourse put on a very suspicious appearance, as the same men were observd arming themselves with Spears Daggers & other weapons whilst the women & children were seen retiring into the woods, this induced the party to lye more upon their guard & use every means to get rid of such treacherous visitors, in order to avoid any serious misunderstanding; for this purpose a shot was first fird over their heads, which did not in the least intimidate them, but one fird directly at the Canoe made them instantly retreat. They afterwards however usd the stratagem of coming on the party whilst on shore, from the woods, in which they were equally unsuccessfull.

---

221. This was the northern end of Dry Strait at the mouth of the Stikine River. There is a very shallow channel between Dry Island and Mitkof Island, but for the most part it would seem to be impassable.

222. Shallow draft vessels can go through Dry Strait at high tide. Once through, they can either go south through Stikine Strait or west through Frederick Sound.

Mr Johnstone proceeded with his party to the Southeastward across Christian Sound & reachd Cape Decision about noon on the day he left the Vessels, he states this Cape to be a rocky point of a moderate height, renderd inconspicuous by being situated within an Island that forms the southeastern boundary of the Sound. From thence the party commencd their examination by pursuing the eastern shore of the Sound to the Northward, which was found to be much broken & intersected with small arms, deep bays creeks & coves, that were interspersd with innumerable Islets & Rocks which also hid the exterior shore & renderd its examination both tedious & difficult on account of its exposure to the Ocean, so that a space of little more than 50 miles employd the party a whole week before they reachd the spacious arm where the other party had commencd their operations,[223] & which was found to be between two & three leagues wide,[224] the southern shore of it trended north eastward for about 20 miles, but this space was also so much broken with small arms & winding inlets branching in various directions, & so interspersd with numerous diminutive islands & rocks, that it occupied the party for six days with its amazing intricacy. One of these branches terminated so continuous to another they had examind near a week before, that they found the Indians could track their canoes across a narrow isthmus from the one to the other. Another narrow winding

223. Along the western shore of Kuiu Island, Vancouver (1798(1984):1383-85 and footnotes) named several features. The first two, Port Malmesbury and Point Harrris, commemorated Sir James Harris who became the first Earl of Malmesbury. The survey party examined Tebenkof Bay, but did not name it. In 1928, the U.S. Coast and Geodedic Survey, named the southern entrance to Tebenkof Bay Point Swaine, in honor of Lt. Swaine of the Vancouver expedition (Orth, 1971:935). Farther north, Point Ellis was named probably in honor of George Ellis who accompanied James Harris on a diplomatic mission. Point Sullivan, Point Kingsmill and Point Cornwallis were apparently named for William Francis Sullivan of the Royal Navy, Vice Admiral Sir Robert Baker Kingsmill and Charles first Marquis Cornwallis, a British Army Commander in the Revolutionary War. The northern point at the entrance to Keku Strait was named Point Macartney, in honor of George, Earl Macartney, governor of the windward islands in the Caribbean (Vancouver, 1798(1984):1388 and footnote).

224. In the south western portion of Frederick Sound are Security Bay and Saginaw Bay, and Keku Strait which is eight miles wide at its entrance.

intricate branch led them to the southward into the great sound where we left off last season, & where they saw distinctly Port Protection to the southeastward of them about 10 or 12 miles.[225] By persevering through this passage they insulated a considerable tract of very broken land between them & Cape Decision that before was supposd to be part of the continent & though it was found but an intricate passage even for Boats on account of its being rocky & shallow & so interspersd with numerous Islets, yet a knowledge of it on the preceeding season would have savd us a great deal of laborious & tedious examination; & how much more would it have shortend our labors had we last year known the passage about 15 leagues inland of this, through which Mr Brown went with his Vessel.[226]

These & other instances ought to teach us to speak with the utmost diffidence of our having all along tracd the continental shore, notwithstanding that every degree of precaution was in general made use of yet such was the expeditious nature of the service, performd often in obscure & inclement weather & such the difficulty of tracing all the windings of such an intricate labyrinth through a region so dreary & broken that it is impossible to pronounce such a laborious task as infallible.

In one of these branches Mr. Johnstone stated that they saw the remains of no less than eight deserted villages,[227] more or less in a state of decay, but all of them uniformly situated on the summit of some precipice or steep insulated rock, which nature had in general renderd inaccessible & art & great labor had made places of strong defense against the hostile intrusions of even a superior foe. These fortresses were constructed by laying a strong platform of wood upon the most elevated part of the rock in such a manner that the edges of it projected so as to overspread the declivity. On

---

225. They were examining Keku Strait whose southern portion is known locally as Rocky Pass. The narrow pass is filled with rocks and has strong tidal currents so that today only a few boats attempt to use it and those that do are often times damaged in the process.

226. Dry Strait.

227. The northern end of Keku Strait was the home of the Kake group of Tlingit. It appears that in the late 1700s there was a great deal of warfare in this area.

these edges a barricade or breast work was generally raisd all round by logs of Timber placd on each other, so as to give strength & security to the whole fabric. These great precautions certainly provd the sanguinary temper & state of warfare which must have persistd amongst the Natives of this part of the Coast. In the vicinity of these places many sepulchres or tombs were noticd, in which the remains of dead bodies were found deposited, these were erectd with a degree of neatness seldom exhibited in their other buildings & they were generally situated near the shore or on some conspicuous point, each consisting of a large square frame closely boarded on all sides & supported on wooden posts about 5 or 6 feet from the ground, within these repositories which were of different sizes, the dead human bodies were laid in boxes wrapped up in skins or in mats, & rangd by the side of each other, for none of them were observd placd over each other. Many of these tombs seemd to have withstood a great length of time & some of the most decayd had evidently undergone recent repairs, from which it would appear that whatever feuds & quarrels might have existed amongst the inhabitants of these villages when living, their remains when dead were not only sufferd to rest unmolested, but taken care of.[228]

These deserted retreats had been passd, & the party approachd near the head of the Arm before they saw any of the Natives, but there in a short space of time a body of them collected upwards of a hundred, amongst whom there were several they had seen some days before; whatever their intentions might be in thus assembling, it was deemd prudent from their number & appearance to keep them at some distance from the boats, this they seemd very unwilling to obey, notwithstanding every sign was made to them to that effect, & their forwardness to close in with the boats increasing with their numbers, the party armd themselves to oppose them & fird off some muskets to warn & intimidate them, this in some measure had the desired effect, as they afterwards kept without the reach of musketry following the boats as they

228. The Tlingit have great respect for the dead and areas where the dead were buried or cremated and their ashes preserved. For these people, it was, and still is, considered a serious offense to disturb a burial site.

were returning back the Arm. Although these natives had some Muskets amongst them, & were well armd with Spears & other weapons, which they seldom go without, yet Mr. Johnstone did not impute their forward conduct to any bad design or hostile intention, on the contrary, he supposd, their ardour for joining the party proceeded entirely from a desire of trafic & obtaining some European commodities in exchange for their sea otter Skins, of which they had a great number of the very best quality; but the situation of the party at that time being in a confind place, in sight of such a numerous tribe of armd Indians, with great reason to apprehend there might be many more in the vicinity, it became necessary to avoid as much as possible a nearer intercourse with them, more especially as it was drawing near the close of the day. They therefore continued on their oars, followd by the Indians at a distance, until they came to a more open situation, when one of the canoes advancd before the rest, & as she approachd the boats, a Chief who stood up in the middle of her, pluckd the white downy feathers from the skin of an eagle he held in his hand, & continued now & then blowing them with his breath into the air, accompanied with songs & other signs of friendship,[229] this induced Mr. Johnstone to invite the Canoe along side of his boat, in order to give the Chief a small present he had prepared, wherewith to dismiss him to his party & decline any further communication. They accepted the invitation with the fullest confidence, though entirely defenseless, not having a single weapon of any kind amongst them, which astonishd our party, & before Mr. Johnstone had time to make his intentioned donation, the Chief presented him in the most disinterested manner with a fine Sea Otter Skin,& then received his present in return as a token of mutual friendship which was ratified on both sides by every ascription likely to be understood; at the same time it was signified to the Chief that as the party was very soon going to rest for the night, they did not wish to be disturbd by any of the Canoes following them any longer, yet after he joind the rest of his tribe, they still

---

229. This was a traditional Tlingit expression of peace and friendship. A scattering of down was considered a sign of peace among many Northwest Coast Indians.

kept following the boats until a musket or two were dischargd towards them, when they gave up their pursuit & all retird out of sight.

Though the latter part of the behaviour of these Natives appeard to be actuated by good faith & peaceable friendly disposition, yet a distrust which prudence suggested inducd the party to increase their distance from them as far as they conveniently could before they stopped to take their repose, on which account they continued rowing on until eleven at night, when they came to a grapnel & slept in the boats, greatly fatigued from the laborious toil of the day, for from the time they set out in the morning, they had been two & twenty hours on their oars, excepting the two short intervals they had stopped to breakfast & dinner.

These intricate arms creeks & bays swarmd with a greater abundance of sea otters & Salmon than had been observd on any party of the coast, the surrounding country though hilly was yet of a moderate height & every where producd a stately forest of pine trees with some Alders & various kinds of underwood.

On the 13th day of their excursion they came out again into the large Arm & pursued its southern shore which was found to trend to the Eastward, & though very rocky & indented, yet it was much more compact in its general direction, as they met but one small cove[230] in a tract of ten or twelve leagues of shore which on account of strong contrary winds heavy rains & boisterous weather occupied them the two following days with all the perseverance they were capable of exerting, as they were now very anxious to meet the other party, least they exhausted state of their provisions should oblige them to return to the Vessels without being able to accomplish their objective. On the evening of the latter day however they had the great satisfaction of meeting Mr. Whidbey & his two boats returning back the southeast arm as we have already stated, & a more joyous meeting than was manifested by both parties on finding that they had thus happily brought their laborious task to a conclusion can hardly be conceivd. Their feelings were instantly testified by the mutual exchange of cheers

230. Portage Bay.

& congratulations, which the surrounding rocks & mountains loudly proclaimd in reverberated echos.[231]

After this juncture, the four boats set out together on their return to the Vessels from which they were about 30 leagues distant, the nearest tract they could pursue, this occupied them two days & a half; in which time, they became greatly stinted for provisions, & on coming into Christian Sound, where they became much exposd, they had to contend with very hard gales from southeast, & a disagreeable turbulent swell that renderd their situation in open boats not only wet & uncomfortable but eminently dangerous; against these difficulties however there was no alternative, but their usually perseverance & exertion, which happily succeeded, & brought them safe to the Vessels on the 19th as already mentioned.

In consequence of having thus finishd our laborious examination of this coast the station which the vessels occupied obtaind the name of Port Conclusion, its Latitude was found to be 56° 15'north & its Longitude [missing][232]

The variation of the compass was also found to be 26° East. The spring tides rose about 16 feet perpendicular height, & it was high

---

231. In his journal, Vancouver (1798(1984):1382) gives an expanded description of this meeting celebrating the end of the search for the Northwest Passage, and claiming of the territory for the King. "In the event of the two parties meeting, and consequently a finishing stroke being put to the examination of the shores of North-West America, within the limits of my commission; Mr. Whidbey had my directions to take possession of the said continent, from New Georgia north-westward to cape Spencer, as also, of all the adjacent islands we had discovered within those limits; in the name of, and for, His Britannic Majesty, his heirs, and successors: this, on the parties stopping to dine, was carried into execution; the colours were displayed, the boats' crews drawn up under arms, and possession taken under the discharge of three vollies of musketry, with all the other formalities usual on such occasions, and a double allowance of grog was served to the respective crews, for the purpose of drinking His Majesty's health."

This was the birthday of His Royal Highness Frederick Duke of York, and so the sound was named Prince Frederick's Sound. Today it is called simply Frederick Sound. The adjacent land was named New Norfolk, but that name is no longer in use.

232. At the conclusion of the survey, Vancouver (1798(1984):1390 and footnote) named Chatham Strait in honor of John Pitt, second Earl of Chatham, who was the first lord of the Admiralty from 1788 to 1794.

water in the harbour on the full & changd 40 minutes after the moon passd the Meridian.

22nd The weather becoming more moderate & the fog clearing away, encouragd us on the evening of the 22nd to weight our anchors & make Sail out of the Port, & though we had to contend with adverse wind, we got clear of it before dark, but we made very little further advance, as we found on the out side light airs mostly from the south east & thick foggy weather, for the night, during which we frequently sounded but had no bottom with a hundred fathoms of line.

23rd Next day the weather continud fair but mostly calm & foggy, so that we remaind still drifting about near the entrance of the harbour. In the evening it cleard up a little, & we were flatterd with a light breeze from North West, which however was of short duration, as it became calm again for the night, & we were drifted about by the influence of the tides, which in the middle of the night carried us so near the shore of Cape Ommanney, that it was deemd necessary for the safety and preservation of the Vessels to hoist out a couple of boats & use the utmost exertions in towing her off from the rocky shore on which the sea broke in a high surf that excited considerable alarm & induced every effort to extricate ourselves from so perilous & critical a situation in this we were at last fortunately aided by a light breeze which happily sprung up from North West, & enabled us to steer clear of the danger that threatend our destruction. The boats were then calld along side to be hoisted on board, in doing this, an unfortunate & melancholy circumstance happend of losing Isaac Wooden one of our best seamen over board, as this worthy man was coming up the ships side from one of the boats, he somehow lost his hold & in his fall unluckily struck his head against the gunwale of one of the boats, by which it was supposd that he was so much hurt, that he instantly sunk, as he was neither heard nor seen by any one after he fell in the water, so consequently no assistance could be given to him, though a boat was immediately dropt astern & every endeavour made to pick him up. He was a quiet peaceable man, much respected by all his shipmates, & when we reflect on the particular period of this unlucky event, just as we were upon the even of returning home, we cannot help being more deeply impressd with regret at his premature death, he might probably a few moments before, in the silent hour of the middle watch, be meditating on the happy prospect which now presented of soon reaching his native country, & anticipating on the pleasure he should enjoy after so long an absence at meeting again his nearest & dearest connections, & cheerfully sharing with them the fruits of his well earned industry.[233]

24th The north west breeze freshend on the 24th & soon enabled us to gain the open Ocean, when we directed our course along the coast to the southeastern shore with a press of sail on the outside of the hazy islets, which are a small group of barren rocky islets about three leagues out from the land abreast of them, & about five leagues nearly due south of Cape Ommanney. In the afternoon we passd pretty close to the entrance of the Port of Bucareli discoverd by the Spaniards in the year 1775,[234] about five or six leagues to the southward of which, we also passd a most dangerous reef of rocks almost level with the surface of the water & nearly five leagues out from the shore abreast of them,[235] these are situated a mile or two to the northward of the Latitude of 55 North and three leagues from Forester's Island, between which & the main we steerd in the evening for the north end of Queen Charlotte's Isles through a channel apparently free of any impediment to Navigation.

---

233. Vancouver (1798(1984):1394) describes the same incident, and then named Wooden Rock (now Wooden Island) in memory of this crew member.

234. Don Juan de la Bodega y Quadra had named it "Puerto y Entrada de Bucareli" in honor of Don Antonio Maria Bucareli y Urua, Viceroy of Mexico (Orth, 1971;164). Today the villages of Craig and Klawock are located at the northern end of this entrance.

235. Vancouver (1798(1984):1395) says, "...from its being so far distant from the main land, it is rendered one of the most dangerous impediments to navigation that we had met with on the exterior coast; and hence it obtained the name of WOLF ROCK." This name is still in use.

25th Next day we had calm & variable light breezes alternately, with weather so thick & foggy that the land was entirely abscurd & we were obligd to make frequent signals to our consort by firing guns to prevent a separation, & though we were sometimes as near to one another as to hear the commanding officers voice on board the Chatham, yet we could not see her from the thickness of the fog: & on the following day we had nearly a continuation of the same thick weather though we were favord with a pretty fresh breeze from the North West, which on this Coast generally produces clear weather.

27th The 27th & succeeding day were mostly calm with dark hazy weather & sometimes thick fog, so that our progress during that time to the south eastward along the coast of Queen Charlottes' Isles from which we were about 6 or 7 leagues distant was so trifling & our views of the land were very indistinct & transient.

29th In the forenoon of the 29th the wind was fresh & squally from the South East, but in the afternoon it veerd to the south westward & became more moderate with thick rainy weather, & for the two following days during which we were crossing the South entrance of the great Channel which divides Queen Charlotte's Isles from the Main. The wind continued light & variable with long intervals of calm & cloudy weather.

Sept 1st On the 1st of Sep^{er} we had sight of the Westernmost of Scott's Islands, & with a moderate North west wind attended with pleasant weather, we next forenoon passd Cape Spitrock & from thence on our way to Nootka saw several canoes out at sea fishing. The same favorable wind continuing to blow pretty fresh enabled us in the evening to anchor in Friendly Cove Nootka Sound where we found three of his Catholic Majesties' Vessels the Princessa Aransasa & San Carlos, together with the Prince Lee Boo commanded by Mr Gordon, who had left China with Mr Brown - the Phoenix bark Mr Meare from Bengal, & the American Brig Lady Washington Mr Kendrick, whose Vessel was under repair.

The Aransasa had been employd during the summer in bringing live cattle provisions & stores from California to this settlement. The Princessa commanded by D^n Fildago, who since we had saw him had been promoted to the rank of Captain of a Frigate, arrivd here the day before from San Blas with Brigadier General Don Jose Manuel Alava on board who in consequence of the death of our much lamented friend Sig^{nr} Quadra, was now appointed Governor of Nootka, & also chargd with the business of giving up this settlement to any person duly qualified from our Court to receive it, on the terms agreed upon by the two governments. The San Carlos had remaind here since the spring of 1793 under the command of Signr Saavadra who also had charge of the settlement, but on arrival of the new government, he deliverd it wholly up to him, & immediately quitted the house on shore to live with his officers on board the vessel.

[This ends the Journal of Menzies for Southeastern Alaska in the year 1794.]

Appendix of
Botanical Collections
Found in Menzies' Journal

This appendix has been prepared by John F. Thilenius, a research plant ecologist with the Forestry Science Laboratory, U.S. Forest Service, in Juneau, Alaska. The plants are listed in order of their occurence in the journals with the page number indicating where the term appears in the text. The botanical references consulted are indicated with [ ].

References

[B] Britton, Nathaniel L. and Addison Brown. *An Illustrated Flora of the United States, Canada and the British Possessions.* New York: Charles Scribner's Sons. 1898. 3 volumes. Obsolete nomenclature.

[C] Hitchcock, C. Leo and Arthur Cronquist. *Flora of the Pacific Northwest.* Seattle: University of Washington Press. 1973. 730 p. Non-Alaska plants.

[H] Hulten, Eric. *Flora of Alaska and Neighboring Territories.* Stanford: Stanford University Press. 1968. 1008 p. Presence and range in Alaska.

[K] Kartesz, John T. and Rosemarie Kartesz. *A Synonymized Checklist of the Vascular Flora of the United States, Canada and Greenland.* Chapel Hill: University of North Carolina Press. 1980. 498 p. Valid taxonomic names and authorities.

[W] Gove, Philip B., editor. *Webster's Third New International Dictionary of the English Language Unabridged.* Springfield: G. & C. Merriam Company. 1976. 2662 p. Vernacular names and terms.

Summer, 1793
British Columbia, Southern Southeastern Alaska

Page 39 and 94. Ledum Palustre—Laborador tea (*Ledum palustre* L. ssp. *decumbens* (Ait.) Hult.) [C727, K193]. Widely distributed in bogs and mires in the Pacific Northwest.

Page 39. Kalmia glauca—Bog Laurel (*Kalmia polifolia* Wang.) [C344, K193]. Commonly found on the ecotone between coniferous forest and bog-mire.

Page 39. Orchis—Key flower (*Amerorchis rotundifolia* (Banks ex Pursh) Hult.) [C705, K310] is the most likely species.

Page 39. Orphys—Either of the two species of twyblade: *Listera cordata* (L.) R. Br var. *cordata* [C704, K313] or *Listera caurina* Piper [C706, K313].

Page 58. ...black & red Whortle berries—Any or all of several shrub blueberries. *Vaccinium membranaceum* Dougl. ex Hook. [C350, K196]; *V. ovalifolium* Sm. [C350, K196]; *V. alaskense* T. J. Howell [C350, K195] are sympatric and have black or blue-black berries. Red huckleberry (*Vaccinium parvifolium* Sm. [C349, K196]) is also sympatric and has red berries. Other species are present and possible.

Page 58. Haws—Crabapple (*Malus fusca* (Raf.) Schneid.) [C222, K400]. The description, "...a kind of wild apple..." makes *M. fusca* the most likely species. Haw is also a vernacular name for hawthorn (*Crataegus* L.) [C209] and highbush cranberry (*Viburnum edule* (Michx.) Raf.) [W1040, C453, K148].

Page 64. Dracoena borealis—More likely spelled Dracaena borealis. This is an obsolete synonym for yellow-flowered clintonia (*Clintonia borealis* (Ait.) Raf.) [B1-428, K24] of eastern North America. The clintonia of the northwestern coast is *Clintonia uniflora* (Schultes) Kunth [C689, K274].

Spring, 1794
Southcentral Alaska, Cook Inlet

Page 94. Birch—Kenai Birch (*Betula papyrifera* Marsh var. *kenaica* (W. H. Evans) A. Henry) [H364, K112] is a relatively small birch of coastal southcentral Alaska. Dwarf birch (*Betula nana* L. ssp. *exilis* (Sukatschev) Hult.) [H365, K111] is also present.

Page 94. Poplar—Black cottonwood (*Populus balsamifera* L. ssp. *trichocarpa* (Torr. & Gray) Brayshaw) [H332, K421] is the coastal subspecies of southcentral Alaska.

Page 94. Alder willow—It is not clear if this refers to a single plant (alder willow) or to two plants (alder and willow). Most likely two, as Menzies often did not use commas to separate words in a series. Sitka alder (*Alnus viridis* (Chaix) DC. ssp. *sinuata* (Regel) Love & Love) [H369, K111] and thinleaf alder (*Alnus incana* (L.) Moench ssp. *tenuifolia* (Nutt.) Breitung) [H370, K111] are ascending shrubs or small trees of coastal regions. Red alder (*Alnus rubra* Bong.) [H36 9, K111] does not occur in southcentral Alaska. Sitka willow (*Salix sitchensis* Sanson ex Bong.) [H361, K428] is commonly sympatric in alder stands.

Page 94. Norway spruce—An apparent reference to the spruce most familiar to Menzies. White spruce (*Picea glauca* (Moench) Voss) [H61, K19]; black spruce (*P. mariana* (P. Mills) B.S.P.)[H62, K19]; the white spruce:black spruce hybrid Lutz spruce (*P. X lutzii* Little [*glauca* X *mariana]*) [H62, K19]; Sitka spruce (*P. sitchensis* (Bong.) Carr.) [H61, K19]) all are present on the shoreline of Cook Inlet. Menzies may have seen any, or all, of the species.

Page 94. Arbutus vitis idea et uva ursi—Apparently a reference to two physically and taxonomically associated species. Arbuts vitis idea may be ligonberry (*Vaccinium vitis-idea* L. ssp. *minus* (Lodd.) Hult.) [H731, K197]. Arbutus is not an obsolete synonym for vaccinium. It is an obsolete synonym for the genus *Arctostaphylos* and the second plant is very likely kinnikinnck (*Arctostaphylos uva-ursi* (L.) Spreng. ssp. *uva-ursi*) [H729,K192]. Both species are trailing, creeping, dwarf-shrubs in the ERICACEAE and often sympatric..

Page 94. Cornus Canadensis—Bunchberry (*Cornus canadensis* L. var. *canadensis*) [H709, K169]; swedish dwarf-cornel (*Cornus suecica* L.) [H708, K169] and the hybrid *Cornus* X *unalaschkensis* Ledeb. [*canadensis* X *suecica*] [H709, K169] all are possible.

Page 94. Pyrola rotundifolia et secunda—Another reference to two taxonomically and physically associated species of wintergreen. If the species were correctly identified, the first is *Pyrola asarifolia* Michx. var. *purpurea* (Bunge) Fern. [H711, K194]; the second, *Orthilia secunda* (L.) House ssp. *secunda* [H713, K194].

Spring, 1794
Southcentral Alaska, Prince William Sound

Page 136 and throughout the text. Pine—Canadian Hemlock & Norway Spruce. As used, "Pine" is synonymous with conifer (PINACEAE). Two species of hemlock are present and sympatric in the coastal forests of Prince William Sound. Both approach the western edge of their distributional ranges. Mountain hemlock (*Tsuga mertensiana* (Bong.) Sarg.) [H63, K20] is abundant at low elevations there, farther east, it is usually found at higher elevation in the forest zone and in muskegs. Western hemlock (*Tsuga heterophylla* (Raf.) Sarg.) [H62, K20] is much less abundant at lower elevations in Prince William sound than in the Alexander Archipelago of Southeastern Alaska. See above for Norway Spruce.

Page 115 and 136. Vaccinium—See above at red and black Whortle berries.

Page 116 and 136. Canadian spruce—See above at Norway Spruce.

Page 118. Betula serrulata—Birches (*Betula* L.) are not very common in Prince William Sound and it is much more likely that the plant Menzies saw was alder (*Alnus* Mill.) which is very abundant there. Betula is also an obsolete synonym for the genus Alnus [B1-512], but no reference was found for Betula serrulata. *Alnus serrulata* Willd. is an obsolete synonym for the eastern North American smooth alder (*Alnus incana* (L.) ssp. *rugosa* (DuRoi) Clausen) [B1-512, K111]. Menzies may have been familiar with smooth alder as it is a Linnaean species (Sp. Pl. 4:336. 1805). Sitka alder (*A. viridis* (Chaix) DC. ssp. *sinuata*) [H368, K111] is the characteristic alder throughout the lowlands and shoreline of Prince William Sound.

Page 118. viola Canadensis—*Viola canadensis* L. ssp. [K469] is not an Alaskan species. The common violets in the lowlands of Prince William Sound are: *Viola glabella* Nutt. [H680, K469]; *V. langsdorfii* (Regel) Fisch. [H681, K469]; *V. epipsela* Ledeb. ssp. *repens* (Turcz.) Becker [H483, K469].

Page 118. Legusticum scoticum—*Ligusticum scoticum* L. ssp. *hultenii* (Fern.) Calder & Taylor [H702, K34] is common on beaches and wetlands of Prince William Sound.

Page 119. ...currants & two species of Whortle berries—Currants of Prince William Sound are: stink currant (*Ribes bracteosum* Dougl. ex Hook.) [H591, K435]; trailing black currant (*R. laxiflorum* Pursh.) [H591, K435]; northern red currant (*R. triste* Pallas) [H593, K435]. See above for whortle berries.

Page 119. Caltha—The marsh marigolds of Prince William Sound are: *Caltha leptosepala* DC. ssp. *leptosepala* [H452, K382]; *C. palustris* L. var. *palustris* [H454, K382]. The first is a large, showy plant and may be the one Menzies saw.

Page 119. Dryas... D. octopetala—*Dryas octopetala* L. ssp. [H630-631, K397] grows on dry, cold barrens either at high elevation or on glacier moraines at low elevation. The "... marshy situation in the woods..." is not correct for this plant and as it was "...not in flower...," Menzies may have mis-identified the plant. It is not possible to determine the species, but it is very unlikely to be dryas.

Page 121. Andromeda ... Andromeda museifriega—*Andromeda polifolia* L. is the only species in North America [K191]. Obviously Menzies' name was not valid. The Alaska plant relates best to *A. polifolia* L. var. *polifolia* [H727, K191].

Page 121. Pothos lanceolata—No reference to a genus Pothos was found. However, Pathos is a vernacular name for ivy-arum (*Scindapsus* sp.) [W1776;W2033]. This suggests a relationship to the arum family (ARACEAE). The only species of ARACEAE in Prince William Sound is the yellow skunk cabbage (*Lysichiton americanum* Hult. & St. John) [H281, K41]. Menzies' description of the habitat and flowering of Pothos lanceolata ("... grows in marshy places in abundance & was now in full bloom.") fits well the habitat of yellow skunk cabbage and its habit of blooming in the early part of May (Menzies saw it on June 8, 1794). This is a wild, best guess on the basis of the limited references available.

Page 135. Carices Mosses & other low vegetables...—This seems to refer to three distinct plant groups in the ground stratum of the understory vegetation. It is impossible to determine if the reference is to sedges (*Carex* L. ssp.) [H215-280, K173-181] specifically, or includes all graminoids (grass-like plants) present.

Page 135. Andromeda carulea A. notifolia & A. museifragia—See above at Andromeda museifragia. The listing of three species raises the doubt that Andromeda as defined by Menzies is the same as the modern definition of the genus. All appear to be members of the ground layer of the vegetation.

Page 135. Empetrum nigrum—Crowberry (*Empetrum nigrum* L. ssp. *nigrum*) [H716, K190] is the subspecies on coastal lowlands in Prince William Sound.

Page 135. Heleborus trifoliata—The genus *Helleborus* sp. L. [B2-52] does not occur in Alaska. The genus *Coptis* L. was once included in Helleborus. Alaska goldthreads are: *Coptis trifolia* (L.) Salisb. ssp. *trifolia* and *C. trifolia* (L.) Salisb. ssp. *groenlandicum* (Oeder) Hult.) [H455, K383].

Page 135. ... a new species of Isoporum—*Isoporum*—This taxon is not in Alaska [Not in K]. [Editor].

Page 135. dwarf Vaccinia—Dwarf vacciniums in the Prince William Sound lowlands are: ligonberry (*Vaccinium vitis-idaea* L. ssp. *minus* (Lodd.) Hult.) [H731, K197] and alpine blueberry (*Vaccinium uliginosum* L. ssp. *pubescens* (Wormsk. ex Hornem.) S. Young) [H734, K197]. Menzies could have seen either.

Page 135. ...two species of Viola—See above at Viola canadensis.

Page 135. Equisetum palustre—*Equisetum palustre* L. [H832, K11] is one of several species of horsetails in the area. There is no way to verify the horsetail seen by Menzies was *E. palustre* L.

Page 135. Plantago macroeaipen—The species name may be incorrectly spelled or transcribed [Menzie's handwriting is not clear at this point, and may be read as "macrocarpen"—Editor] *Plantago macrocarpa* Cham. & Schlecht [H832, K323] is present on the shoreline of Prince William Sound.

Page 136. Rubus sarmentosus—Rubus is a very large and complex genus. Rubus sarmentosus is neither a recognized species nor a synonym. Sarmentose means, "producing long, slender, runners", and Menzies may have seen a low growing or prostrate Rubus with this characteristic. *Rubus pedatus* Sm. [H601, K408]; *R. chamaemorus* L. [H602, K406]; *R. arcticus* L. ssp. *stellatus* (Sm.) Boivin [H603, K405] all have this growth form and are in the area.

Page 136. Rubus Nootcagensis—The taxonomic name Rubus nootagensis (or R. nootkatensis) does not exist. Thimbleberry (*Rubus parviflorus* Nutt. var. *parviflorus* [H605, K408] and salmonberry (*Rubus spectabilis* Pursh. var. *spectabilis*) [H604, K409] are the large, erect subspecies of the area. Menzies could have seen either or both.

Page 136. Menziesia ferruginea—Rusty menziesia (*Menziesia ferruginea* Sm.) [H720, K194] is a relatively common shrub in the understory of the spruce-hemlock forest throughout southcentral and southeastern Alaska.

Page 136. Sedum busifolium—Roseroot (*Sedum integrifolium* (Raf.) A.Nels. ex Coult. & A. Nels. ssp. *integrifolium* [H561, K170] is the only sedum in coastal areas of southcentral Alaska. [From the   handwriting, the term may be *Ledum* . *Ledum palustre* L. ssp *decumbens* _(Ait) Hulten (K193, H717) is found in Prince William Sound—Editor]

Page 136. ...two new species of Vaccinium—See above at black and red Whortleberries.

Page 136. willows—Tall-shrub or small-tree willows are: Sitka willow (*Salix sitchensis* Sanson ex Bong.) [H361, K428]; Alaska willow (*Salix alaxensis* (Anderess.) Colville var. *alaxensis* and *S. a.* var. *longistylis* (Rydb.) Schneid.) [H356, K421]; Barclay willow (*Salix barclayi* Anderss.) [H353, K422]; undergreen willow (*Salix commutata* Bebb) [H353, K422].

Page 136. alders—See above at alder willow.

Page 136. Pines—See above at Pine...Canadian & Norway Spruce. See above at Norway spruce.

Page 136. Thuja —Menzies refers to western redcedar (*Thuju plicata* Donn ex D. Don) [H64, K18] which he had seen in British Columbia. It is not present in Prince William Sound. Another CUPRESSACEAE, Alaska yellowcedar (*Chamaceyparis nootkatensis* (D. Don) Spach), [H65, K18] occurs in Prince William Sound, but not in the area visited by Menzies.

Page 136. Gaultheria—Menzies had seen salal (*Gaultheria shallon* Pursh) [H728, K193] in British Columbia. It occurs only in the extreme southern part of the Alexander Archipelago of southeastern Alaska, not in Prince William Sound.

Page 136. ...several species of Jungermannia—In Menzies' time the genus *Jungermannia* L. included nearly all of the leafy HEPATICAE (liverworts). Some modern bryophyte taxonomists do not recognize the genus.

Page 136. Dodecatheon meadea—American cowslip (*Dodecatheon meadia* L.) is a Linnean species (Sp. Pl. 144 1753 [B2-594] and may have been familiar to Menzies. The coastal lowland shootingstar is (*Dodecatheon maacrocarpum* (Gray) Taylor & MacBryde) ([H747, K379].

Page 136. ... dwarf new species of Raspberry—See above at Rubus.

Page 139. ...Birch...scrubby pines, bushy alder, & low brush wood—See above where appropriate.

Summer 1794
Southeastern Alaska

Page 162. Selena acaulis—Moss campion (*Silene acaulis* (L.) Jacq. ssp. *acaulis*) [H441, K153] occurs on glacier moraines near sealevel and is not necessarily an "Alpine plant."

Page 162. Pulmonaria maritima—*Pulmonaria maritima* L. [B3-59] is an obsolete synonym for *Pneumaria maritima* (L.) Hill [K118] which, in turn, is an obsolete synonym for *Mertensia maritima* (L.) S. F. Gray spp.. *Mertensia maritima* (L.) S. F. Gray var. *maritima* [H781, K118] is the lungwort on the beaches in southeastern Alaska.

Page 168. Ledum latifolium—*Ledum groelandicum* Oeder [H718, K193]

Page 168. Caltha... Caltha celiarius ... Caltha palustria—See above at Caltha.

Page 181. Tobacco—A species of wild tobacco (*Nicotiana attenuata* Torr. ex S. Wats.) [C411,K457] is endemic to dry, open, sandy, habitats east of the Pacific Coast mountain ranges in the Pacific Northwest and British Columbia. Because the tobacco observed by Menzies was cultivated it is unlikely it was the native species. Most probably, tobacco had been obtained either as seed, or seeds had been in tobacco the natives had obtained in trade. Cultivation of crop plants appears to be a learned activity for the natives of coastal Alaska and the idea of growing tobacco may have been passed on to them either by European traders, or during trading exchanges with natives from the east. [Turner, (1972) says that *Nicotiana quadrivalis* Pursh. [syn. N.bigelovii (Torr.) Wats.] was cultivated by the Tlingit and Haida Indians and provides an extended explantion of the possible introduction of tobacco on the Northwest Coast—Editor.]

Page 193. Sampire—Sampire [W2008] is the vernacular name for glasswort (*Salicornia europaea* L.) [H401, K161]. The species is endemic, widely distributed, and common on seashores and halophytic wetlands of southeastern Alaska. The antiscorbutic properties were known and it was eaten for that property.

At right: Photograph of a pressed
specimen of Menziesia ferruginea,
a plant named in honor of Archibald Menzies.
The note on the bottom indicates the sample was
collected on the "Northwest Coast of America Mr. Menzies."
(Courtesy British Museum of Natural History.)

Northwest Coast of America Mr Menzies

Isotype Menziesia ferruginea in
collina Cistae? overende at
Burke Channel, B.C. by Menzies
I Kovan 95

Bibliography

Anderson, Bern

1960   *The Life and Voyages of Captain George Vancouver*: *Surveyor of the Sea*. Seattle: University of Washington Press.

Boas, Franz

1911 (1971) The Tsmshian Language. *Handbook of American Indian Langauges*. Facsimile reproduction. Seattle: Shorey Book Store.

Barbeau, Marius and William Beynon

1987   *Tsimshian Narratives, 2: Trade and Warfare*. Edited by George F. MacDonald and John J. Cove. Mercury Series, Directorate Paper No. 3. Ottawa: Canadian Museum of Civilization.

Colnett, Captain James

n.d.   "Voyage to the N W Side of America." Unpublished journal aboard the *Prince of Wales*, October 16, 1786 to November 7, 1788. Manuscript in the Public Records Office, Kew, Richmond, Surrey, England. Adm. 55/146. Juneau, Alaska: Alaska State Library. Microfilm.

de Laguna, Frederica

1934   *The Archaeology of Cook Inlet, Alaska*. Philadelphia: University of Pennsylvania Press.

1956   *Chugach Prehistory*: *The archaeology of Prince William Sound, Alaska*. Seattle: University of Washington Press.

Emmons, George Thornton

1991   *The Tlingit Indians*. Edited with additions by Frederica
            de Laguna and a biography by Jean Low. Anthropologi-
            cal Papers of the American Museum of Natural History,
            #70. Seattle: University of Washington Press.

Galloway, D. J. and E. W. Groves

1987   "Archibald Menzies, MD, FLS (1754-1842), aspects of
            his life, travels and collections." *Archives of Natural
            History*, Vol. 14, No. 1 pp. 3-43. London, England.

Groves, Eric W.

1992   "Archibald Menzies: an early botanist on the west coast
            of North America." Paper presented at the Vancouver
            Conference on Exploration and Discovery, April 23-26
            1992,Vancouver, British Columbia.

Howay, F. W.

1973   *A list of trading vessels in the maritime fur trade, 1785-
            1825*. Edited by Richard A. Pierce. Kingston, Ontario:
            Limestone Press.

Keithahn, E. L.

1940   "The Authentic History of Shakes Island and the Clan."
            Wrangell, Alaska: Historical Society. Reprint. *Wrangell
            Sentinel*, 1981.

Lamb, W. Kaye

1992   "Banks and Menzies: Evolution of a Journal." Paper
            presented at the Vancouver Conference on Exploration
            and Discovery, April 23-26, 1992, Vancouver, British
            Columbia.

Naish, Constance and Gillian Story

1976   *English-Tlingit Dictionary: Nouns*. Sitka, Alaska:
            Sheldon Jackson Museum.

Naish, John

1992   "The Health of Vancouver and his men." Paper pre-
            sented at the Vancouver Conference on Exploration and
            Discovery, April 23-26, 1992, Vancouver, British
            Columbia.

Newcombe, C. F. (editor, annotator)

1923   *Menzies' Journal of Vancouver's Voyage: April to October, 1792.* With biographical note by J. Forsyth. Archives of British Columbia, Memoir No.V. Victoria, British Columbia.

Orth, Donald J.

1971   *Dictionary of Alaska Place Names.* Geological Survey Professional Paper #567, Washington, D.C.: United States Printing Office.

Price, E. Grenfell (editor)

1971   *The Explorations of Captain Cook in the Pacific as told by selections of his own journals, 1768-1779.* New York: Dover Publications.

Shaw, George C.

1909   *The Chinook Jaragon and How to Use it.* Seattle: Rainier Printing Co., Inc. Facsimile reproduction. Seattle: Shorey Book Store, 1965.

Sheriff, John   (master's mate aboard the *Chatham.*)

n.d.   Unpublished journal kept while on the voyage with Captain Vancouver August 18,1791 to June 6, 1795. Original journal at the Public Records Office, Kew, Richmond, Surrey, England Adm. 53/334.

Speck, Gordon

1970   *Northwest Explorations.* Portland, Oregon: Binfords and Mort, Publishers.

Turner, Nancy J. and Roy Taylor

1972   "A review of the Northwest Coast tobacco mystery." *Syesis*, Vol. 5, pp. 247-257. (Victoria, British Columbia).

Vancouver, George

1798 (1984)   *A Voyage of Discovery to the North Pacific Ocean and Round the World 1791-1795.* Edited and annotated by W. Kaye Lamb. Four volumes with introduction and appendices. London: The Hakluyt Society, 1984.

Wagner, Henry R. & W. A. Newcombe (editors)

1938   "The Journal of Jacinto Caamano, part 1" Translated
            from the Spanish by Captain Harold Grenfell, R.N.
            British Columbia Historical Quarterly, Vol.2, pp. 89-
            222.

Williams, Frank and Emma Williams

1978   *Tongass Texts.* Transcribed and edited by Jeff Leer.
            Fairbanks, Alaska: Alaska Native Language Center,
            University of Alaska, Fairbanks.

Index

The letter "n" following a page number indicates that the reference is a footnote.